Mithras Reader Volume III

An Academic and Religious Journal of Greek, Roman

and Persian Studies

Editor: Payam Nabarz

Papers and Contributions by: Prof. Ezio Albrile, Dr. Israel Campos Méndez, Robert F. Mullen MA, Dr. Ranajit Pal, Csaba T. Szabó, Sheda Vasseghi, Dr. MasatoTōjō, Hassan Hashemi Zarjabad, Dr. Farhang Khademi Nadooshan, Dr. Seyed Mehdi Mousavi, Dr. Javad Neyestani, Dr. Syed Sadrudin Mosavi Jashni, Prof. Barbara Kaim, Dr. Reza MehrAfarin, Dr. Seyyed Rasool Mousavi Haji, Dr. Javad Neyestani, Masoud Rashidi Nejad, Amirhossein Salehi, Akashanath, Ana C. Jones, Lesley Madytinou, David Rankine, Harita Meenee, Melissa Gold, Jane Raeburn, Farida Bamji, Katherine Sutherland, and Dr. Payam Nabarz.

Mithras Reader: An Academic and Religious Journal of Greek, Roman and Persian Studies, Volume III.

ISBN: 978-0-9556858-3-5

Editor: Payam Nabarz Copyright © 2010.

The Copyright of each article is retained by their respective authors.

Published in 2010 by 'Web of Wyrd Press'
An imprint of BECS Ltd.

http://www.webofwyrdpress.com

For mailing list: http://www.myspace.com/webofwyrdpress

All rights reserved. No part of this book may be reproduced or utilised in any form or by any means, electronic or mechanical, including photocopying, recording, or by any information storage and retrieval system, without permission in writing from the publisher.

Table of Contents

Acknowledgments	4
Editorial	5
Contributors Biographies	8
Part 1: Academic Papers	14
A Journey to the Hypercosmic side of the Sun by Prof Ezio Albrile	15
Internet and the Resurrection of a God: the Neo-Mithraic Communities by Dr. Israel Campos	28
Aristotle and the Natural Slave: The Athenian Relationship with India by Robert F. Mullen, M.A.	35
The Dawn of Religions in Afghanistan-Seistan-Gandhara and the Personal Seals of Gotama Buddha and Zoroaster by Dr. Ranajit Pal	62
Dacia and the cult of Mithras by Csaba T. Szabó	84
Sun Tzu and the Achaemenid Grand Strategy by Sheda Vasseghi	98
Zen Buddhism and Mithraism by Dr. Masato Tōjō	114
A New Archaeological Research of the Sassanian Fire Temple of Rivand in Sabzevar, by Hassan Hashemi Zarjabad, Farhang khademi Nadooshan, Seyed Mehdi Mousavi, Javad Neyestani, Syed Sadrudin Mosavi Jashni, Barbara Kaim	144
The Zoroastrian Holyland of Haetumant by Reza MehrAfarin, Seyyed Rasool Mousavi Haji, and Javad Neyestani	180
The Archaeological Evidence in Tarik Dareh (Dark Valley), in Hamadan, Iran, by Masoud Rashidi Nejad and Amirhossein Salehi	196
Part 2: Arts	203
Kephra by Akashanath	204
Modern Altars by Ana C Jones	210
Part 3: Religious Articles, Poems, and Stories	212
Into The Looking Glass Tragic Reflections of Life by Lesley Madytinou	213
Solomon in Olympus: The Enduring Connection between King Solomon and Greek Magic by David Rankine	229

Orphic Hymn to Aphrodite translated by Harita Meenee	**234**
The Athenian Festivals of Demeter by Melissa Gold	**236**
The Lioness by Jane Raeburn	**246**
Anahita: Lady of Persia by Payam Nabarz	**256**
Origin of the Gathas of Asho Zarathustra by Farida Bamji	**268**
Mehrgan by Farida Bamji	**272**
A Prayer for Initiation by Katherine Sutherland	**274**

Acknowledgments

The front cover painting *Kephra* by Akashanath, the four sons of Horus icons were derived from http://en.wikipedia.org/wiki/File:Four_sons_of_Horus.svg by Jeff Dahl, using the Creative Commons Attribution-Share Alike license. The cover is therefore also a Creative Commons Attribution-Share Alike license and the image is available by contacting Akashanath. This does not apply any other part of the Journal; the copyright of each article is retained by their respective author.

The inside cover photo shows *Demeter and Persephone with Triptolemus*, a copy of stone panel from the Telesterion at Eleusis; the original is in the National Museum in Athens; photo taken July 2006 by Melissa Gold.

To Alison Jones for helpful comments on this manuscript.

Mithra is twentyfold between two friends or two relations;
Mithra is thirtyfold between two men of the same group;
Mithra is fortyfold between two partners;
Mithra is fiftyfold between wife and husband;
Mithra is sixtyfold between two pupils (of the same master);
Mithra is seventyfold between the pupil and his master;
Mithra is eightyfold between the son-in-law and his father-in-law;
Mithra is ninetyfold between two brothers;
Mithra is a hundredfold between the father and the son;
Mithra is a thousandfold between two nations;
Mithra is ten thousandfold when connected with the Law of Mazda,
and then he will be every day of victorious strength.
- Hymn to Mithra (Mehr Yasht 116-117).[1]

---

[1] Translated by James Darmesteter (from Sacred Books of the East, American Edition, 1898), Avesta.org.

Editorial

This is the third volume of the Journal; it has been two years since the last volume. This time was used to bring together this volume which in quality and breadth of the papers is unique, and, the Journal itself is in fact larger than the previous two volumes put together; furthermore, now it is in an A4 format. The other differences in this volume are that it covers several different approaches and sources to Greek, Roman and Persian studies. There are papers which look at the Eastern sources and links with India, China and Japan as well as papers considering the Western sources. The Achaemenid 'Persian Royal Road' and, the 'Silk Road' are some of the ways in which knowledge and trade travelled in both directions between East and West. The spread of religious memes and technology in the ancient the world did not stop at the national borders or at the Hellespont.

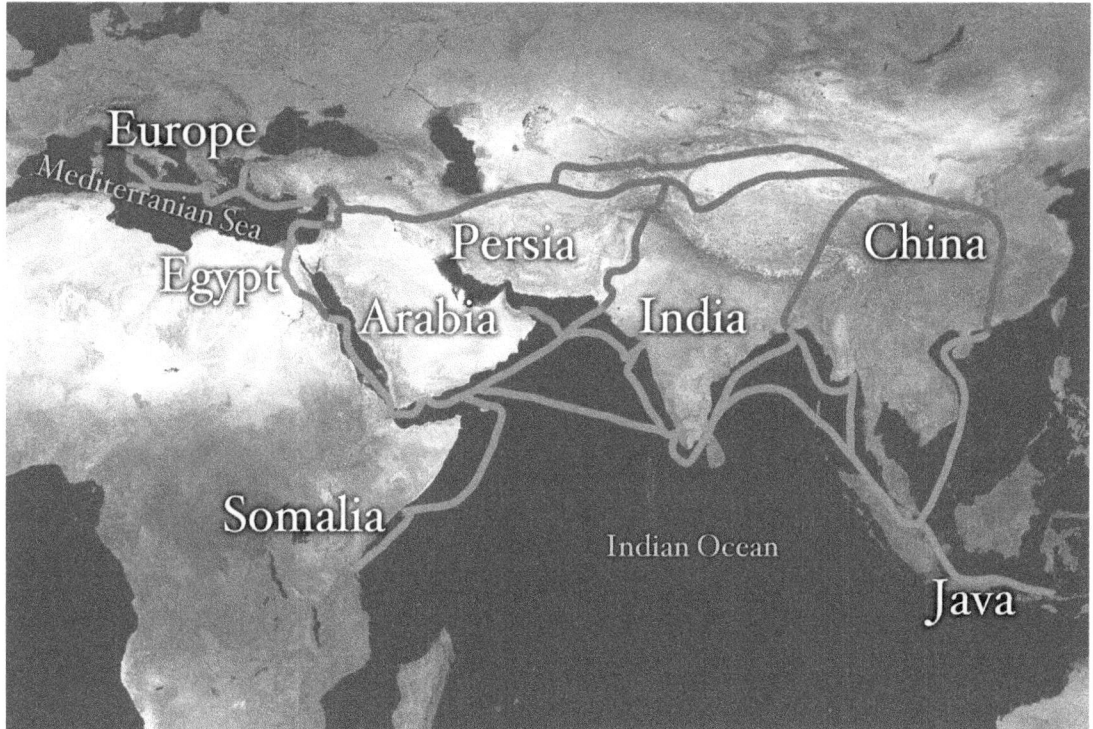

Figure: The Silk Road (Land routes are red, water routes are blue)[2]

The papers and material in this issue provide numerous examples of the knowledge different cultures had of each other in the ancient world, and, their potential influences on each other as the result. To add my own example to the list of East-West influences on each other in this issue, I would like to bring the readers' attention to the fact that some early Islamic coins imitated those used in Persian Sassanian (Zoroastrian) and Byzantine (Christian), empires. Some

---

[2] Map from http://en.wikipedia.org/wiki/File:Silk_route.jpg

Islamic coins still showed the Zoroastrian fire altar on one side and head of the Sassnian king on the other, but had Arabic text from the Quran added to them.

The reverse of this process can be seen in the gold coin of Offa, the King of Mercia in England (757 -July 796). The coin shows 'Offa Rex' on one side and an Islamic text from the Quran on the other, the coin is similar to an Islamic Abbasid period dinar coin. The old trade routes allowed the flow of goods and knowledge for hundreds of years, and, coins were the universal language spoken by all, be they Zoroastrian, Christian, Moslem, Buddhist or any other faith.

Payam Nabarz

Editor.

Papers and Articles Submission Guidelines.

Mithras Reader: An Academic and Religious Journal of Greek, Roman and Persian Studies is dedicated to all the religions of the classical world. We invite submissions of academic papers from researchers and spiritual articles from practitioners of the religions of the classical world. We also welcome classical world based art work; both modern interpretations, and traditional forms.

Occasional articles covering the non-religious aspects of the ancient Greco-Roman or Persian world will be considered, for example dealing with geopolitical, cultural, or relevant military history. The Journal is divided into three sections. Part 1 contains the academic papers; Part 2 art work inspired by the classical world, also sculptures and paintings; in Part 3 there are articles by modern practitioners and independent scholars, rites, hymns, stories and poetry. Authors should state in which section they wish their papers to be included in. Please also include a short biography.

Authors receive one complimentary copy of the issue in which their article appears. The Journal pays no royalties or remuneration to the authors. All papers, articles, materials featured in the journal remain the copyright of their authors and artists and not the publishers. Authors can publish their material in other publications too.

As a 'Reader' Journal, it is the opinions of the writers that are expressed rather than peer reviewed views. Authors who wish to publish their material in the part 1 of the journal (the academic section), need to state their academic qualifications, their publication record in the field and/or at which university the research was undertaken.

Authors, who are not academics in the field or previously published, can still submit material for part 3. Materials in part 1 are papers, while materials in part 3 are articles.

The Journal is available both in printed format and as an electronic download. If you wish to submit your work please have a look at the last issue, and obtain a copy of it, so you become familiar with journal's format and style. Please see:
http://www.webofwyrdpress.com

Authors are solely responsible for obtaining copyright permission for all previously published or copyrighted materials that are used / included in their submissions.

Materials are to be submitted in good English and should not normally exceed 9000 words, and should be presented in 12 point Garamond font. If English is not your first language please have your work read by a professional English translator before submitting your work, as a translation service cannot be provided.

Materials are to be submitted electronically as .doc or .rtf files, and images should be submitted as JPEG files unless otherwise discussed, and should be provided at the size intended for production at a resolution of 600 dpi. References should be numbered in the text and appear as numbered footnotes. The bibliography should be located at end of the article.

To contact us, or send your submissions, please email us at: nabarz@hotmail.com

Payam Nabarz

Editor.

Contributors Biographies

In Part 1 Academic Papers

Prof Ezio Albrile (Torino 1962) is Professor of religious history of Iran and Central Asia at the CESMEO Turin. He studies the interference between Iranian pre-Islamic religion and Hellenistic dualism (Hermeticism, Gnosticism, Manichaeism and others).

Dr. Israel Campos Méndez is an Assistant Professor in Ancient History at the University of Las Palmas of Gran Canaria (Canary Islands, Spain). His lines of research are related to History of Religion, and in particular to the Cult of Mithra in Ancient Iran and Roman Empire. His Ph. D. was entitled: 'The God Mithra: Analysis of the processes of adjustment of his worship from the social, political and religious frame of the Ancient Iran to that of the Roman Empire'. He has written two books in Spanish about the cult of Mithra in Ancient Persia, and many others papers and articles about Zoroastrian Religion and the Mithraic Mysteries.

Robert F. Mullen is completing his doctoral studies in Philosophy and Religion with a concentration in Asian and Comparative Studies. His current project is a study of the body in Buddhist thought. His specific interests lie in the Tantric systems of India and Buddhist philosophical traditions, as well as the German existentialists of the early 20th century. Robert's article "Holy Stigmata, Anorexia, and Self-Mutilation: Parallels in Pain and Imagining," was recently published by the European Journal for the Study of Religions and Ideologies, 9:25, 2010. "JSRI volume 9, no. 25, Spring 2010"

Dr. Ranajit Pal is a Ph. D. from the Indian Institute of Technology, Kharagpur (1973). He is a life member of the Bhandarkar Oriental Research Institute, Pune, and the Indian Society for Greek and Roman Studies, Bareilly. He has published several papers and books including *"Non-Jonesian Indology and Alexander"* and *"Gotama Buddha in West Asia"* (in Japanese). His website address is http://www.ranajitpal.com

Csaba T. Szabó (Romania, Cluj-Napoca, 1987) is graduate student at the University of Babeş-Bolyai, Faculty of History, specializing in Provincial Archaeology and Ancient History, particularly on the cults of roman Dacia. His examination-paper is about the local cult of Mithras and the examination of the Mithraeum, as an architectural and sacred place. The author was the President of the Association of Hungarian History Students from Cluj (2008-2010) and regularly publishing in the Historia section of the Szabadság (Liberty), the most well-known newspaper of the region.

Sheda Vasseghi has a Masters in the Ancient History of Persia and a Masters in Business Administration. Ms. Vasseghi focuses on Iranian national identity. Her special interest encompasses Iranian philosophy as it applies to modern day social, political, and religious issues. She believes history provides the answers to current problems, and lack of knowledge in the field leads to poor decision-making by citizens and policymakers. Ms. Vasseghi is a regular contributor to political and history magazines on Iran's affairs. She is currently working on textbooks covering ancient Iran for K-12 students. Ms. Vasseghi is on the Board of Azadegan Foundation and a member of www.persepolis3D.com

Dr. Masato Tōjō Born in Niigata City, Japan in 1957. Earned the degree of Ph. D. in Information Technology from Dept. of Information Technology (now Information Science), Graduate School of Engineering, The University of Tokyo in 1985. Japanese committee member of ISO/IEC JTC1 SC18 WG9 from 1992 to 1996. Chairman of Mithraeum Japan (Founded in 1997). Author of books: *Qewl -Holy Book of Mithra* (MIIBOAT Books, 2006), *Mithraic Theology* (Kokushokankōkai, 1996), *Dictionary of Gods of the World* (Gakken, 2004), *Esoteric Astrology of Mithraism* (MIIBOAT Books, 1998), *Let's Read the Secret Doctrine* (Shuppanshinsha, 2001), *Encyclopedia of Tarot* (Kokushokankōkai, 1994).

Specialty: Cognitive psychology, computer linguistics and artificial intelligence. Making the investigation on pictograms and language processing mechanism of human brain a start, began study on mystic symbolism. The study gradually shifted to the study of Iranian religious tradition and its history, especially Mithraism, Maitreya (Miroku), Shiism and Sufism.

Dr. MasatoTōjō Official Site:

http://homepage2.nifty.com/Mithra/english_index.html
http://homepage2.nifty.com/Mithra/index.html

Hassan Hashemi Zarjabad is a PhD Student, Dept of Archaeology, Tarbiat Modares University.

Dr. Farhang khademi Nadooshan is an Associate Professor, Dept of Archaeology, Tarbiat Modares University, Tehran, Iran.

Dr. Seyed Mehdi Mousavi is an Assistance Professor, Dept of Archaeology, Tarbiat Modares University.

Dr. Javad Neyestani is an Assistance Professor, Dept of Archaeology, Tarbiat Modares University.

Dr. Syed Sadrudin Mosavi Jashni is an Assistant Professor, Department of Political Thought, Imam Khomeini and Islamic Revolution Research Institute and Department of Indian Studies, Faculty of World Studies, University of Tehran.

Prof. Barbara Kaim, Department of Near Eastern Archaeology, Institute of Archaeology of University of Warsaw.

Dr. Reza MehrAfarin was born in the land of Haetomant, (Sistan). He received his BA in English language translation from Allameh Tabatabaee University. Being interested in Iranian culture and civilization, continued his studies in archaeology in Tarbiat Modarres University and received his MA and Ph.D from this University. Now, he is Assistant Professor in the University of Sistan and Baluchestan. His research and teaching interests include the art, religion and archaeology of Medes, Achaemenid, Parthian and Sassanid era. He has worked in many research projects at the Miras-e Farhangi-ye Iran (Iran Civilization heritage) including archaeology digs and field surveys in Sistan and other old sites of Iran and also published many articles and a few books about archaeology, art and religion of Iran.

Dr. Seyyed Rasool Mousavi Haji was born on December 30, 1967, in Savadkouh, Iran. He received his Ph.D in Archaeology in 2003 from Tarbiat Modarres University of Iran. He is teaching as an Assistant Professor in Archaeology Department in University of Sistan and Baluchestan. And He also is the Dean of the Faculty of Art and Architecture. He published two books and several articles about the archaeology of Sassanian and Islamic periods. His main fieldwork are: Archaeological survey in Sistan plain in 2007 and 2008, archaeological survey in

Zahedane Kohne (capital of Sistan during 5 to 9 A. H.) in 2002 and excavation to estimate size of the Zahedane in 2007.

Dr. Javad Neyestani is a Faculty member and director of Archaeology Department of Tarbiat Modares University Member and author of the Great Islamic Encyclopedia Member of Scientific Advisors Group and author of Art and Architecture of Islamic Encyclopedia.

Masoud Rashidi Nejad is a MA of achaeology, Department of Archaeology, Faculty of Humanities, Tarbiat Modares University and instructor of the Islamic Azad university of Hamadan Branch, Mail: mrashidinejad7@gmail.com.

Amirhossein Salehi is an instructor at Semnan University of Tourism. He is currently a PhD student at Tarbiat Modares University in Tehran.

In Part 2 Arts.

Akashanath is a ceremonial magician with a background in Thelema and the Golden Dawn system. He is also a Sanyasin of the Adinath Sampradaya and a practitioner of English rune magick.

Ana C. Jones was born in Brazil; she is trained as a teacher and electrical engineer. In 1989 She came to live in England with husband and their three children. Her interest in Traditional Astrology led her to complete C. Warnock's Renaissance Astrological magical course, plus two others of the same calibre. At the moment she is studying Alchemy from Adam McLean courses, Hermetic Magic with the OMS and Mithraism from several sources. She practices Traditional British Witchcraft and Stregoneria. Finding inspiration among her studies and practices to express herself through her drawings, paintings and sculptures.

In Part 3 Religious Articles, Poetry, Stories.

Lesley Madytinou has been a believer in the Hellenic religion and a private student of all things Hellenic, both ancient and modern, for fourteen years. She lives with her husband on the island of Lesbos in Hellas where they are involved in the translation of ancient and modern texts into English for various local and international Hellenic organisations. Her articles have been published in journals and magazines concerned with the indigenous religions of Europe.

David Rankine is an author and esoteric researcher whose expertise covers a wide range of topics, including the Western Esoteric Traditions, especially Greco-Egyptian magic, the Qabalah, and the Grimoire tradition. He has been writing since the 1980s and is the author of twenty-three books, including Hekate Liminal Rites (with his author wife Sorita d'Este), The Veritable Key of Solomon (with Stephen Skinner) and The Book of Treasure Spirits. His published work in recent years has been characterised by the publication of previously unavailable or inaccessible material on the grimoires and other areas of magic. He is a keen believer in the propagation and dissemination of rare texts, and is a member of both Societas Magica and ESSWE (European Society for the Study of Western Esotericism). Website: www.ritualmagick.co.uk

Harita Meenee is a Greek independent scholar of classical studies and women's history. She has presented cultural TV programs and has lectured at universities in Greece and the US. She is the author of five books, as well as of numerous articles published in Greek, British and American magazines. Website: www.hmeenee.com

Melissa Gold graduated from the University of North Carolina at Chapel Hill in zoology, then pursued botany and obtained her Masters of Museology at the U of T. More recently she studied classical languages at the University of Toronto and has entered the Clergy Ed program of Hellenion. She leads rituals for the Hellenic Spirit in Toronto. hellenicspiritcanada at gmail.com

Jane Raeburn is an American writer and computer scientist. She is the author of '*Celtic Wicca*', co-author of '*Building a Magical Relationship*', and editor of the poetry anthology '*The Pagan's Muse*'. She produces an annual series of poetry readings in cooperation with the Southworth Planetarium in Portland, Maine. This piece is a chapter from a novel in progress, tentatively titled The Lioness.

Payam Nabarz is author of *The Mysteries of Mithras: The Pagan Belief That Shaped the Christian World*' (Inner Traditions, 2005), '*The Persian Mar Nameh: The Zoroastrian Book of the Snake Omens & Calendar*' (Twin Serpents, 2006), and *Divine Comedy of Neophyte Corax and Goddess Morrigan* (Web of

Wyrd Press, 2008). He is also editor of *Mithras Reader An academic and religious journal of Greek, Roman, and Persian Studies. Volume 1(2006), Volume 2 (2008)*. His latest books are *Stellar Magic: a Practical Guide to Rites of the Moon, Planets, Stars and Constellations* (Avalonia, 2009) and, *Seething Cauldron: Essays on Zoroastrianism, Sufism, Freemasonry, Wicca, Druidry, and Thelema* (Web of Wyrd Press, 2010). For further info visit: www.stellarmagic.co.uk & http://www.myspace.com/nabarz

Farida Bamji is a poet and more of Farida's work can be seen at:

- http://groups.msn.com/ZoroastrianPoetryGroup
- http://groups.msn.com/creatingawareness
- http://groups.msn.com/ahunavargroup

Katherine Sutherland is a poet and author, her collection *Underworld*, a reworking of the Persephone myth, was recently published (Web of Wyrd Press, 2010). She has papers published in the following anthologies: *Both Sides of Heaven: Essays on Angels, Fallen Angels and Demons* (Avalobia, 2009), *From a Drop of Water* (Avalobia, 2009), *Hekate: Her Sacred Fires* (Avalobia, 2010).

Part 1: Academic Papers

The Luxor Obelisk in Paris, photo by Payam Nabarz.

Part 1: Academic Papers

A Journey to the Hypercosmic side of the Sun by Prof Ezio Albrile

In a little Nag-Hammadi Gnostic text called *Hypsiphrone*, «She of High Mind», that occupies the final four pages of Codex XI (69,21-72,33; Robinson 1984: 453), we find traces of Iranian influences. Hypsiphrone is described in the company of her brothers, and she proceeds to deliver a revelatory discourse concerning her katabasis from the place of her virginity into the world (70,20-21) and her conversations with Phainops, the «Bright-eyed one». The name of this personage recalls the teachings of the Zoroastrian Magi about the *gyān wēnišn*, the «Eye of the Soul», the *illuminatio matutina*, that is the «Inner vision» of Pahlavi texts (Gnoli 1979: 419 n. 162). This concept, according to the Proemium of Diogenes Laertius, evokes the doctrine of the εἴδωλα, typical of the Democritean-Epicurean mentality (Brillante 1986: 30 ff.).

These preliminary remarks are opportune since the Platonic tradition attested in the *Chaldaika logia* (= *Chaldaean oracles*) – a collection of visionary sayings of the second century A.D. – speaks about the existence of two Suns, one manifest in its physical splendor and the other related to the inner space (Ulansey 1994: 257-264). According to these reports the Chaldaean distinguished between two fiery bodies: one having a noetic nature, the other being the visible Sun.

According to Proclus, the Chaldaeans call the «Solar world», located in the hypercosmic region, «Entire Light» i.e. «Inner Light» (Brisson 2000: 109 ff.). On the other hand Porphyrius stated that Hypercosm's Soul is the Demiurge (Fr. 41 [Sodano 1964]): this means that the Demiurge is the late, visible outpouring of the hypercosmic reality. Again, there are some affinities with the Psychē of the Gnostic tradition, shattered in the dark world of *hylē*. Also, the Chaldaean consider the «Inner Fire» as the «Father» or «Hypercosmic Paternal Abyss», a place located over the Stars. We note that a certain Iranian cosmology places the Sun beyond the Stars, and we find this evidence particularly in the Mysteries of Mithras. The Hypercosm is in fact an inner condition achieved through hard cultual practices. In an admirable page *On the hieratic art*, the Neoplatonic Proclus helps us to understand a probably «entheogenic» rites (Bidez 1936: 93-97), where two mysterious botanical variety are used: the Heliotropion (that moves in accord with the Sun) and the Selēnotropion (that moves in accord with the Moon), two mythical «plants» that disclose the way towards the «Inner Light» (Faraggiana di Sarzana 1985: 241; cfr. Festugière 1968: 8-9).

The most important source for our knowledge of the Platonic tradition of the existence of two Suns is the *Chaldaean oracles*, the collection of sayings ascribed by a father and son both named Julian. These oracular sayings were, as is well known, seized upon by Porphyry and later Neoplatonists as constituting a divine revelation (Saffrey 1981: 209 ff.). For our purposes, the most important element in the Chaldaean teachings is that of the existence of two Suns. The Chaldaeans distinguished between two fiery bodies (Lewy 1956: 151-152): one a noetic nature and the other corresponding to the visible Sun. The former was said to conduct the latter. Again, Proclus states that the supramundane Sun was known to them as «time of time….» (Saffrey 1984: 73 ff.; cfr. Brisson 2000: 109 ff.).

The *Chaldaean oracles* were the product of a Middle Platonic milieu, since they are permeated by concepts and images known from Platonizing thinkers ranging from Philo to Numenius (Lewy 1956: *passim*). It is thus likely that the Chaldaean concept of a Hypercosmic Sun is at least partly derived from the famous solar allegories of Plato's *Republic*, in which the Sun is used as a symbol for the highest of Plato's Ideal Forms, that of the Good. In Book VI of the *Republic* (508A ff.) Plato compares the Sun to the Good, saying that as the Sun is the source of all illumination and understanding in the visible world, the ὁρατός τόπος, the Good is the supreme source of being and understanding in the world of the forms, the νοητὸς τόπος or «Intelligible world». Plato then amplifies this image in his famous allegory of the cave at the beginning of Book VII of the *Republic*. In this famous passage, Plato symbolizes normal human life as life in a cave, and then describes the ascent of one of the cave-dwellers up out of the cave where he sees for the first time the dazzling light of the Sun outside the cave.

Thus in Book VI of the *Republic* we see the image of the Sun used as a metaphor for the Form of the Good – the source of all being which exists in the «Intelligible world» beyond the ordinary «Visible world» of human experience – and then in Book VII, in the allegory of the cave, this same image of the Sun is used even more concretely to symbolize that which exists outside of the normal human world represented by the cave. In addition, as has often been noted, there seems to have been a connection in Plato's imagination between his allegory in Book VII of the *Republic* of the ascent of the cave dweller to the sunlit world outside the cave and his myth in the *Phaedrus* (247 B-C) of the ascent of the Soul to the realm outside of the cosmos where «True Being» dwells.

No earlier myth has told of a place beyond the heavens, a ὑπερουράνιος τόπος, but this is not the first occasion on which the true Being, the οὐσία ὄντως οὖσα, has been given a local habitation (Ulansey 1994: 258). In the passage of *Republic* VI which introduces the famous comparison of the Form of the Good to the Sun we have a νοητὸς τόπος contrasted with a ὁρατός τόπος (508C): but a spatial metaphor is hardly felt there.

A truer approximation to the ὑπερουράνιος τόπος occurs in the simile of the cave in *Republic* VII, where we are plainly told that the prisoners' ascent into the light of day symbolizes the ascent of the Soul to the noetic, τὴν εἰς τὸν νοητὸν τῆς ψυχῆς ἄνοδον (517B); in fact, the νοητὸς τόπος of the first simile has in the second developed into a real spatial symbol.

So there is a connection in Plato's mind between the ascent from the cave in the *Republic* and the ascent to the «Hypercosmic Place» in the *Phaedrus*. Because the movement upward had found its fullest expression in the allegory of the cave in the *Republic*. Now in the *Phaedrus* the dimension of the above is stated according to the new cosmic co-ordinates. For the νοητὸς τόπος, the «Intelligible Place» in the *Republic* (509D; 517B) now becomes the ὑπερουράνιος τόπος, , the «Place beyond the Heavens» (Friedländer 1958: 194).

What is, of course, important to see here is that there exists already in Plato the obvious raw material for the emergence of the idea of the Hypercosmic Sun: when the prisoners escape the cave in the *Republic* what they find outside it is the Sun, but the vision of what is outside the cave in the *Republic* is linked in Plato's mind with the vision of what is outside the cosmos in the myth recounted in the *Phaedrus*. It would therefore be a natural and obvious step for a Platonist to imagine that what is outside the cosmic cave of the *Republic* – namely, the Sun, the visible symbol of the highest of the Forms and of the source of all being – is also what is to be found outside the cosmos in the Hypercosmic Place described in the *Phaedrus*. An intermediate stage in the development of the concept of the Hypercosmic Sun between Plato and the *Chaldaean oracles* can be glimpsed in Philo's writings (for example *De op. mund.* VIII, 31 [Colson 1929: 25]; cfr. Wolfson 1947: 294-324).

Philo refers to the existence in the intelligible sphere of a ὑπερουράνιος ἀστήρ, a «Hypercosmic Star» which he links with the image of sunlight, and which he sees as the ultimate source of the light in the visible heavens (cfr. Boyancé 1963: 33-51). Philo's formulation here is, of course, strikingly similar to the Chaldaean concept of the Hypercosmic Sun, because the Chaldaeans distinguished between two fiery bodies: one of a noetic nature and the visible Sun (Klein 1962: 68 ff.). The former was said to conduct the latter. As we stated, according to Proclus, the Chaldaeans call the «Solar world» situated in the supramundane region «Entire Light» (Lewy 1956: 151; Boyancé 1936: 65-77). The course that goes from Plato through Middle Platonism to the *Chaldaean oracles* continues beyond the time of the *Chaldaean oracles* into early Neoplatonism, for we find the concept of the existence of two Suns clearly spelled out in the writings of Plotinus, in a context that makes it clear that for Plotinus one of these Suns was «Hypercosmic». In his *Enneads*, Plotinus speaks of two Suns, one being the normal visible Sun and the other being an «Intelligible Sun» (*Enn.* IV, 3,11, 14-22 [Faggin 1992^3: 578]).

What is especially interesting is that in the same third chapter of the fourth Ennead, a mere six paragraphs after the passage just quoted, Plotinus explicitly locates the intelligible realm – which he has just told us is the location of a second Sun – in the space beyond the heavens (*Enn.* IV, 3,17, 1-6 [Faggin 1992³: 586]). In any event, we here find Plotinus first positing the existence of an «Intelligible Sun» besides the normal visible Sun, and then locating the intelligible realm spatially in the region beyond the outermost boundary of the heavens (Majercik 2001: 265 ff.).

Finally, to return to the *Chaldaean oracles*, the fact that the Chaldaean concept of the «Hypercosmic Sun» was at least sometimes taken in a completely literal and spatial sense is shown by a passage from the Platonizing Emperor Julian's *Hymn to Helios*. According to Julian, in certain unnamed mysteries it is taught that «the Sun travels in the starless heavens far above the region of the fixed stars» (*Orat.* IV, 148A [Wright 1962: 405]). Given the fact that Julian's thinking was steeped in the Neoplatonic philosophy of Iamblichus who was deeply committed to the *Chaldaean oracles* as a source of divinely inspired knowledge, and given the fact that the doctrine of the Hypercosmic Sun is an established teaching of the *Chaldaean oracles*, it is virtually certain that Julian is referring here to the teaching of the *oracles* (Turcan 1975: 124).

The passage from Julian, therefore, shows that the Hypercosmic Sun of the *Chaldaean oracles* was understood as being hypercosmic not in a merely symbolic or metaphysical sense (Eitrem 1942: 54 ff.), but rather in the literal sense of being located physically and spatially in the region beyond the outermost boundary of the cosmos defined by the sphere of the fixed stars.

As stated from the beginning, we have shown that in the late second century C.E. there is in the *Chaldaean oracles* the doctrine of the existence of two Suns: one the normal, visible Sun, and the other a Hypercosmic Sun. The evidence from Julian shows that the hypercosmic nature of this second Sun was understood as meaning that it was literally located beyond the outermost sphere of the fixed stars. The fact that the *Chaldaean oracles* emerged out of the milieu of Middle Platonism suggests that the doctrine of the Hypercosmic Sun found in the *oracles* did not develop overnight, but that it has roots in the Platonic tradition, most likely, as we have seen, going back ultimately to Plato himself: specifically, to the allegory in the *Republic* of the ascent beyond the world-cave to the sunlit realm outside and the related myth of the *Phaedrus* describing the ascent of the Soul towards its ultimate vision of the ὑπερουράνιος τόπος, the Hypercosmic Place beyond the heavens. An intermediate stage between Plato and the *Chaldaean oracles* is to be found in Philo's reference to the ὑπερουράνιος ἀστήρ, the Hypercosmic Star which is the source of the light of the visible heavenly bodies, and slightly later than the *Chaldaean oracles* we find Plotinus making reference to two suns, one of them being in the intelligible realm which he places spatially beyond the heavens.

We may say, therefore, that it is likely that there existed in Middle Platonic circles during the second century C.E. – and probably much earlier as well – speculations about the existence of a second Sun besides the normal, visible Sun: a Hypercosmic Sun located in that «Place beyond the Heavens», the ὑπερουράνιος τόπος described in Plato's *Phaedrus*.

We see here, of course, a striking parallel with the iconography of the misteries of Mithras in which we also find two Suns, one being Helios the Sun-god (who is always distinguished from Mithras in the iconography) and the other being Mithras in his role as *Sol invictus*, the unconquered Sun. On the basis of this explanation of Mithras as the personification of the force responsible for the precession of the equinoxes this striking parallel becomes readily explicable. For, as we have seen, the Hypercosmic Sun of the Platonists is located beyond the sphere of the fixed stars, in Plato's ὑπερουράνιος τόπος.

As is well known, Porphyry, quoting Eubulus, explains in the *Cave of the Nymphs* that the Mithraic cave in which Mithras kills the bull and which the Mithraic temple imitates was meant to be an image of the cosmos (*De antr. nymph*. VI [Simonini 1986: 44]). And it is linked with the Soul's journey that goes toward proper location precisely in that same «Hypercosmic Realm» where the Platonists imagined their Hypercosmic Sun to exist (see also Macrobius, *Sat*. I, 17-1, 23, 21[Marinone 1967 : 242-304], for the Porphyry's prayer to the Sun). A Platonizing Mithraist (of whom there must have been many – witness Numenius, Cronius, and Celsus), therefore, would almost automatically have been led to identify Mithras with the Platonic Hypercosmic Sun, in which case Mithras would become a second Sun besides the normal, visible Sun. Therefore, the rock-birth of Mithras is a symbolic representation of hypercosmic nature of the Soul. Capable of moving the entire universe, Mithras is essentially greater than the cosmos, and cannot be contained within the cosmic sphere (Beck 1988: 2-3). He is therefore pictured as bursting out of the rock that symbolizes the cosmos – not unlike the prisoner emerging from the cosmic cave described by Plato in *Republic* VII), breaking through the boundary of the universe represented by the rock's surface and establishing his presence in the Hypercosmic Place indicated by the space into which he emerges outside of the rock. The place where turn itself the Soul in the afterlife (Ulansey 1994: 262-263).

During their journey, the Souls gazing down from an unspecified place discern, extended from above through the heaven and the earth, a beam of light like a pillar that is compared with the rainbow probably on account of its transparency. To this they came after going forward a day's journey, and they saw there at the middle of the light the extremities of its fastenings stretched from heaven; for this light was the girdle of the heavens like the under-girders of triremes, holding together in like manner the entire revolving vault (Brendel 1977: 52 ff.).

Most likely this rainbow-like pillar of light is to be understood as the super-celestial sight of the Milky Way which, in Pythagorean concepts at least, is conveyed as an outermost circle of fire and the force surrounding the whole (cfr. Cicer. *Somn. Scip*. III). At any rate, from this passage, leaving aside the known difficulties of verbal and contextual interpretation, we derive the following: the sky is held together from the outside by bands as a barrel is by staves (Adam 1902: 446 ff.). In the *Timaeus* (36 B-C) the cosmos is actually constructed as a sphere from two such rings, perhaps circles of the heavens like the sidereal equator and the ecliptic (Taylor 1928: 146-148; 160 ff.). These intersect like the strokes of a χ □ (*chi*) in the letter forms of the fifth century B.C.

If one translates these descriptions into the imagery of the monuments, the result is a well-known sight: it is the picture of the celestial sphere with crossed bands that medieval art took over from Roman antiquity. With a cross attached on top, it was sanctioned as the orb of the Holy Roman Empire. Thus, this significant and much used symbol can claim to illustrate a concept of the heavens already known to Plato, although at first we understood it to be a Hellenistic invention (Casadio 1997: 45 ff.); it was merely transformed by schematic rectangularity of the bands into an ornamental and popularized illustrative shape. The Zodiac and celestial equator, if these are meant, do not intersect perpendicularly but obliquely (Pfeiffer 1916: 56-58). Plato's comparison with a *chi* therefore did not necessarily gainsay the letter forms of his time (Kirchhoff 1887[4]: 95).

This calls to mind the terminology employed in earlier Greek philosophy to elucidate the character of Ananké, Necessity (Onians 1953[2]: 332-333), especially in its Pythagorean manifestation. Ananké – the cohesive force of the outer limits – was also sought, apparently, in the fiery periphery of the cosmos, as she could be the sphere of fixed stars and the outermost layer of the world (cfr. Boyancé 1946: 3 ff.; Todini 1971: 21 ff.). In this she resembles the World Soul that had been postulated in the *Timaeus*.

In the Plato's *Republic* Necessity play a central role. A passage in the story of Er (*Rep*. 617 B) do we learn that the giant spindle is moving in her lap, hence she is seated. However, the description concentrates first only on this spinning implement which not only symbolizes the single concrete outward appearance of the world but its manifold mobility, the inner mechanism of the great *machina mundi* (Brendel 1977: 54). Therefore Ananké cannot be intertwined with it as law, but appears suddenly as principal cause, a *primum movens* of the whole as divine person (Adam 1902: 452). The picture is thereby completely changed. It will change again just as suddenly, when (*Rep*. 617 D), derived from a different concept, the same Ananké takes part in the judgment of the dead and the election of the Souls. To understand the passage, it is essential to recognize its metamorphic character. The images flow into each other like the freely shifting scenes of a dream, and, like a genuine dream, they base their unreality in general on separate elements of reality which in return become individually recognizable as historically comprehensible concepts.

Such an element is the image of the universe surrounded by bands. Anankē, the spinner who is quite unexpectedly introduced as the cause of their movement, must be seen in a similar light. It is the story of Er Armenios the Pamphylian, the slain man visits the next world and returns to life. The purpose of the latter version is to describe the justice of the afterlife, not to emphasize the resurrection of Er. Classical writers identify the supernatural traveler as Zoroaster (Kroll 1894: 28).

The transformation of one image into the other is described just before (*Rep.* 616 D). The first words seem to continue the context: we learn that Anankē's spindle is attached to the same shaft from which the bands of heaven start whereby our contemplation is suddenly directed upwards and we become simultaneously acquainted with the reasons for the just mentioned rotation of the world. Here now the cosmos has been changed, from one word to another, as it were, into a spinning implement which is entirely new. It is indeed that part onto which the thread, weighted by the whorl, is spooled as it emerges from the loose material of the distaff; it is the only movable part. The conclusion one might naturally derive from this image would be that the world is the web of Necessity (Peterson 1948: 199ff.; Rudolph 2000; 149 ff.; Albrile 2005: 5 ff.).

Yet this is nowhere stated nor is it what was intended by the Platonic concept. In fact, not the web but the whorls are the subject of the discussion; thus the idea has taken a new turn which is equivalent to a sudden interruption of the hitherto coherent concept. The break, if this is what we may call the interlocking of the visions, happens just in that passage where the discussion of the theory of the spheres begins (*Rep.* 616 D). The metamorphosis of the impersonal image of the cosmos into the mythical personification precedes this and is accordingly its prerequisite, although not its real cause as will be demonstrated momentarily. First we must study the figure of the spinning woman because she creates the predominant, higher idea for all that follows (Brendel 1977: 55-56).

The Greeks knew the spinner as goddess of fate but called her Moira, also Aisa, not Anankē (Gundel 1914: 48). She belonged from early times not so much to myth as to poetic tradition, even as early as Homer (*Il.* XX, 127 ss.). The lyric fragment has Aisa, exactly like Plato's Anankē, operating an adamant spindle. On the whole she seems to have remained a rather abstract personality whose origin could be easily remembered by her name (Eitrem 1931: 2449). However, the plurality of two, three or more Moirai, is at home in the myth where they are nymph like, indistinct beings bearing a striking resemblance even in art to the sisterly groups of Nymphs or Horai.

The act of spinning is originally foreign to them (Eitrem 1931: 2480) and it is noteworthy that they existed for a long time on monuments without any attributes; their influence is exerted by their magic presence. In Homer Aisa is once surrounded by the κλῶθες (*Od.* VII, 197 ss.; Onians 1953[2]: 335), perhaps the combination of Fate-goddess and women spinning most similar to the Platonic group, as the name clearly indicates. Moreover, we must consider that all these beings, following an old religious tendency, are always concerned with the individual fate of humans and gods, something that appears only later in Plato's account. On the contrary, his Anankē has indeed a hyper-individual and hyper- human character which already indicates how far removed from this domain his story is, its wealth of references surpassing it; the basic concept is different and though there is often a reminiscence of the concept of the Moirai and a connection with them in poetry and religious belief, we can neither grasp it clearly nor understand it fully from this concept alone (Brendel 1977: 57-58).

These recall the cult at Hierapolis that was not organized before Hellenistic times, but the goddess, known as Atargatis or by some other name, definitely originates earlier (Garstang 1929: 305-307). Conceptually she incorporates various elements, including the ancient image of the spinning goddess (Cumont 1901: 2236-2243). At an early stage she was associated with the great mother sanctuaries of Asia Minor.

Some Hittite reliefs expressing the same religious idea should probably be included in this broader context. Here again we find the seated mother or matron with κάλαθος, mirror and spindle (Garstang 1929: 230; 224). The basic idea, expressed by venerable attributes, is generally the same. Even theological speculation, unfortunately understandable only at a later stage, has preserved a notion of the homogeneity of these beings and by preference made them the object of mystic contemplation. Much is to be learned from this for the conflation of goddess of fate, cosmic mother and heavenly queen in the image of the Syrian goddess and similar figures (Cumont 1901: 2239).

Only thereby is the totality of those global and governing qualities rendered in a divine spinner; these qualities are the essence of the Platonic Anankē and can only be realized by a universal goddess. Here she is enthroned as cult image in full view, a celestial goddess, a spindle in her hand, endowed with almost unlimited power over all things living and dead; here she proves to be a genuine and ancient image of the myth. As far as she is called Aphrodite – one of her many names – she is Urania (Cumont 1901: 2240), and as such she can eventually be found again in the Greek domain of Orphic hymns. As celestial Aphrodite she is the mother of Anankē and mistress of the three Moirai (*Orph. Hymn.* LV, 1-10 [Ricciardelli 2000: 144]), elsewhere the eldest of the Moirai (cfr. Paus. I, 19, 1). Since Plato himself did not use the name Aphrodite in connection with Ananke̅, we do not have to enter into the Greek domain for the time being. But it does serve to reveal how this image of the spindle goddess could become a part of the existing concepts of the powers of fate in the story of Er, that is, simply by representing the Celestial being. It is possibly recognizable in her the primal mother or rather one of the primal mothers of the Platonic Ananke̅ (Dieterich 1891: 101-103).

Thus, the account of the apparently dead, later resurrected man was an oriental fairy tale which Plato explicitly introduced through the narrator, and it is not surprising to come across, traces of a celestial or mother religion from Asia Minor; this being a further proof of the validity of Plato's statement about its place of origin which was in any case beyond doubt (Eisler 1910: I, 97-99). If, however, the basic mythical concept from which the vision of Ananke̅ evolved could be found there and named, then, going back to the text proper, it is almost possible now to set the dream image visibly side by side with its counterpart in mythical reality.

On these monuments the celestial sphere nowhere resembles the spindle but rather the distaff, since it occasionally even displays crossed bands which obviously served to hold the clew of loose wool together. One would think that the analogy with the celestial globe would be perfect. If instead Plato transferred the mythical comparison to the spindle, whose corresponding appearance in art is hardly demonstrable, there must be a reason, and that is: when they are in use, the distaff is motionless, whereas the spindle turns. That, however, is the point of the myth; the concept is to proceed from the visual impression of the world as sphere to an understanding of the revolving spheres. Therefore not even the image of the turning spindle is sufficient, for when the distaff is empty, owing to the fully wound clew, the spindle approaches a spherical shape (Onians 1953^2: 334-335). The spindle passes through the centre, a miniature counterpart of the axis of the universe; again at the top we find the hook made of adamant which distinguishes the image of the spindle. In Pythagorean speculations about the appearance of the world there may even have been an analogy for it (cfr. Stob. *Ecl*. I, 256).

Archeological evidence shows that an example of Ananke̅'s spindle from Ephesus corresponds more closely with Plato's view mentioned above (Schuhl 1930b: 62; pl. 6). This object does have concentric circles decorating the surface, but of course it is all one piece. A disc-like whorl made of bone, in the British Museum may prove that the ornamentation with concentric circles continues over a long period (Brendel 1977: 65; pl. XXI). How remarkably well such top-like implements can serve as images of the celestial sphere is shown by comparing them with one of the schematic diagrams of the sky which, to illustrate the structure of the universe, remained in use up to the late Middle Ages. The Platonic metaphor of hemispherical bowls fitting into one another is confirmed by the disc-like surface produced, but the rest of the arrangement presented as real is not.

This is Plato's unique invention, and it served solely as illustration of the theory of the sphere in its special form. It arises from the possibility of relating a real object, constructed like the mechanism of the cosmos, to the image of the mythical spinner, which is always known as a superordinate concept (Schuhl 1930a: 249). This mechanism goes back itself to the Manilius' verses: *Quippe etiam mundi faciem sedesque movebit / Sidereas, caelumque novum versabit in orbem* (*Astr.* I, 4, 267-268 [Breiter 1907: 98]), where the universe is spherical and the Demiurge makes it round as a ring (*Timaeus* 33 B ; cfr. *Laws* 898 A-B). And this implies the existence of an artificial sphere that imitated the sky and its movement (Schuhl 1930a: 247-248). Also it is possible that the works *Sphaera graecanica* and *Sphaera barbarica* were something like this, because the name of Neopythagorean writer Nigidius Figulus recall *orbem ad celeritatem rotae figuli torqueri* (*Schol. ad Lucan. in Phars.* I, 369; Carcopino 1930: 73 n.1), that is the image of the potter's wheel.

Both statements are allegorically valid for the universe; these images are not parts of a systematic deduction but of a slowly developing, dream-like and mythical vision. Therein lies their inner unity. Properly speaking, each of them, but especially the image of the spindle, is a didactic metaphor created by deliberately interpreting a cosmography together with mythical, basic ideas; it is a mythico-poetic allegorical interpretation. Winding in a round motion, the Soul comes back to the Hypercosmic Place i.e. the Inner Sun: the idea will be appropriated by the *Corpus hermeticum* (Festugière-Nock 1954: 18) and later by in the Renaissance Platonism of Giovanni Pico della Mirandola's *Heptaplus* (Garin 1942: 270).

BIBLIOGRAPHICAL REFERENCES

Adam, J. a. c. (1902) *The Republic of Plato*, I-II. Cambridge (Mass.).

Albrile, E. (2005) Fragments of a Forgotten Αἰών. An outline on a Gnostic Myth. *Kervan. Rivista internazionale di studii afroasiatici*, 2, 5-10. Torino.

Beck, R. (1988) *Planetary Gods and Planetary Orders in the Mysteries of Mithras* (EPRO 109). Leiden.

Bidez, J. (1936) Proclus Περὶ τῆς ἱερατικῆς τέχνης. *Annuaire de l'Institut de Philologie et d'Histoire Orientales et Slaves*, 4 (Mélanges Franz Cumont), 85-97. Bruxelles.

Boyancé, P. (1936) *Études sur le songe de Scipion*. Paris.

Boyancé, P. (1946) Les Muses et l'armonie des sphères, in AA.VV., *Mélanges dédiés à la mémoire de F. Grat*, I, 3-16. Paris.

Boyancé, P. (1963) Études philoniennes. *Revue des Études Grecques*, 76, 33-51. Paris.

Breiter, Th. a c. (1907) *M. Manilii Astronomica*, I: *Carmina*. Leipzig.

Brendel, O.J. (1977) *Symbolism of the Sphere. A Contribution to the History of Earlier Greek Philosophy* (EPRO 67). Leiden.

Brillante, C. (1986) Il sogno nella riflessione dei presocratici. *Materiali e discussioni per l'analisi dei testi classici*, 16, 30-47. Pisa.

Brisson, L. (2000) La place des *Oracles Chaldaïques* dans la *Théologie platonicienne*, in A. Ph. Segonds – C. Steel (a c.), *Proclus et la theologie platonicienne*, Actes du Colloque international de Louvain (13-16 mai 1998) en l'honneur de H. D. Saffrey et L. G. Westerink, 109-162. Paris.

Casadio, G. (1997) Dall'Aion ellenistico agli Eoni-Angeli gnostici. *Avallon*, 42, 45-62. Rimini.

Carcopino, J. (1930) *Virgile et le Mystére de la IVe Églogue*. Paris.

Colson, F.H. a c. (1929) *Philo*, I . London.

Cumont, F. (1901) Dea Syria, in *PWRE*, IV, 2236-2243. Stuttgart.

Dieterich, A. (1891) *Abraxas. Studien zur religionsgeschichte der späteren Altertums*, Festschrift H. Usener. Leipzig-Berlin (repr. Aalen 1973).

Eisler, R. (1910) *Weltenmantel und Himmelszelt*, I-II. München.

Eitrem, S. (1931) Moira, in *PWRE*, XV, 2449-2497. Stuttgart.

Eitrem, S. (1942) La théurgie chez les néoplatoniciens et dans les papyrus magiques. *Symbolae Osloenses*, 22, 49-79. Oslo.

Faggin, G. a c. (1992³) *Plotino Enneadi*. Milano.

Faraggiana di Sarzana, Ch. a c. (1985) *Proclo I Manuali I testi magico-teurgici. Marino Vita di Proclo*. Milano.

Festugière, A.-J. (1968) Contemplation philosophique et art théurgique chez Proclus, in U. Bianchi (a. c.), *Studi di Storia Religiosa della Tarda Antichità*, 7-18. Messina.

Festugière, A.-J.–Nock, A.D. a c. (1954) *Corpus Hermeticum*, III. Paris.

Friedländer, P. (1958) *Plato I. An Introduction*. New York.

Garin, E. a c. (1942) *Giovanni Pico della Mirandola De hominis dignitate, Heptaplus, De ente et uno*. Firenze.

Garstang, J. (1928) *The Hittite Empire*. London.

Gnoli, Gh. (1979) Ašavan. Contributo allo studio del libro di Ardā Wirāz, in Gh. Gnoli-A.V. Rossi (a c.), *Iranica* (IUO – Seminario di studi Asiatici, *Series Minor* X), 387-452. Napoli.

Gundel, W. (1914) *Beiträge zur Entwicklungsgeschichte der Begriffe Ananke und Heimarmene*. Giessen.

Kirchhoff, A. (1887^4) *Studien zur Geschichte des griechischen Alphabets*. Berlin.

Klein, F.N. (1962) *Die Lichttterminologie bei Philon von Alexandrien und in den hermetischen Schriften. Untersuchungen zur Struktur der religiösen Sprache der hellenistischen Mystik*. Leiden.

Kroll, W. (1894) *De oraculis Chaldaicis*. Breslau (repr. Hildesheim 1962).

Lewy H.(1956) *Chaldaean Oracles and Theurgy: Misticism, Magic and Platonism in the later Roman Empire*, Le Caire (nouvelle édition par M. Tardieu, Études augustiniennes, 1978).Paris.

Majercik, R. (2001) Chaldean Triads in Neoplatonic Exegesis: Some Reconsideration. *Classical Quarterly*, 51, 265-296. London.

Marinone, N. a c. (1967) *Macrobio Teodosio I Saturnali*, (repr. 1987). Torino.

Nardi, B. (1977) Luce, in AA.VV., *Dizionario delle Idee*, 647a-649a. Firenze.

Onians, R.B. (1953^2) *The Origins of European Thought about the Body, the Mind, the Soul, the World, Time and Fate*. Cambridge-New York-Melbourne.

Peterson, E. (1948) La liberation d'Adam de l'Ἀνάγκη. *Revue Biblique*, 55, 199-214. Jerusalem.

Pfeiffer, E. (1916) *Studien zum antiken Sternglauben* (ΣΤΟΙΧΕΙΑ II). Leipzig-Berlin.

Robinson, J. a c. (1984) *The Nag Hammadi Library in English*, Second edition. Leiden.

Rudolph, K. (2000) *La gnosi* (Biblioteca di cultura religiosa 63). Brescia.

Saffrey, H.D. (1981) Les néoplatoniciens et les *Oracles Chaldaïques*. *Revue des Études Augustiniennes*, 27, 209-225. Paris.

Saffrey, H.D. (1984) La devotion de Proclus au Soleil, in AA.VV., *Philosophes non chrétiens et christianisme*, 73-86. Bruxelles.

Schlachter, A. (1927) *Der Globus, seine Entstehung und Verwendung in der Antike* (ΣTOIXEIA VIII). Leipzig-Berlin.

Schuhl, P.-M. (1930a) Un mécanisme astronomique dans la quatrième Églogue de Virgile. *Revue Archéologique*, Ser. V, 31, 246-252. Paris.

Schuhl, P.-M. (1930b) Autour du fuseau d'Ananké. *Revue Archéologique*, Ser. V, 32, 58-64 (pl. VI-VII). Paris.

Sodano, A.R. a. c. (1964), *Porphyrii in Platonis Timaeum commentaria*. Napoli.

Taylor, A.E. (1928) *A Commentary of Plato's Timaeus*. Oxford.

Todini, U. (1971) La cosmologia pitagorica e le Muse enniane. *Rivista di Cultura Classica e Medioevale*, 13, 21-38. Roma.

Turcan, R. (1975) *Mithras Platonicus. Recherches sur l'hellénisation philosophique de Mithra* (EPRO 47). Leiden.

Ulansey, D. (1994), Mithras and the Hypercosmic Sun, in J.R. Hinnells (a c.), *Studies in Mithraism* (Storia delle Religioni 9), 257-264. Roma.

Wolfson H.A. (1947) *Philo. Foundations of Religious Philosophy in Judaism, Christianity and Islam*, I. Cambridge (Mass.).

Internet and the Resurrection of a God: the Neo-Mithraic Communities by Dr. Israel Campos[3]

University of Las Palmas of Gran Canaria, Spain.

Abstract

The atmosphere of spiritual agitation that was present in the first centuries of the Roman Empire that allowed the spread of the mystery religions has been reproduced in Western society over the twentieth and early twenty-first. In this context is possible to find the revival of religious models inspired by religiosity before the triumph of Christianity. Within this perspective, we have identified several groups of people joined around the god Mithra; these groups have formed a neo-pagan cult whose main characteristic is the use of the Internet as a dissemination tool.

Religion has traditionally been an element of expression of inner feelings that human societies have expressed in connection with divinity throughout history. The vehicles of expression of this religiosity have been adapted from time to time, into ways of expression that each society has seen as its own. Myths, legends, images and temples have had a special role; however, the Internet today is the most significant vehicle of dissemination used by those wishing to share and disseminate their religious beliefs.

In the dominating sociological context that has developed during the last thirty or forty years, it has become customary to see, from time to time, the emergence of new patterns of expression of religious feeling, most of which seek to overcome the traditional religious systems based upon a still strong and recognizable religious institution, such as the Catholic Church. These new currents have been often branded under the sociological parameters of "New Religious Movements" (NRM), as an attempt to provide a theoretical framework to the large number of individual or group initiatives who have found in spirituality, with all its potential variants of expression, the tool to search for answers to their personal concerns. It is important to clarify that the emergence of these alternatives to the "traditional religions" is not an innovation of our time, but in the last quarter of the twentieth century it has become a rising

---

[3] This article is a revision and expansion of a paper presented at the International Online Conference "Human @ Religion @ Internet" in 2007

phenomenon, with a faster diffusion rate and a surprising adaptive instinct capable to use very efficiently the communication resources that modern society provides (Leon 2001; Ramos 2004). Sects and heresies are well-known in Ancient History; these terms were used to refer to those groups that diverged from the mainstream model of religion. In the early days of Christianity, those concepts always presumed a derogatory connotation, and thereafter the term "paganism", was viewed with a sense of confrontation against the Christian religion. However, an overall review of the history of Christianity in Europe provides us immediately with a lot of evidence that argues that many "pagan" elements managed to survive clandestinely, fed by individuals or groups who tried to maintain a relationship with these remote cults and religions. This is one of the reasons that explain the prevalence of "Neo-paganism" and its "revolutionary" role within the, more general, New Age movement. As noted by W.J. Hanegraaff (1996: 77) "neo-paganism covers all those modern movements which are, firstly, based on the conviction that what Christianity has traditionally denounced as idolatry and superstition actually represents / represented a profound and meaningful religious worldview and, secondly, that a religious practice based on this worldview can and should be revitalized in our modern world". Therefore, the roots of the neo-pagan movement can be found in its confrontation with Christianity, as a religion that starred in the triumph of monotheism against the Graeco-Roman polytheism, and that has conditioned the way of life and the expression of religiosity of individuals from that time. Although Neo-paganism is just a part of a whole set of new religious formulations that are covered under the general term New Age, one particular feature of neo-pagans, compared to many other members of NRM, is the disposition of being avid readers, because they find in academic literature and semi-scholar pamphlets the information they need to give substance to their inventions and practices and the foundations of their former cults.

NEO-MITHRAIST GROUPS

The religious groups that we want to discuss in this communication are included, correspondingly, in the Neo-Pagan definition given above. During the last four years we have been tracking several information sources that confirm the formation of several groups around the world organized under the invocation-avocation of an ancient divinity of Iranian origin called Mithra. The particularity which connected these testimonies was that the Internet had become the main way of communication between their members. The cult of god Mithra had its origins in the ancient Iranian religious pantheon and then found a special place in the Zoroastrian religion, practiced by the Iranian people of the Achaemenid, Arsacid and Sassanid dynasties – and nowadays by small groups of Zoroastrians dispersed throughout the world (Hinnells

2005:125). During the days of glory of the Roman Empire, a cult of mysteric nature emerged around (a Romanised version) of this god. It had a wide distribution and enjoyed acceptance among the male population until its persecution by the Christian authorities. Archaeological evidence point to the V century A.D. as the final date of this cult, because after that date no more dedicated temples have been found anywhere in Europe. The cult of Mithra was forgotten, and, although there are signs showing that certain aspects of it were Christianised, it was not until the Renaissance when the statues representing this divinity reappeared, and when scholars started to wonder about the religion which existed around this god. Until the late XIX c. there was not a single rigorous study interpreting Mithra and the characteristics of its ancient worship. After that date, in parallel to the increasing interest about the Mysteries of Mithra, several individuals also started to show some interest about the "revival" of this religion (Guthrie 1918). Some authors have sought evidences of Mithraic elements in some ceremonies performed at Masonic lodges; others have considered that Mithra and his cult have indirectly shaped ceremonies in some sects like the Ordo Templi Orientis or great Wiccan rite (Nabarz 2005: 14).

We have chosen the term "Neo-Mithraists" because the defining characteristics of the different groups involved in the re-birth of the Mithra cult, which fully coincide with the elements described before in relation with Neo-paganism of the New Age. It has been generally perceived that the ultimate reason that attracts these individuals to the cult of Mithra is to find an answer to fatigue caused both by today's society and traditional religious models. However, they show not only a religious or experiential interest, but also training and academic knowledge of the religion's elements in which they want to actively participate. The most visible groups of neo-Mithraists can be easily located around five distinct territories (Great Britain, Germany, France, Spain and Italy), although, the physical location, despite affecting the particular characteristics of involvement, organisation or incidence, is not really decisive, since their active presence on Internet, can overcome any geographical limitations.

INTERNET AS A DISSEMINATION TOOL.

As mentioned above, one of the main features shared by these different groups of new followers of the god Mithra is that Internet has become their main instrument of organisation, communication and dissemination. Therefore, they are directly connected with an element that also characterises the way in which, in our day, there is a rising expression of religious feeling. The use of the Internet as a channel to express and find answers to the personal search in connection with a religion is in continuous growth, since the Internet is a new way to offer a "new and improved form of community" (Foltz 2003: 322).

From the perspective of this research, we must emphasize the huge number of websites dedicated to spread knowledge (of debatable rigour) around the god Mithra and the characteristics of his religion (there are about 840,000 entries in Google and 169,000 for "Mithraism"). In most cases we find that many of them are inspired by a revisionist motivation, with the clear intention of proving the "benefits" of Mithraism, compared with revenge and "evil" that has been present in the Catholic tradition:

http://www.jesusneverexisted.com/Mithraism-spanish.html
http://www.edwardjayne.com/Christology/mithra.html

The resources of public expression of these neo-Mithraic communities reside primarily in their official websites, where, through a variety of links, provide descriptions of what the cult of Mithra represents for them, what are their reference books, some ceremonies or organisational forms and their contact details. This informational structure is clearly present in the different portals available for groups settled in Germany, Spain and France:

·Los Amigos de Mithra [http://lam.mitra.free.fr/doc.htm] (with Spanish and French version)
·La Casa del dios Mithra, [http://personales.com/espana/madrid/DiosMithra/]
·Orden del dios Mithra, [http://ordendeldiosmithra.iespana.es/]
·Mithras - Der Kult Wiederbelebt., [http://www.datacomm.ch/olhaenzi/roem.civ13.html]

For Italy and the UK, the reference is a bit more complex, since for the Italian case it is possible to find two different forms of Mithraic expression: a website that attempts to rebuild the main features of the ancient cult of Mithra, with bibliographical references and external links [http://www.mithra.it/home1.htm], and a section within the website of the *Associazione Yoga e Terapia Naturali* [http://www.rajayoga.it/scuolamithra.html] entitled *Scuola Mithraica*, which provides a range of exercises to perform an "initiation in Mithraic grades" . For the English case, a website is available with information about the Mithraic history and then some suggestions for meditations in relation to the different grades of initiation:
[http://www.bizstore.f9.co.uk/indexmithras.htm]. A more recent website comes from Japan: [http://homepage2.nifty.com/Mithra/english_index.html], The Mithraeum Japan Official Website contains a lot of texts in Japanese and English with references to a modern way of worship to Mithra, and links to many of the websites cited before. It is very interesting that in order to identify the neo-pagan character of this group, there has been a translation into a Japanese manga character in relation to the myth related to Mithra:
[http://homepage2.nifty.com/Mithra/HP_Mithra_Myth_Comics_English.html]

In parallel to the role of promotion, dissemination and proselitization exerted by these virtual portals, we have found two additional instruments in English and Spanish that are being actively used as a complement in the organisation and consolidation processes of the new followers of the god Mithra: the main theme of several email distribution lists is eminently Mithraic. In English we found the *Mithras List*, [http://groups.yahoo.com/group/mithras/] which is described as: "a list for discussion of all things related to the god Mithras. Topics include the Mithraic Mysteries, Mithraic history, archaeology, iconography, and more. Serious scholarly discussion is welcome, as are religious topics from those interested in practising Mithraism as a living religion". Interestingly, this list aims to merge, in the same area, the academic debate with the personal experience of current followers of the Mithraic cult. The list began in 2001 and now has 614 members of both sexes mainly located in America, Australia and Europe. With a much more restricted focus, led directly to those in the work of recovering from the Mithraic Mysteries in an experiential way, we can find a list called Mithraeum. In this case, it has 143 members and was started in 2001 by an American who was the founder of the "Nova Roma" movement and the "Julian Society ". In Spanish, we can find the Official Forum of the Order of the Lord Mithra, whose declared objective is "to promote Restoration of the Mithraic Religion. But all this from the Respect, the Tolerance and the Freedom inherent in the Mithraism, and the Respect to other religions". This forum was created in 2001 and has 43 members: [http://es.groups.yahoo.com/group/ForoDelDiosMithra/], The importance of these *fora* surpasses that of the websites mentioned above, since although the latter act as a "windows" for general information about the cult and the neo-Mithraists groups, it is through active mail dialogues that the feelings or religious experiences are spread from member to member thus creating progressively a sense on of "community".

DISCUSSION

The data that we have collected in connection with the defining characteristics of the neo-pagan Mithraic groups and their diffusion over the Internet, allow us to pose two basic questions. The first one is to what extent can these groups be considered truly "Mithraists" as compared with the features of the cult of Mithra during the Roman Empire? The second question, considering Internet communication capabilities, is it possible to consider that these neo-Mithraists really constitute a religious community? Answering in detail these two questions would require a longer debate, well beyond the limits of this paper. For that reason we will summarize the discussion into the following ideas. The Mithraic religion in Roman times was a cult carried out exclusively by men who gathered to hold a liturgy itself and to develop the ceremonies of initiation. The structure was very hierarchical and communities used to be registered in the city where their temple was located. In the case of the neo-Mithraists, we have found that they accept the presence of women (a cultural and social imposition in western societies, although there were also mysteric cults in Rome that were mixed). The issue of hierarchy is represented nowadays by the importance attached to the grades of initiation, but it is not linked to the performance of a recognised explicit authority. There are moderators on the lists, but this fact does not appear to be linked to membership in the higher grade of "pater", who were the leaders in ancient Mithraic communities. In the reconstruction of the personality of Mithra evidence in some of these groups, it is possible to see the influence of a mixture of elements that highlight the dual identity of Mithra as a Persian and Roman god, while in the Roman cult, this issue had been totally minimised in order to avoid problems with the Roman authorities. On the question of whether via the Internet and its related instruments can be considered as a religious "cyber-community", we coincide affirmatively with what other researchers, as L. Dawson (2004) or H. Campbell (2005), have asserted in favour of accepting the reality of this communal fact on the Internet. The websites and, particularly, the active mailing lists serve as an instrument of communication and dissemination of news and experiences, but it is very difficult to quantify the degree of personal belonging and individual involvement that must exist in any community experience (Hackett 2006). The way in which these new groups of worshippers of Mithra have been structured suggests that most of them have focused on creating helpful spaces where stories of individual relationship with the God can be shared with the rest of the "community" members. Although it is very difficult to recognize the sincerity of religious beliefs of individuals, it is clear that in these cases of new followers of Mithra, there are elements that go beyond religious devotion. Some elements are recognized from the esoteric curiosity or belligerent response to Christian beliefs. These aspects must be added the first stage of deeper understanding of the resurrected god, thus at some point we may consider these neo-Mithraic groups as creating a new religion.

Dr. Israel Campos Méndez

Facultad de Geografía e Historia

Universidad de Las Palmas de Gran Canaria

c/ Pérez del Toro, 1, 35002 – Las Palmas de G.C.

Spain

e-mail: icampos@dch.ulpgc.es

Sources

- Campbell, Heidi. 2005, *Exploring Religious Community online: we are one in the network*. Peter Lang Publishing, New York.

- Dawson, Lorne. & Cowan, Douglas. 2004, *Religion Online, Finding Faith on the Internet*. Routledge New York.

- Foltz, Franz. 2003, "Religion on the Internet: Community and Virtual Existence". *Bulletin of Science, Technology & Society*, 23.4: 321-330

- Guthrie, K.S. 1918, *Mithraic Mysteries Restored and Modernized. Drama of Interior Initiation*. Kessinger Publishing, New York

- Hackett, Rosalind. 2006, "Religion and the Internet". *Diogenes*, 53 : 67-76

- Hanegraaff, Wouter, 1996, *New Age Religion and Western Culture: Esotericism in the Mirror of Secular Thought*. State University of New York Press, New York..

- Hinnells, John. 2005, *The Zoroastrian Diaspora: Religion and Migration*. OUP Oxford, Oxford.

- León, Osvaldo. 2001, "Movimientos Sociales en la Red, online" [http://alainet.org/publica/msred/] (accessed January 20, 2010)

- Nabarz, Payam, 2005, *The Mysteries of Mithras. The Pagan Belief That Shaped the Christian World*. Inner Traditions, Vermont.

- Ramos, Manuel. 2004, "Aproximación sociológica al uso de Internet de los Nuevos Movimientos Religiosos como nuevos movimientos sociales", *Scripta Nova*, VIII, 170(39) agosto 2004, online [http://www.ub.es/geocrit/sn/sn-170-39.htm] (accessed January 20, 2010)

Aristotle and the Natural Slave: The Athenian Relationship with India by Robert F. Mullen, M.A.

California Institute of Integral Studies.

> Those who live in a cold climate and in Europe are full of spirit, but wanting in intelligence and skill; and therefore they retain comparative freedom, but have no other political organization, and are incapable of ruling over others. *Whereas the natives of Asia are intelligent and inventive, but they are wanting in spirit* [thymos], *and therefore they are always in a state of subjection and slavery.* But the Hellenic race, which is situated between them, is likewise intermediate in character, being high-spirited and also intelligent. Hence it continues free and is the best-governed of any nation, and, if it could be formed into one state, would be able to rule the world" (My italics.)[4]

It is the purpose of this article to inquire into Aristotle's views of the non-Athenian citizen during the culmination of the 200 year reign of the Achaemenid-Persian Empire, whose influence and cultural integration provided an open channel for philosophical contacts between Greece and India from Pythagorean academics through Aristotle's tenure as tutor to Alexander. How did Aristotle's sociopolitical concept of slavery within the Greek *polis* affect his interpretation of *thymos*,[5] and how did his appraisal of Asia relegate the Indian civilization, among others, to the role of "other" and make them "natural" material for slavery as a result of his opinion that the Indic [Asiatic] peoples lacked a fully developed *psuchē* (soul).

Aristotle's justifications are researched and appraised to illuminate why the Greek aristocrat believed that Asia's [India's] collective population was bereft of a fully developed *psuchē* (soul). I will analyze interpretations of the origins and evolution of *thymos* in order to focus its relational applications. I have narrowed my research to Indo-Greco relationship because of my predisposition to that line of comparative study, understanding an evaluation of the totality of Asian civilizations would be far too considerable an effort for purposes of this article. Specificity will be based on pre-Socratic definitions of *thymos* and evidences of Greek historical affiliations with India.

---

[4] Aristotle, 1984 *Politics*. VII.7.1327 24-33.

[5] The Greek words *thymos* and *thumos* are employed intermittingly among various referential and historical materials with the sources for this paper. For purposes of coherency, *thymos* will be used throughout.

There is more than ample evidence of strong epistemological and cultural associations between the neighboring countries.[6] Was Aristotle, in justifying his claim that a stable and effective *polis* required natural slaves for production, seeking a philosophical and moral source for the "need," and discovering it in anyone "other-than-Greek" who fulfilled notions of incompleteness? As evidenced, Aristotle differentiated between Europe and Asia, citing the former's lack of intelligence and political insight, while complimenting the latter for intelligence but declaring them *lacking in spirit*. Were Aristotle's famous words an example of attuned ignorance of Indic epistemological co-dominance by way of the arrogance of a "master racist?" Was Aristotle so steeped in the heroic historicity of *thymos* exemplified by the mythological Greek-warrior *übermensch*, he was unwilling to ignore a patriotic symbolism that coerced his vision of *other than Athenian citizen* as inferior beings?

The awareness of how the divisive concept of "otherness" with its intentional conceit of superior truths to support nationalistic aspirations, which contributes to false alliances, and nationalistic and xenophobic policies, offers significant contributions to the psychology of social and political science as they relate to prejudice, judgment, diasporas, and the subsequent annihilation, assimilation and/or incorporation of diversity.

This article speculates that Aristotle did not take any nation's maturity into account when he ascribed potential slavery status, but rather, made a pure political consideration as a result of: (1) his belief in the superiority of Greek/Macedon polis governmental structure; (2) his need to support this political structure with slave labor from *other-than-Greek* territories, and; (3) his belief that there was no greater form of wholesome manliness than that which resided in the very perfect soul of the Homeric Greek warrior.

It is crucial to focus on the relationship of Indic and Greek thought in the centuries prior to the publication of *Politics*. McEvilley provides generous possibilities of cultural cross-currency, offering comparative corroboration, among others, between the *Rigveda* and Thales of Miletus; Anaximander's *aperiōn* (the indefinite) and early Upaniśadic texts; Anaximenes' concept of "divine air" and the *Atharva Veda*, and the *Chāndoga* and *Bṛhadāraṇayaka Upanishads*.[7]

How much Greco-Indic thought evolved via dialectic between great minds in the halls of hospitable inns, or in sparring debates under oasis laden fig trees scattered along the Persian Royal Road of Persia (Fig. 1). This royally constructed road for commerce brought the Ionians "into direct contact" with merchants and thinkers from the east.[8] Scholarship evidences even

---

[6] McEvilley 2002, p. 9; Gunderson 1980, p. 2.
[7] McEvilley 2002, pp. 29-35.
[8] Burkert 1992, p. 14.

earlier latitudinous assimilation, pointing to the "Greek adoption of Phoenician script" around 900 B.C.E. via a route transversing the Red Sea,[9] as well as evidence of jewelry found at Knosses, providing vestigial evidence of religious practice "directly imported from the east,"[10] circa 800 BCE.

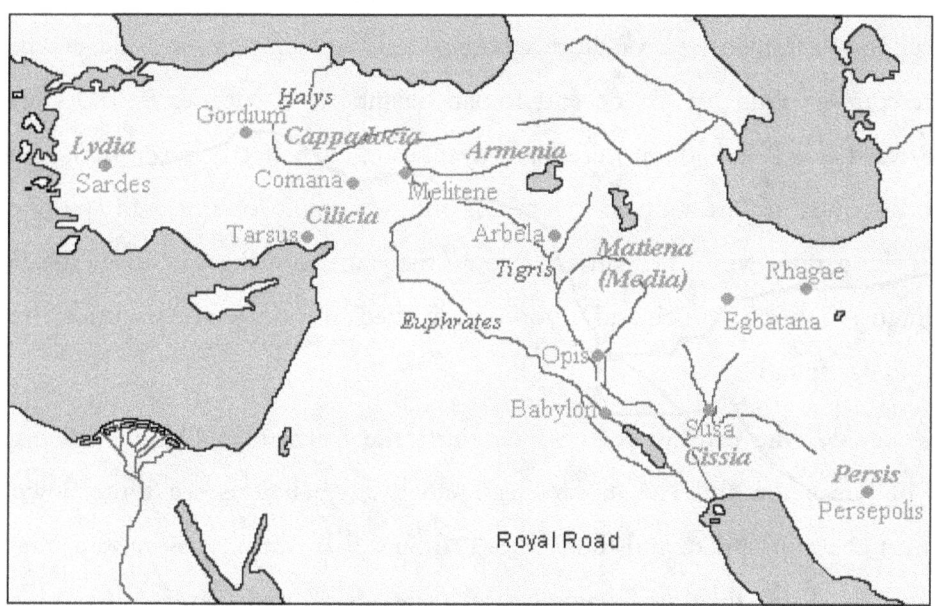

Figure 1: The Royal Road (courtesy: "darkwing.uoregon.edu")

Earlier Asian-Athenian Assimilation

There are numerous examples lending credence to philosophical interrelationships between B.C.E. India and the pre-Socratics, and this article offers concrete substantiation of discourse and exchange through oral and written association.

Avenues of interrelationships are the historical trade routes that provided continued contact between Asia and Greece from pre-historic times to the Alexandrian conquest, commencing at the height of the Achaemenid-Persian Empire (circa 545-490 B.C.E.), which encouraged the free flow of thought under the calculated benevolence of the Persian government.

In 606 B.C.E., Ninevah was the center of trade in Western Asia. Rawlinson describes "Ionian traders, Jewish captives, Phoenician merchants from distant Tarshish, and Indians from the Punjāb," converging on crowded and chaotic marketplaces.[11] Similarities of developing thought indicate the exchange and juxtaposition of ideas between early Indian and Greek

---

[9] Burkert, 1992, pp. 29,30.
[10] Ibid, p. 54.
[11] Rawlinson 1916, p. 7.

"philosophers," a borrowing or syncretic assimilation of neighboring knowledge, sometimes historically challenged but providing "justification for further research."[12]

Early Trade Routes

The myths of India's great isolation, coupled with her predisposition to aural tradition and textual absence supports the theory of a culture whose iconoclastic epistemology developed via philosophical intercourse within her Greco and Ionian neighbors. Centuries before Darius I constructed his Royal Trade Route, there were many avenues of exchange between India and the Southwest where discourse on art, culture, calendars, numbers, philosophies, and spiritualities prevailed. One of the earliest was a Persian Gulf route that ran from the mouth of the Indus River to the Euphrates towards Antioch and beyond, which tied India to East Asia and existed as far back as the 3rd millennium B.C.E.

Other routes include "the caravan road which skirts the Karmanian Desert and reaches Antioch by way of Ktesiphon and Hekatiompylus," and the treacherous sea route down the Persian and Arabian coasts to Aden, and the Red Sea to Suez.[13] It is a fair assumption that the great minds of their day shared their developing consciousness with others from India to Greece to Egypt to Mesopotamia.

The center of the Persian Empire, concentrated in what had been Babylonia, flourished with Cyrus the Great after his armies conquered the neighboring islands of Sardes, and Ionian city-states including Thales' and Anaximenes' home of Miletus, as well as Colophon, Ephesus, and Samos "where the pre-Socratic philosophers would very soon be active."[14] Soon thereafter, the Persian king annexed the area north and south of the Hindu Kush (Fig. 2), an area encompassing eastern Afghanistan, northern Pakistan, India, and a portion of western China. Forty years later in the main court in Persopolis (*Parsa:* The City of Persians) and throughout his kingdom, Darius I opened the doors to traders, poets, physicians, and other thinkers of the day. "Craftsmen of all kinds, as well as mercenaries"[15] found sanctuary, residence, and centers of studies for peoples of all the major Mediterranean civilizations. This opened further opportunities of travel further into Asia as "political contacts became more frequent" between India and the Greek states.[16]

---

[12] Dillon 2000, p. 540.
[13] Rawlinson 1916, p. 2.
[14] McEvilley 2002, p. 6.
[15] Burkert 1992, p. 24.
[16] Gunderson et al 1980, pp. 14, 15.

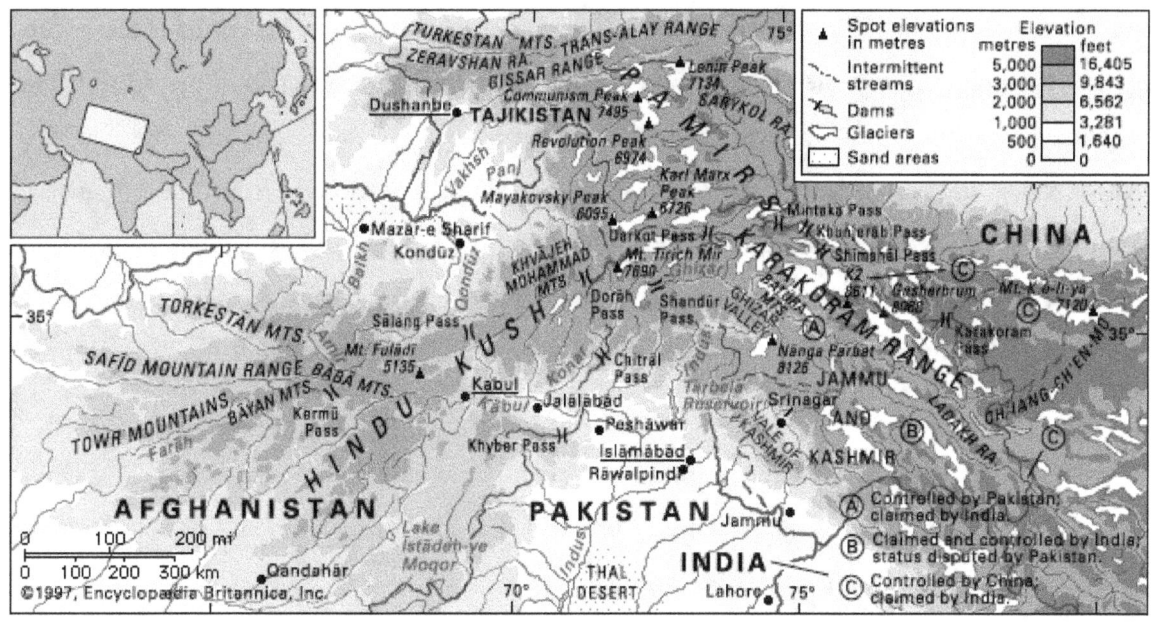

Figure 2: Hindu Kush (courtesy: "history.upenn.edu ")

To place chronology into perspective, historians cite the golden years of Persian-Greco-Indic interaction between 545 and 490 B.C.E. Anaximander was in his prime in 540 B.C.E. and Socrates was born about 20 years after the beginning of the great empire's decline. These dates include the heart of the of pre-Socratic philosophical theorizations of Pythagoras, Heraclitus, Empedocles, and others.[17] Indian dates are less concrete due to the lack of written transmission, but most surmise that the earliest *Vedic* texts orally originated circa 2,000 B.C.E., although little was scripted by pre-Socratic times. Portions of the great epics including the *Valmaki Ramayan* and *Mahabharata* flourished during the Persian era, as did the *Upanishads* (esoteric teachings), and *Brahamas* (commentaries on Sanskrit chants)—all whose contributions to Indic philopsychology and pre-Aristotelian thought cannot be minimized.

The Persian Empire's Indic-Greco interrelationship in Babylonia and Persepolis, as well as in Darius' mercenary military provided direct contact on lands "erected on the ruins of the Assyrian Empire."[18] Following are examples of the fruits of said interactions, some historically strong, others lacking direct authenticity but supportive of the "whole" in historical context.

Hecataeus (c.550-476 B.C.E.)

Hecataeus was a wealthy native of Miletus who tried to dissuade his fellow countrymen from revolting against the Persian conquerors. When the cities of Asia Minor, including Miletus, were defeated, he became ambassador to Darius' brother, Artaphenes. Hecataeus encouraged the

---

[17] McEvilley 2002, p. 18.
[18] Ibid, p. 6.

proliferation of the belief in *The Hyperboreans*, which played a large part in contemporary Greek legend. Originating from the *Uttarakuru*, a pseudo-mythical nation existing somewhere beyond the Himalayas, this proto-Indic civilization is glorified in *Vedic*, *Brahmanic*, and Buddhist texts. The Greeks believed that *Uttarakuru* shamans wandered down from the Himalayan mountaintops to Greece, [19] where they were attributed legendary status to include Orpheus and Pythagoras.[20] This migration took place from the early 6th century B.C.E.—where there are early references to Orpheus and Abaris—and continued to the death of Pythagoras.

In *Perigesis*, Hecataeus reported on fact, travel, and legend. He provided descriptions of the vast geographic terrain of the Persian Empire including "the Hindu Kush, and India." [21] Scholars credit Hecataeus with two books, each organized in the manner of a *periplus*, or coastal survey: one of "Europe," and another book on Asia.

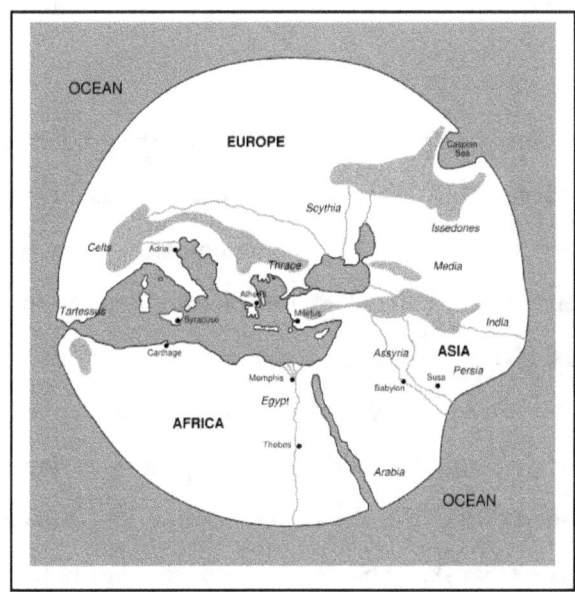

Figure 3: Hecataeus' Map   Courtesy: "mlahanas.de"

Herodotus and Heraclitus

According to extant materials, Herodotus is the first Greek to offer extensive observations on India. In the earliest books *The Histories* between 431 and 425 B.C.E, he writes of Democedes, a Greek physician to Darius through circumstances that kept him in relative captivity. It is rumored his freedom was granted when he was able to cure the queen's breast ulcer, and he frequently emigrated to Croton, the site of the Pythagorean schools, carrying with him wondrous

---

[19] Rawlinson 1916, p. 25.
[20] West 1971, p. 214.
[21] Gunderson et al 1980, p. 14.

stories of India garnered from his travels.[22] Herodotus wrote of India as far as the Panjab, which was the end of the world. He described dark-skinned "Ethiopian" Dravidians, and blond Aryans of the north. Herodotus also made a "very interesting reference to a religious sect whose members killed no life, lived a strict vegetarian diet, and had no houses," whom future historians hypothesized might be a reference to practices of Buddhism or Jainism.[23]

Heraclitus, another Greek pre-Socratic, lived in Ephesus, located on the west coast of Turkey. He taught distinctive theories on universal flux, the unity of opposites, and elemental physics. Although only fragments remain of his book, the philosopher was extolled by many historians including Plutarch, Aristotle, and Sextus Empiricus. Heraclitus had an early understanding that the soul, an evolving conceptual force, "possesses depths which cannot be grasped."[24] Heraclitus was active around 485 B.C.E. during the period when Darius was planning his historical attack on the Greek mainland at Marathon. "Darius saw himself as a new Threatona, the mythical Iranian hero who was said to have slain a three-headed monster; for him—and through him—history was regenerated, for it was in fact the revivification—the reactualization—of a primordial heroic myth." The similarities to Homeric mythology and that of India are too powerful to be ignored.[25]

The battle of Marathon, as well as the one at Attica included mercenaries and slaves from India. West notes the connections between Heraclitus' and Indic religion, offering substantial proof of comparative thought between the Greek philosopher and the *Brihadāranyaka Upanishad*.[26]

Ktesis and revisionism

An additional example of the early pre-Socratic Indic-Greco interrelationship is found in the small corpus of Ktesis (Ctesias). While it is true is that Plutarch called Ktesis an ambitious, inaccurate "liar" in reference to his accounts of India,[27] Ktesis did have peripheral knowledge through close sources, and wrote extensively of the civilization in his book, *Indika*. However, resulting from these personal denigrations by Plutarch and other detractors, the exactitude of his

---

[22] Ibid, p. 145.
[23] Rawlinson 1916, p. 22.
[24] Long 1973 pp. 3, 4.
[25] Eliade 1954, p. 37.
[26] West 1971, pp. 201, 202; McEvilley 2002, p. 44.
[27] Gunderson et al 1980, p. 16.

accuracy is not taken seriously by scholars. Rawlinson writes of Ktesis' inclusion of "grotesque legends," and declares his other writings to be "equally unreliable and uncritical."[28] However, there was enough veracity amidst self-promoting mythos to engender some authentic representations of India.

In the case of India's contributions, even when evidence of assimilation and comparison seems overtly conclusive, the exact chronology of Indian participation is often arguable because of their reluctance to put early historical and religious perspective into writing. "This accounts for the vagueness and inaccuracy of the accounts of India which filtered through to the West in early times."[29] However, we must assume a number of these contemporary great minds had ample opportunities to share their developing consciousness from India to Egypt, Persia to Greece. McEvilley masterfully sums up the theoretical relationship:

> The early period of philosophy in Greece and India contained many shared elements: the Problem of the One and the Many as the originative philosophical topic; the meltdown of polytheistic pantheons in the Cosmic Person; the merging of cosmogony into natural inquiry; material substrate monism as a first solution beyond myth; ... the definition of an ontological absolute; the rejection of the world of experience in favor of that absolute—and more."[30]

In investigations into specific references to Asia by Aristotle or Plato, there is a surprising dearth of concrete evidence. According to the digital website, *Perseus*, Plato referred to Asia a few times but offered little of relevance to philosophy, mathematics, politics, or the sciences. Aristotle used the word sparingly: in *Rhetoric* regarding the great war, and in *Politics*, including the statement on *thymos*. Persia is mentioned a few times, but again, little affecting philosophy or conceptual thinking.[31] There is argument that Aristotle was not aware of India's contribution to his Athenian philosophical thought, since it wasn't until the 20th century that Western philosophy began to acknowledge Indic philosophical, mathematical, numerical, linguistic, and astronomical influence. In 1971, West reminded us of this self-aggrandizing deficiency "In a tidy world, I daresay, a Greek thinker would be fully explicable from Greek material. The facts are otherwise."[32] Even today, much of ancient Mediterranean philosophical foundational accuracy is still at the mercy of classical scholarly divisiveness.

---

[28] Rawlinson 1916, p. 27.
[29] Rawlinson 1916, p. 2.
[30] McEvilley 2002, p. 59.
[31] Perseus 2010.
[32] West 1971, p. 201.

Anaximander, Anaximenes, and Parmenides

Aniximander's cosmos comes into being out of the eternal and limitless *apeiron* (boundless, indeterminate) according to the decree of time. In *Physics* 23.13, Aristotle writes "Things perish into those things out of which they have their being, according to necessity."[33] Contemporary Indian philosophy also posits that worlds come out of the infinite and perish back into it. "'All these beings arise from Akasa *(space)* alone and are finally dissolved into Akasa; because Akasa alone is greater than all these and Akasa is the support at all times" (*Chāndoyga Upaniśad* 1.9.1). West offers Zaehner's translation of the *Maitri Upaniśad* 6. 17: "In the beginning this (world) was Brahman, the One unbounded…unbounded in every direction…Space is his self…Out of this space he causes all that consist of thought alone to awaken. By this He thinks (into existence) this (material world) and into Him it disappears."[34]

Two hundred years before Aristotle, Anaximenes revised Thales of Miletus' theory of water as the principle form of matter-in-nature by stating, "that changes in the one substance [*aer, mist*] produces the variety of forms through condensation and rarefaction."[35] Rarified air becomes fire, condensed air a mist that precipitates rain, which soaks to the earth and is compressed into minerals. In V.x.5 and V.x.6 of the *Chāndogya Upanishad*, Swami Swahananda translates: "They come to Akasa, and from Akasa to air. Having become air, they become smoke. Having become smoke they become the white cloud. Having become the white cloud, they become the (rain-bearing) cloud. Having become the cloud they fall as rain."[36] The idea of a basic constituent of the universe was not a new one. Hesiod and Homer combined earth and water as the matter of man.[37] The thoughts were evolving, the influence was prevalent, the relationships are evident, and we are to draw our own conclusions from evidentiary totality.

Scholars offer numerous examples of comparative Parmenidean and Indic thought including the idea of opposites: "Here, on the one hand, aetherial flame of fire, gentle, very light, everywhere the same as itself … But not the same as this other, which in itself is opposite: dark night, a dense and heavy body."[38] This is comparable to the atheistic dualism of Indian *Sāmkhya*: atheistic in its denial of the existence of an absolute deity, dualistic in its belief in the two external alternate existences of *prakriti* (basic universal matter) and *purusha* (the individual soul).

---

[33] Ibid, p. 91.

[34] Ibid, pp. 93, 94.

[35] McEvilley 2002, p. 35.

[36] Uddālaka 2007, pp. 29-30

[37] West 1971, p. 199.

[38] Parmenides 2007, B.8.1-2.

For Parmenides, the mixture of light and dark in our bodies determine our thoughts and perceptions. In the *Samkhya* all mental functions—perception, imagination, thinking, willing—are not performed by the soul, but via mechanical processes of the material aspects of the body.[39] In *Parva naturalia*, Aristotle posited a single unified sense faculty, located in the heart, "by which the data of sense are coordinated,"[40] and wherein self-awareness, imagination, and dreaming reside.

"In the *Chāndogya Upanishads,* Uddālaka offers phrasing similar to Parmenides, who states that non-Being does not exist, and hence cannot be brought into causal accounts. A and not-A are mutually exclusive as are Being and non-Being. In VI-ii-1-2, Uddālaka writes: "Some say that, in the beginning, this was Non-being alone, one only, without a second. From that Non-being arose Being ... in the beginning (before creation), there was Being alone, one only, without a second."[41] Uddālaka is said to have lived around the 9th century B.C.E., Parmenides 300 years later. McEvilley labels the philosophical relationship "virtually identical."[42]

Pherecydes of Syros, a Pythagorean contemporary, was an initial supporter of metempsychosis (*transmigration of the soul, reincarnation*), sharing his belief that souls enter a succession of bodies. References do not offer the concept of the soul's ability to enter animals, but some scholars point to Pythagorean similarities, whose philosophy did include such transference, an impression common amongst many "primitive peoples."[43] The difference between folk metempsychosis, and the burgeoning philosophies of India and Greece are the two civilizations' further elaboration on the distinct progress of the soul's evolution throughout karmic rebirth.

Pythagoras, long credited with the geometric theorem of the hypotenuse of a right-angle triangle, shares his claim to originality with Baudhayana, who discovered the same theorem at least two decades before that of the mathematician of Samos.[44]

Buddhism, like other formidable philosophical organizations, was evolutionary of prior and Indian concepts. "Buddhism arose out of such independent sects, [and] incorporated what is considered to be the best from all, both the orthodox and the heterodox."[45] It is primarily these texts and sects that would have influenced comparative thought within the *Academy* in Athens. In

---

[39] West 1971, p. 223.
[40] Long 1973, p. 6.
[41] Uddālaka 2007, p. 34
[42] McEvilley 2002, p. 58.
[43] West, 1971, p. 61.
[44] Sampad and Vijay 2002, p. 60.
[45] Raju 1973, p. 148.

addition to the sources already provided, there is evidence of the Indic-Greek philosophical interrelationship of unfolding actuality during the lives of Socrates, Plato and Aristotle, emphasizing Buddhist perspective and influence from approximately 550 B.C.E up to Aristotle's death in 382 B.C.E.

Socrates

Most Greek philosophy was of a great lineage stemming from the earliest pre-Socratic to Aristotle. Reports by Diogenes Apolloniates, and later by Porphyry, a Neo-Platonist student of Plotinus, point to Socrates' relationship to Archelaus, a pupil of Anaxagoras. Anaxagoras, "the first to bring the philosophy of nature from Ionia to Athens," according to Diogenes, can be traced though the Ionian philosophers Empedocles, Parmenides, Pythagoras, Anaximenes and Anaximander. Later accounts by Porphyry and Diogenes state that Socrates studied both under the physicist Anaxagoras and, upon his death, with Archelaus—plausible confirmation of the purity of the lineage.[46]

We have briefly set the scene for the emergence of Socrates' philosophy, so let us likewise for Buddha. The greatness of the Brahmanical thinkers declined after the death of emperor Janamejaya and the flooding of Hastinūpura in the 8th century B.C.E. Religion took a back seat to the studies of "ritual, law, linguistics, astronomy, and geometry."[47] Although a portion of her northwest was under the thumb of the Persian Empire, India was not subject to much foreign assimilation: "her people were too proud and warlike to brook long the burden and reproach of foreign thralldom,"[48] and Darius was always careful to allow his dominions to maintain their own ideologies under his well-crafted, non-interference policy.

At the time of Siddhartha's arrival, rather than a unified India, sixteen major states called the *16 Mahajanapadas* existed in northern India, exhibiting multiple methods of governance. Economic progress including the "exploitation of natural resources and the development of industry,"[49] easy access to trading, and the aggregation of Indian physicians, mercenaries, mystics, traders, craftsman, and thinkers in Persepolis, Babylonia, and Ionia, tugged away at India's veneer of isolationism, motivating new schools of thinking by new age philosophers called *śramaṇas* of which Buddha was, arguably, the more successful.

---

[46] Ibid, p. 305.
[47] Warder 1980, p. 28.
[48] M'Crindle 1974, p. 5.
[49] Warder 1980, 28, 30.

Forerunners to Buddhism and Jainism, the *śramanas* cultivated a pessimistic worldview of the *sangsara* as full of suffering and advocated renunciation and austerities. They rejected the autocratic superiority of the Brahmans, ridiculing the archaic rituals, and deconstructing the Veda by pointing out its contradictions and unethical traditions. Some *śramanas* went so far as to charge the Brahmans as conspiratorial enemies of the people.[50] The *śramanas* searched for cosmological answers through logic, theoretical scrutiny, and argument. While rejecting many of the contemporary values of Indian society, they evolved concepts regarding the attainment of happiness and salvation. Besides Buddhism and Jainism, the other philosophical schools that flourished were the *Ājīvaka, Lokāyata,* and *Ajñāna*.

Socrates and Buddha

In the broadest sense, Buddha and Socrates were both philosopher kings. Alan Weber offers mutually affecting comparisons of the two. "Like the spiritual habits and practices of the Buddha, what Socrates practiced and called philosophy was done solely as a means to salvation, or liberation."[51] Like Buddha, the philosopher viewed the soul as overly attached to the desires of mortality. "It must purify, or detach, itself from the bodily,"[52] in order to achieve liberation from *sangsara*, the endless cyclical birth, death, and rebirth to which conditioned beings are subject. In *Phaedo*, Plato quotes Socrates as saying: "... those who care about their souls and do not devote themselves to the body disassociate themselves firmly from these others and refuse to accompany them on their haphazard journey."[53]

While Buddha exemplified the art of meditation, Socrates could also be seen, standing in enstatic contemplation on various street corners. In *Phaedo*, wisdom is described essentially the same as that in Buddhism. "Wisdom is not a form of acquired knowledge, but is a state of mind, or state of the soul."[54] Concerning Socrates' attitude towards death, Plato revealed his mentor, "holds nothing to the supreme equanimity of the Buddha."[55] "But no soul which has not practiced philosophy, and is not absolutely pure when it leaves the body, may attain to the divine nature; that is only for the lover of learning."[56] Similarities are found centuries earlier in

---

[50] Ibid, p. 34.
[51] Webber 1985, p. 10.
[52] Ibid, p. 22.
[53] Plato 1954, 82D.
[54] Webber 1985, p. 10.
[55] Dillon 2000, p. 526.
[56] Plato 1954, 82BC

Uddālaka's *Chandogya Upanishad*. "And as in this case he (the man attached to truth) is not burnt, (similarly a man of knowledge is not born again)."[57]

Socrates didn't fear death because he believed that his own philosophic realization was the stepping stone to liberation and the full "attainment of wisdom:"[58] "when it [the soul] investigates itself, it passes into the realm of the pure and everlasting and deathless and changeless ... this condition of the soul we call Wisdom."[59]

Buddha and Socrates were great and generous teachers, passing on the esoteric depths of their psychagogy to those attuned in perception. The teaching of the Buddha is primarily based on two truths: that of a personal everyday world and a higher truth which surpasses it. Was Aristotle aware of the similarities? Was he aware of the emerging Indian orthopraxy at that time? Would knowledge of the teachings and wisdom of Buddha and his contemporaries have mattered one way or another in relation to his pronouncement of the *thymotic* deficiency of the Indian peoples?

Plato

What is the "allegory of the cave," if not the epitome of the role of the Bodhisattva? "Then our job as lawgivers is to compel the best minds to attain what we have called the highest form of knowledge, and to ascend to the vision of the good as we have described, and when they have achieved this ... return again to the prisoners in the cave below and share their labors and rewards, whether trivial or serious."[60] According to the Buddhist *Abhidharma* (elements of wisdom according to schematic classifications appearing in the Pali Buddhist Suttas), phenomena lacked reality, and associating them to levels of authenticity produces suffering. For Plato, phenomena are shadows on the wall of the cave. Once one has seen beyond, one can understand the futility of attachment, yet it is a blessed duty, "not to "linger there" in the presence of the Real," but to return to the cave to shed light on the ignorance that rules "darkly as in a dream by men who fight one another for shadows."[61]

The similarities between Plato's *Theory of Ideas* and the *Abhidharma* are emphasized in multiple comparative studies. Although the *Abhidharma* was not written until the fourth century, the concept of *dharma* as an account of the elements and their different classifications, originates

---

[57] Uddālaka 2007, VI-xvi-3
[58] Webber 1985, p. 41.
[59] Plato 1954, 79D.
[60] Plato 2003, 7:518cd.
[61] McEvilley 2002, pp168-9

from the *Sarvāstavādin* school, "one of the earliest, if not the earliest of Buddhist sects. The Sarvāstavādin *dharma*-list recognized seventy-five impersonal "elements" or ultimate constituents of phenomena."[62] Plato's similar list is extinct but is outlined in his *Theory of Ideas*, where reality is made up of two realms: the physical world experienced by our five senses; and the eternal world of forms or ideas. In both traditions, phenomena are regarded as ultimately unreal. The foundation of the *dharmas* is concreted in a unifying, ultimate reality. Likewise for Plato and his *Idea of the Good*, which is the indispensable unity behind his Ideas. "This Good," Plato wrote, "is beyond being."[63]

Webber contrasts Plato's philosophy to Buddha's Four Noble Truths, as well as the metaphysics of the *Abhidharma*, *Madhymika*, and *Vijnanavada* schools, positing that Plato's works should be regarded as "wisdom literature," and a "philosophy of liberation," comparable to that of Buddhism. "The Buddhist and the philosopher are ethical absolutes; for both, the absolute principle is not an object of divine revelation, a commandment to be believed, but an object of attainment."[64]

Reincarnation and Purification

The soul reentering another being after the death of the bodily host was not an original notion when Plato discussed the early Greek mystery association with reincarnation in one of his earlier books, the *Meno*. He also wrote in *Phaedo* "that a philosopher "duly purified" may live forever without a body, thus avoiding transmigration."[65] One of the two *sūtras* in the *Madhyamaka* asks Buddha about the inequality of men's circumstance. "His answer is that all this depends on action (*karma*)."[66] Buddha then goes on to explain how various actions determine the circumstances of the next incarnation.

Reincarnation is discussed in some aspect in the *Republic, Phaedrus, Timaeus*, and the *Laws*. In fact, although not represented in the *Rigveda* or in Homer,[67] it certainly registered quickly thereafter in both cultures. The true Greek concept of the doctrine, which includes purification of the soul as an active (*karmic*) principle necessary for progression "is found, outside Greece, only in India."[68] Dillon opines that: "Both the Orphics and Heraclitus seem in fact to have held

---

[62] Ibid, p. 167.
[63] Webber 1985, p. 4.
[64] Ibid, pp. 10, 11.
[65] Ibid, p. 20
[66] Ibid, p. 188.
[67] McEvilley 2002, p. 112.
[68] Dillon 2000, p. 535.

a doctrine of the process of reincarnation that was spelled out in the early Upanishads."[69] Reincarnation is mentioned, albeit briefly, in the latter part of the *Vedic* writings, then relatively "taken for granted."[70] It is the concept of purification, "combined with the doctrine of metempsychosis" that makes this theory unique to the Indians and Greeks. The search for purity or the "Good" becomes "the requisite for progress toward ultimate release from the cycle of rebirths."[71] Unlike other notions of rebirth, doctrines found in both Greece and India determine that "it is not chance but the moral quality of one's past behavior" that is causal to the form of rebirth."[72]

Porphyry indicates that reincarnation was introduced into Greece by Pherecydes of Syros (circa 650 B.C. E.), who is credited "with the ability to remember his past incarnations."[73] As Pythagoras' purported teacher, he was the seminal link to the lineage that included Socrates, Plato and Aristotle, all of whom incorporated the Orphic, Pythagorean, Empedocledian doctrines of cyclical rebirths from which the soul struggles to gain release.

The *Satapatha Brahmana* (Brahmana of one-hundred paths), circa 1000 B.C.E., is an ancient Hindu sacred text, which describes *Vedic* rituals, and includes creation myths and the Deluge of Manu. Orally transmitted for centuries until committed to writing around the time of Plato and Aristotle, section 12.9.3.12 offers what McEvilley believes is an Iron Age description of metempsychosis. "The god of death causes to be born again from out of the immortal womb."[74]

Plato claimed that the soul is subject to normal bodily decay, yet does retain some "memory" of the "Good" and, providing it is willing to follow an ethical path of virtue in its new life, it can eventually return to its pre-existent state of purity and wisdom. On the other hand, that same soul is subject to eternal damnation should it choose a path of "non-Good." In regards to metempsychosis, "the overall concept of the process is rather astonishingly similar in both the Greek and Indian sources of this period."[75]

The philosophers of Buddha's period taught that the goal was not that of continued progressions of rebirths as much as the orthopraxic consciousness required in order "not to be reborn at all."[76] A systematic method had to be developed for an eventual cessation of rebirth,

---

[69] Ibid, p. 41.

[70] Warder 1980, p. 25.

[71] Dillon 2000, p. 535.

[72] McEvilley 2000, p. 99.

[73] Ibid, p. 104.

[74] McEvilley 2002, p. 113.

[75] Dillon 2000, p. 535.

[76] Warder 1980, p. 36.

which required a reassessment of the thousands of years of doctrine, text, and rituals. Buddhist doctrine advocates seeking liberation from *sangsara*, "freedom from all bodily existence."[77] That too was the ultimate goal of the contemporary Greek philosophers, who believed their vocation to be the ultimate spiritual activity. Socrates determined that, "All who Have duly purified themselves by philosophy live henceforth altogether without bodies, and pass to still more beautiful abodes."[78] The ultimate goal of reincarnation is transcendence to cessation through right action (*karma*), and adherence to the Good. The soul, susceptible to remaining "overly attached to the mortal nature,"[79] must separate itself from worldly desires in order to realize its true nature. Plato's dualism is evident in *Phaedo*, where he writes of the dichotomous substances of soul and body. "It is the aim of the soul, which is simple in essence and immortal, to rid itself of the body, for while it is embodied the soul cannot attain perfect knowledge."[80]

Aristotle

Most of Aristotle's writings credit the hierarchy of Greek philosophers for the foundations of his own creativity, a myopic viewpoint of Greek superiority that had developed over time, and a source for speculation that Aristotle's opinions were grounded on inherent "nativism." It is important to underscore that, in its origination, the Greek concept of soul was little more than Homer's breath of ghostly smoke which held aspirations no greater than a pale and taciturn eternity in Hades. This perspective is exemplified by the early doubters in the *Phaedo* who question their master's visionary aspects of immortality: "[W]hat you have said to me about the soul,' Cebes responds to Socrates, 'leaves the average person with grave misgivings."[81] Socrates replies that not only is the soul immortal, but it also continues to value the truth after death and separation.

The earlier Greeks perceived their world in a temperament of awe and wonder. As philosophy evolved, and became more practical and codified, cosmic existence began to fade into the philosophical, as investigation and discourse prevailed. Socrates offers many arguments to assure his colleagues of his philosophic rationale of the soul's immortality. He writes of the essential essence of heat within fire as the essence of the soul within the impure bodily host. (Yet when the fire dies, whither goes the heat?) Socrates' corroborations are metaphysical responses which Aristotle later tries to turn into evidence through particularized application.

---

[77] Webber 1985, p. 19.
[78] Plato 1954, 114c.
[79] Ibid, p. 223.
[80] Long 1973, p. 3.

Plato's concept of soul in *Phaedo* evolves somewhat in the *Republic* from an "uncompromising dualism" to a tripartite of oneness within the dualism "in which a unitary self is attainable if harmony can be established" among reason (*logos*), emotion (*thymos*), and bodily appetite (*epithumia*).[82] The soul then becomes the source and monitor of bodily and psychological regulation, exhibiting unrestrained anger and pride, and all the negative components of developing *thymos* while "adorning [the *psuchē*] not with borrowed beauty but with his own – with self-control, and goodness, and courage, and liberality, and truth."[83]

These three parts of the Platonic soul are not separate entities but interacting waves and particles of unification. His reason (*logos*) has the ability to facilitate evaluation, perception, and learning, while moderating the bodily functions. In *Phaedrus,* Plato famously analogizes the tripartite human soul as the warrior and his horse-drawn chariot. The driver is reason (*logos*) holding the reins of passion (*thymos*) and appetite (*epithumia*). The thymotic horse is heroic, an unsoiled, moral stallion guided by reason, a lofty being fierce by nature. Alongside him struggles the other steed, "a shaggy, recalcitrant beast which tries to drag the chariot down from its heavenly course."[84] "The vicious horse is heavy and to the extent it was not trained well it sinks earthward and weights the charioteer down."[85] "Appetite" (*epithumia*) is primarily concerned with the urges and impulses "due to our feelings and unhealthy cravings," which include "food and drink and sex and the like."[86] In the *Bhagavid-Gita*, Krishna is the driver of Arjuna's chariot, as they advance midway into the Valley of *Kurukshetra*, interpreted by many as the internal faculties of good and evil that battle within each of us.

The pre-Socratic and Platonic notions of the soul envisioned it as a separate entity that did not require a body in order to exist. Aristotle posited that the soul was responsible for moving the body, could not survive without it, and was thus mortal. He agreed with Plato that the soul was dualistically separate from the body, but did not support Socrates' claim that the soul continued to exist after death. Aristotle's soul does not collapse into oblivion after the termination of the host, nor ascend into transcendent solidarity. It returns to the collective from which it later remerges to enter a new host as its life force. He believed that the soul, as life force, is present in every living thing. Aristotle categorized the soul: the lower level providing nurturing characteristics for plants, another level for animal instinct, and the highest level for the

---

[81] Plato 1954, 70a.

[82] Long 1973, p. 4.

[83] Plato, 114e-115a.

[84] Long 1973, p. 4.

[85] Plato, *Phaedrus* 2003, 246e-254e.

[86] Plato, *The Republic* 2003. 439d; 580e.

human ability to be rational. He created ten classifications of organisms, from zoophytes to vertebrates; each with their own companion soul ascribed to the potential actuality of the classified being, the higher the biologic classification the more formidable the soul. Many of his beliefs are culminations of thought originating with Pythagoras and Empedocles: the philosopher who recognized the reincarnate soul of a dog as his former friend, and the historian who could remember past lives including that of a fish and bird. Aristotle was dedicated to practicality; he was a scientist. He did not see the world clearly through mystical Socratic eyes, as personified by his statement in *Nicomachean Ethics* that death is "the most terrible of things."[87] But he also could not dishonor centuries of Greek philosophical history. While Aristotle's interpretation of *thymos* varies dramatically throughout his writings, in *De Anima* he does indicate, following Plato's outline, that the "nonrational desiring part of the soul" includes *epithumia* (appetite) and *thymos*."[88] What he means by *thymos* is more complex than simply "spirit." He maintained a special belief that the highest soul, the apex Greek soul, is abounding in *thymos*, the deliberately sought Homeric courage for the sake of what is noblest.[89] Barbara Koziak provides a masterful, comprehensive study of the various interpretations of *thymos* Aristotle might have employed. According to her extensive study of Aristotle's *Rhetoric, De Anima, Eudemian* and *Nichomachaen Ethics*, and the most revealing *Politics*,[90] Koziak provides evidence that Aristotle understood many distinct yet interrelated meanings for *thymos;* among them: (1) the traditional Homeric concept of the rage that motivated the less-than-deliberate *courage* of Achilles; (2) the more controlled and justifiable emotion of anger; (3) as appellation for the soul's capacity to feel emotions as an inherent part of that human nature that controls the universal drive toward the particular goods of honor and freedom from tyranny…a [spirited] desire from which courage results in the fight for independence and self-government; and (4) as homage to the Homeric Greek as hero encapsulated in myth and nationalistic conceit.[91]

Homer

In literary terms, *thymos* originated in Homer's epics, most English texts exclusively translating it as the word "spirit." Both epics concern themselves with the great defining moment of Greek heroics, the Trojan War, where protagonist and antagonist alike were trained for the honor and glory of war, desiring nothing more than to be deemed courageous, trained for

---

[87] Aristotle 1999, 115a 26-27.
[88] Brady 2005, p. 196.
[89] Ibid, p. 200.
[90] Koziak 2000, p. 82.
[91] Ibid, pp. 82-87.

the spiritedness, that inestimable, deliberate, emotional "blood"-curdling, "breath"-taking action on the battlefield.[92] War was a social structure for warriors and their protectorates, who valued "honor and glory above all else."[93] "In defending like a dog for its master, *thymos* defends something higher than itself."[94]

Greek thought evolved an intriguing division of supramental life into two souls, the *thymos* (active soul) and the *psuchē,* (the immanent soul, independent from the body). Later evolutes of *thymos* were associated with the heart and liver. Breath was identified with the immediate soul; the soul became the life-force. The liver was the foundation of emotions; the heart, the place of desires. "*Thymos*" works hand-in-hand with both reason and appetite. It is our desire or appetite for recognition of value that drives us to be virtuous, courageous—to be leaders of men. An appetite for recognition of our virtue is "reasonable" for a Good existence. When it does not appropriate what it feels it deserves it becomes indignant. *Thymos* has become the Western psychological mean between *megalothymia*, (the need to be thought of as superior), and *isothymia*, (the need to be merely recognized as equal). *Thymos* is an intimate ally of *logos* as it provides the requisite passion to Homeric courage, but any thymotic reaction beyond the mean would, naturally, be in conflict with reason.

These evolutions of thought, combined with the Platonic tripartite of the soul, and Aristotle's nationalistic fervor, give ample evidence of the evolution of *thymos*, which became a permanent possession of the complete man. Socrates credits *thymos* as the characteristic of the philosopher as he ascends from the unconsciousness bewilderment of things unexplained to the rational, concrete aspect of understanding and self-awareness.

Koziak speculates that Platonic *thymos* as discussed in the *Republic*, essentializes four specific truths, their differences completed by their sameness: the Homeric association with the good warrior, "its characteristic expression as anger," its extolling of courage and justice, and its manliness.[95] *Thymos* is "commanding and invincible."[96]

Aristotle and Slavery

"Man is by nature a political animal," so reads the famous phrase from *Politics*, but to take it out of full context is to miss some revelation. "From these things therefore it is clear that the

---

[92] Long 1973, p. 2.
[93] Koziak 2000, p. 58.
[94] Harvey 2001, p. 45.
[95] Ibid, p. 65.
[96] Bentley 1999, p. 109.

city-state is a natural growth, and that man is by nature a political animal, and a man that is by nature and not merely by fortune, without country, is either low in the scale of humanity or above it."[97] Its prevailing influence in Aristotle's ethical philosophy cannot be over-emphasized. It positions the state as paramount to the individual. This "ideal" *polis* is not that of a democracy, but that of a timocracy, the of the majority of male Greek citizens of property. Men do not of themselves deliberately chose their own value, but are, by nature, set upon a certain course, cast by fate's determination. The majority of men are naturally subordinate unless "fortunate" enough to be citizens of the *polis*; although a very few, i.e., the ascetic philosopher, anchorite, and mystic, can survive "above" it all. The "formed-by-nature" hypothesis is essential to Aristotle's rationalization for the subordination of those designated for slavery. These people who "lack certain things" essential for living the excellent life are also burdened with a "much restricted capacity for development." Another candidate for slavery is the individual who does not aspire to take advantage of the "resources at his disposal."[98] That would simply indicate faulty determination.

Aristotle believed that man's "capacities and aims" were ultimately rewarded only by participation within the *polis*. The individual's eudemonia must "involve the good of fellow members of a community."[99]

"Now it is evident that the form of government is best in which every man, whoever he is, can act best and live happily," he explains in *Politics*.[100] To Aristotle, true happiness is eudemonistic—possessing a good guardian spirit. However, unless the slave desires to be a slave, he is not blessed with eudemonia. By calling this individual a "natural slave," implies that it is for his own good; being a slave is his "flourishing," his indeliberate endgame. One might argue, few men would deliberately chose to be a slave; Aristotle counters by proposing that one thing that is lacking in *thymos* is the ability for deliberation.

The natural slave

"Citizens, in order to live well politically and practically [within the *polis*] need slaves."[101] "That state or the political community, which is the highest of all, and which embraces all the rest, aims at good in a greater degree than any other, and at the highest good."[102]

---

[97] Aristotle, *Politics* 1984, 1:1253.5-5.
[98] Bentley 1999, p. 112.
[99] Irwin 1999, p. xxiii.
[100] Aristotle *Politics* 1984, 7.2.1324a22-23
[101] Garver 1984, p. 180.

The *polis* could not survive without the foundation of slavery. Because he is a political animal, the Athenian citizen requires the foundation of the *polis* "for the full actualization of his potentialities."[103] Some label this "conflicting idealism," that of maintaining a "free political community that rested on a slave economy."[104] I am uncomfortable calling a timarchy of male, Greek, citizen landowners a "free political community," nor do I advocate slavery should not have been part of the equation. It was a matter of fact, and the ethical morality of slavery is beyond the scope of this paper. Farms, as they were then maintained, could not have produced effectively for the *polis* without slavery. The armies and mercenaries needed the support of slaves to wage war, and one might argue, the Battles of Marathon and Attica, and the successful overthrow of the Persian Empire by Alexander would not have succeeded without slavery.

Plato did not attribute the lack of *thymos* as primary prerequisite for slave mentality and believed the slave lacked *logos* (reason) . He could possess true belief, but not the reasonable awareness to understand what makes that truth valid; "he can neither give nor follow a rational account."[105] Without *logos,* the slave is unable to understand Plato's concept of the Good, which is essential for full self-determination. He has no choice but to subject his understanding of his beliefs to that of an authority, and to become subordinate to the dominance of the knower.[106] Aristotle attributed the problematic not to the full lack of *logos* but to "incomplete" *logos*. Possessed of a rational soul, a natural slave's comprehension of reason was only partial, "incomplete," due to the lack of *thymos* which prevented "full development of reason."[107]

The determining factor in Aristotle's adaptation of the "natural" aspect of slavery; accepting the subaltern as a design of nature, an inferior "otherness" blessed by the gods, was his belief in the majesty of the Athenian *polis*. Slavery is "natural because it follows a pattern that pervades all nature."[108] "For all things which form a composite whole and which are made up of parts…a distinction between the ruling and the subject element comes to light… originating from nature as a whole."[109] To confirm the naturalness of slavery, Aristotle evidenced how it is good for the master, who requires the slave to maintain his (the master's) economic and political presence within the *polis*, as well as good for the slave whose *thymotic* deficiency is supplemented by his master's intellectual superiority. "For that which can foresee by the exercise of mind is by nature

---

[102] Aristotle *Politics* 1984, I.1.1252a4-57

[103] Garver 1984, p. 190.

[104] Vlastos 1973, p. 153.

[105] Vlastos 1973, p. 148.

[106] Ibid, p. 150.

[107] Garver 1994, p. 185.

[108] Vlastos 1973, p. 160.

[109] Aristotle *Politics* 1984, 1.4.1254a28-31

lord and master, and that with its body give effect to such foresight is a subject, and by nature a slave; hence master and slave have the same interest."[110] It is not necessary to feel sorry for the slave because he is incomplete (*ateles*), "They can perform given tasks perfectly well, but cannot live by themselves."[111]

In Review

In discussing the varied uses of *thymos* and theorizing why Aristotle applied this particular singularity to the Asiatic—specifically the peoples of India—we will attempt to "select the best and most dependable theory that human intelligence can supply, and use it as a raft to ride the seas of life."[112]

> Spirit [*thymos*] as the Homeric hero is concerned with bravery and courage; "for those who act on spirit also seem to be brave—as beasts seem to be when they attack those who have wounded them—because brave people are also full of spirit. For spirit is most eager to run and face dangers; hence Homer's words, 'put strength in his spirit,' 'aroused strength and spirit,' and 'his blood boiled.' All these would seem to signify the arousal and impulse of spirit.[113]

Here Aristotle betrays his admiration for the Homeric Greek warrior, someone who faces death, not with *logos* or discrimination, but with a bloodthirsty taste for killing and revenge. Later he amends this by declaring that the beast is fighting, not as much for himself, but in defense of his own species, a logical result of passionate duty. The great Greek hero who brims with *thymos* is the warrior willing to give up his own life in defense of what is good, that good being that of the sociopolitical structure of the *polis*.

This desire for national preservation is intrinsic. "And nature provides for the characterization of "one's own" as oneself and one's species."[114] Aristotle is not alone in believing that fighting for one's nationality is superior to fighting for the entire species of man. "*Thymos* is transformed such that the courageous person is moved by the desire to protect the community rather than himself only insofar as the courageous person understands himself as part of that whole." In *Nicomachean Ethics* III.8.1117a3-5, Aristotle writes: "The [bravery] caused by [*thymos*] seems to be the most natural sort, and to be [genuine] bravery once it has also

---

[110] Aristotle *Politics* 1984, 1.1252a31-34
[111] Garver 1994, p. 178.
[112] Plato 1954, 85d.
[113] Aristotle 1999, III.8.1116b.25-31
[114] Brady 2005, p. 201.

acquired decision [*prohairesis*] and the goal."[115] This was exclusion of warriors of India and other Asiatic nations because they fought for "lesser" forms of community.[116]

Alexander's foray into India was chronicled by many historians, all reporting a fierce and formidable foe. Alexander was met with a most determined resistance, and could only subdue the opposition through "wholesale massacres and executions." "The people were not only of a most martial temperament, but ... had they been but united...the Macedonian army was doomed to utter destruction."[117] Those that had been clever enough to know they could not compete with his vast numbers, waited for Alexander and his army to depart before quickly uniting under Candraguptra, the Mauryan leader, to recapture "all the territories" within the Hindu Kush.[118] The Indians were obviously no pushovers.

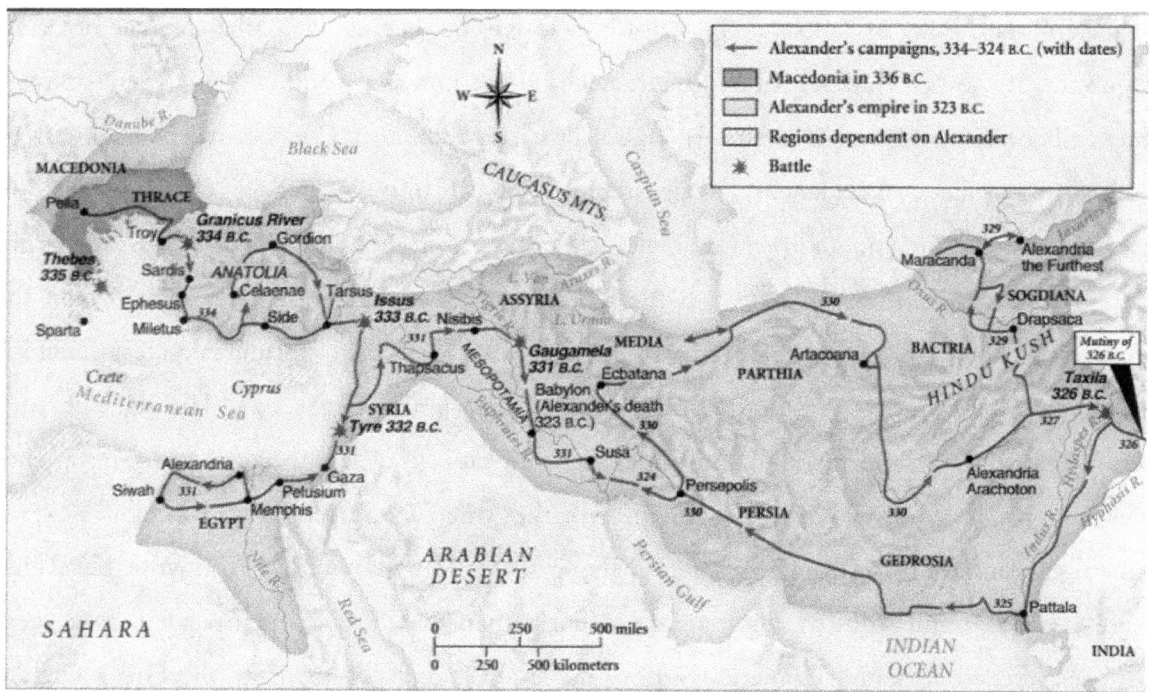

Figure. 5: Alexander's Empire (courtesy "usu.edu")

Aristotle did not live to witness this defeat, nor would it have changed his estimation. Long writes that, "Aristotle takes the mind to be in one respect analogous to a blank wax-tablet on which anything can be imprinted. This makes the mind fully open to receiving ideas, but it has "no actual existence until it thinks."[119] It also allows the blank slate to be filled with what one chooses to impart, a foundation which can easily be selective to what accuracies are imported. The power of the subjective suggestive is another of paramount importance.

---

[115] Garver 1994, p. 167.
[116] Brady 2005, p. 203.
[117] McEvilley, 2002, pp. 858-859.
[118] Ibid, pp. 858-859.

<u>Conclusion</u>

Thus did Aristotle adapt a biopolitical model that provided the normative, male, Greek citizen-landowner with a soul of utmost completeness and deliberative capacity. Anything "other" was outside of that value. These "others" were assigned actualities that manifested their "natural" incomplete potentialities, and who they were destined to be as a result of this need for completion. They were naturally subordinate and, in the dominant imagining, less civilized and suitable for slavery. It is my conclusion that the principal reason for Aristotle's denigration of the Asiatic and thus the Indic civilization was his belief in the sanctity of the Greek warrior, and not just primary justification for acquiring the slave population necessary for valorization and political sustainability of the *polis*. It is not conclusive, but seems likely, that he was not fully cognizant of the vast tradition of Indic influence on the prevailing and evolving philosophy of Greece because of his innate desire to "nationalize" the superiority of the male, Greek citizen land-owner. There is evidence to suggest philosophical amnesia, due largely to his fervent personal nationalism, and androcentric belief in Greek citizen racial superiority. Aristotle might have been aware of their acumen in battle, but since they were fighting for "other" than the Greek polis, their efforts were somewhat negligible. His egocentricity formulated an unflinching belief in the superiority of the governmental structure of the Greek *polis*. His self-righteous certitude as to the inferiority of all non-Greek city-state citizens as less-than-adequate stewards of their own being, led him to justify his support for the Athenian/Macedonian "superior" political structure with slave labor from other-than-male-Greek-citizen-landowners. His mythic belief that there was no greater form of wholesome manliness than that *thymos* which resided in the very perfect Greek soul of the Homeric warrior made any being "other than" the Greek citizen-warrior deficient in true courage and inferior to the complete "Aristotelian" soul.

---

[119] Long 1973, p. 6.

Sources

Aristotle. 1984. "De Anima." *The Complete Works of Aristotle, V1*. Ed. Jonathan Barnes. Princeton, N.J.: Princeton University Press.

----. 1984. "Politics." *The Complete Works of Aristotle, V1*. Ed. Jonathan Barnes. Princeton, N.J.: Princeton University Press.

----. 1999. *Nicomachean Ethics*. Tran. Terence Irwin. 2nd ed. Indianapolis, Ind: Hackett Pub. Co.

Arendt, Hannah. 1958. *The Human Condition*. Chicago: University of Chicago Press.

Ashliman, D.L. 1925. "The Jakata Tales. The Future Buddha as Judge." 30 January 2002. Source: *Buddhist Birth-Stories; or, Jataka Tales*, edited by V. Fausbøll and translated by T. W. Rhys Davids (London: George Routledge and Sons, 1925), pp. xiv-xvi. First published 1880. Accessed 3 November 2007. <pitt.edu/~dash/jataka.html>.

Bentley, Russell. 1999. "Loving Freedom: Aristotle on Slavery and the Good Life." *Political Studies* 47.1.

Brady, Michelle E. 2005. "The Fearlessness of Courage." *Southern Journal of Philosophy*. 43.2.

Burkert, Walter. 1992. *The Orientalizing Revolution : Near Eastern Influence on Greek Culture in the Early Archaic Age*. Cambridge, Mass: Harvard University Press.

Dillon, Matthew. 2000. "Dialogues with Death: the Last Days of Socrates and the Buddha." *Philosophy East & West*. 50.4; 4.

Eggeling, Julius. 1900. "The Satapatha Brahmana, Part V." *Sacred Books of the East*. Vol. 44. Accessed 13 November 2007. <http://www.sacred-texts.com/hin/sbr/sbe44/index.htm>.

Eliade, Mircea. 1954. *The Myth of Eternal Return*. New York: Penguin Group.

Eusebius. 1912. *Preparation for the Gospel*, (per Arius Didymus) XV, 20, 2. Tran. John Burnet. Accessed 18 May 2010.

<http://en.wikisource.org/wiki/Fragments_of_Heraclitus#Fragment_12>

Fukuyama. Francis. 2006. *The End of History and the Last Man*. New York: Free Press.

Garver, Eugene. 1994. "Aristotle's natural slaves: incomplete 'praxeis' and incomplete human beings."*The Journal of the History of Philosophy*. 32.n2.

Gunderson, Lloyd L., et al. 1980. *Aristotle's Letter to Aristotle about India*. Meisenheim am Glan: Hain.

Harvey, Martin. 2001. "Deliberation and Natural Slavery." *Social Theory and Practice*. 27:1.

Heraclitus. 1995. *Greek Philosophy*. Tran. Hooker. Accessed 7 October 2007. "http://www.wsu.edu/~dee/GREECE/HERAC.HTM"

Irwin, Terence. 1999. "Forward. *Nicomachean Ethics*. Indianapolis: Hackett Pub. Co.

Koziak, Barbara. 2000. *Retrieving Political Emotion : Thumos, Aristotle, and Gender*. University Park, Pa. Pennsylvania State University.

Long, Anthony A. 1973. "Psychological Ideas in Antiquity." *Dictionary of the History of Ideas*. Vol. 4. New York: Scribner's.

Mansfield, Jaap. 1992. "Heraclitus Fr. B 85 DK. (Possible Translations of a Fragment by Heraclitus Based on Interpretations of the Greek Word 'thumos')." Mnemosyne 45.n1.

M'Crindle, John Watson. 1974. *The Invasion of India by Alexander the Great*. New Delhi: Today and Tomorrow's Printers & Publishers.

McEvilley, Thomas. 2002. *The Shape of Ancient Thought*. New York: Allworth Press.

Parmenides, and Allan Randall. 2006. *On Nature (Peri Physeos)*. 2006. Elea.Org. Accessed 17 October 2007. <elea.org/Parmenides>.

Perseus Digital Library. "Greek and Roman Materials." Copyrights: Varied. Tufts University. Accessed November 2010. <perseus.tufts.edu/ cache/perscoll_Greco-Roman.html>.

Plato. 2003. *The Republic*. Tran. Henry Desmond Pritchard Lee. London ; New York: Penguin Books.

----. 1954. "Phaedo." *The Last Days of Socrates*. Trans. Hugh Tredennick and Harold Tarrant. New York City, New York: Penguin Books.

----. 2003. *Phaedrus*. Tran. Stephen Scully. Newburyport, MA: Focus Philosophical Library.

Raju, P.T. 1973. *Structural Depths of Indian Thought*. Albany: State University Press.

Rawlinson, H. G. 1916. *Intercourse between India and the Western World from the Earliest Times to the Fall of Rome*. Cambridge, U.K.: University Press.

Romm, James S. 1989. "Aristotle's Elephant and the Myth of Alexander's Scientific Patronage." *American Journal of Philology*. Vol. 110.n4.

Sampad and Vijay. 2002. *The Wonder that is Sanskrit*. Ahmedabad, India: Mapin Publishing.

Stocks, J. L. 1927. "The Composition of Aristotle's Politics." *The Classical Quarterly*. Vol. 21, No. 3/4.

Stone, Brad Elliott. 2006. "Curiosity as the Thief of Wonder." *KronoScope*. 6:2.

Vlastos, Gregory. 1973. *Platonic Studies*. Princeton, N.J.: Princeton University Press.

Uddālaka and Swami Swahananda. 2007. "Chandogya Upanishad." Accessed August 2, 2007 *Advaita Vedanta Library*. Accessed 1 November 2007.

<geocities.com/advaitavedant/chandogya.htm>.

Warder, Anthony Kennedy. 1980. *Indian Buddhism*. Delhi, India: Motilal Banarsidass.

Webber, Alan. 1985. *Philosophy and Liberation: a Cross-cultural Comparison of Classical Buddhism and Platonic Philosophy.* Diss. University of California, Irvine, 1985. ProQuest Digital Dissertations. Accessed 5 Nov. 2007. <http://resources.ciis.edu:2051/>.

West, M. L. 1971. *Early Greek Philosophy and the Orient.* Oxford: Clarenden Press.

Woodbury, Leonard. 1971. "Socrates and Archelaus." *Phoenix.* 25:4.

The Dawn of Religions in Afghanistan-Seistan-Gandhara and the Personal Seals of Gotama Buddha and Zoroaster by Dr. Ranajit Pal

Bhandarkar Oriental Research Institute, India.

Abstract: This paper points to the Nepalese frauds in Buddhist history and holds that Buddhism, Zoroastrianism and early Judaism originated in India-Iran-Afghanistan. The Amorites are posited in the Harappan civilization. Gaumata is identified with Gotama. Names such as Tiŝŝa, Ŝedda-ŝaramana and Ŝuddyauda-ŝaramana in the Persepolis tablets show that Gotama Buddha was born in Seistan-Baluchistan. It is claimed that PFS79 and PFS1243 were the seals of Gotama and Zoroaster (Dāmidata) respectively.

Introduction

The rough outlines of the histories of early Buddhism and Zoroastrianism are clear but for the discerning reader many questions remain unanswered. Although Buddhism is said to have been born in Nepal (or Eastern U. P.), this has no archaeological basis. No Nepalese Buddhist Canon[120], Nepalese Buddha icon, or any early Nepalese Buddhist relic is known, which contrasts sharply with the radiant Buddhist finds from Gandhara, Bamiyan and Seistan.

The history of Zoroastrianism is mired with greater uncertainties[121]. Zoroaster remains a mythical figure with no relics. While M. Boyce, a leading writer on Zoroastrianism, places him around 1700-1500 B.C., E. Herzfeld, T. C. Young Jr. and J. Duchesne-Guillemin put his date in the sixth century B.C.[122] which coincides with the rise of Buddhism and as both the religions were heresies[123] against old Vedic type creeds, there is the possibility of a link. This was

---

[120] J. N. Farquhar, *Outline of the Religious Literature of India* (Oxford, 1920) 275.

[121] W. B. Henning writes, " ...there is scarcely a point on which there is unanimity; Zoroaster's time and place, the religion he inherited from his forefathers, the message he brought, his aim, his community, the development of his church, the history of the Avesta - each scholar will dissent from his fellows on one point or another". W. B. Henning, *Zoroaster, Politician or Witch Doctor?* (Oxford, 1951).

[122] Similar to the Vedic Indra and the Buddhas, the term Zoroaster may have designated many individuals in different periods. Gotama was the last of the Buddhas and the last Zoroaster may have been his elder contemporary.

[123] B. K. Ghosh, quoted in D. P. Mishra, *Studies in the Proto-History of India* (New Delhi, 1971) 38.

suspected by Sir Charles Eliot but was soon forgotten. There were many Buddhas[124] before Gotama which implies that Buddhism was as old as Zoroastrianism. In fact, after correcting some obvious errors, they can be seen to be sister religions which *belonged to the same milieu* but which later separated. At Merv and other sites Zoroastrian and Buddhist artifacts are found side by side. Moreover, many knotty problems of Zoroastrianism can be resolved in reference to Buddhist history. Data from the Persepolis tablets and other sources suggest that Buddhism evolved from Eastern Judaism.

The Afghans are a warlike people and Afghanistan today is a cauldron of intense conflicts but the message of love and amity of Asoka, who was Diodotus-I of Bactria[125], once took the world by storm. The mute archaeological relics, including more than 10,000 recently discovered Buddhist text fragments, reveal Afghanistan's glorious past[126]. On the surface there is just a hint of a Jewish heritage[127] but a detailed study leads to great surprises. Josephus wrote that Aristotle saw a link between the Jews and Indians (Book I:22.). This is usually doubted and traced to Clearchus of Soli and Megasthenes[128] but Aristotle can be seen to be right. In the 18th century B.C. *Abraham and the Jews*[129] went from this area, not Sumer. J. Tod, an early historian of Rajasthan wrote[130];

> Mr. Elphinstone scouts the idea of the descent of the Afghans from the Jews; and not a trace of the Hebrew is found in the Pashtoo, or language of the tribe, although it has much affinity to the Zend and Sanscrit. I cannot refrain from repeating my conviction of the origin of the Afghans from the Yadu, converted into *Yahudi,* or 'Jew'. Whether these Yadus are or are not *Yuti* or Getes, remains to be proved.

Archaeology has changed the historical scenario since the days of Tod, but both he and Elphinstone seem to be correct. Afghans and Indians are offsprings of the Yadus who were the forefathers of Abraham. The Hebrew term *Yehudi* corresponds to the Latin *Judaeus* which

---

[124] The Isigili Sutta of the Majjhima Nikaya names a line of pre-Gotama Buddhas. A recently found Bamiyan fragment written in Greek script names six pre-Gotama Buddhas. See K. Kogi http://www.shin-ibs.edu/documents/pwj3-4/06KD4.pdf

[125] Ranajit Pal, 'An Altar of Alexander Now Near Delhi', *Scholia*, vol. 15, p78-101.

[126] An Afghan scholar, Viradeva, was one of the first Acharyas of the famous Nalanda University.

[127] The lone Synagogue at Kabul and four others at Herat provide a silent reminder of a rich past that is now completely forgotten.

[128] A. Momigliano, "Alien Wisdom", Cambridge, 1975, p. 85.

[129] Tacitus' theories on Jewish origin contains grains of truth but ignores that the garden of Eden was in the East. The Jews were linked to the Amorites who are placed in the west but were also in India. A. Koestler gave a new definition of Jewish origins which has been ignored.

[130] James Tod, 'Annals and Antiquities of Rajasthan', Madras, 1873, p. 214.

resembles Jadu or Yadu, an ancient clan mentioned in the RigVeda and other texts. Alexander is said to have prostrated before the Jewish high priest Jaddua whose name echoes Yadu. B. G. Tilak, M. Shendge and others[131] have alluded to similarities between *Yahweh* and *El* and the RigVedic *Yavah* and *Ila* which supports Aristotle's view. Notably, the names of Abraham and Serai resemble the Indian deities Brahma and Saraswati. The common homeland of Buddhism, Zoroastrianism and Judaism seems to vindicate Max Muller and has crucial implications in the history of religions.

The Dreadful Nepalese Forgeries

The greatest hindrance in the history of early religions is the allusion to a Gotama of Nepal. It is most important to note is that the antecedents of Buddhism are found in the Indus-Saraswati area and South Iran, not Nepal. The primacy of the North-west is shown by that the great Asoka was Diodotus-I of Bactria. The peerless Buddhist monuments of Bamiyan hint at a Buddhist heartland in this vicinity. Recently a huge collection of more than *ten thousand Buddhist fragments* have been found at Bamiyan, a large part of which is now in the *Schoyen collection*. This sensational find has been compared with the *Dead Sea Scrolls*. The colossal Buddha statue of Yun Kang and the thousand Buddhas of China also highlight the crucial role of the Silk-route in the transmission of ideas from the Buddhist heartland of Seistan-Bamiyan-Gandhara. Nothing in the history, archaeology, literature, or art of early Nepal has the faintest hint of Buddhism, and it is uncanny that the patently absurd story of the rise of Buddhism in Nepal has survived scholarly scrutiny for nearly a century. Sir Aurel Stein, who almost single-handedly established the material basis of Buddhism, found nothing in Nepal. The largest number of Buddha images is from Gandhara, not Nepal or eastern India where one should expect them in the Jones-Cunningham theory[132]. Although most historians unwittingly swallow the absurd Nepalese fables, C. Humphreys voices concern[133],

> The Lumbini gardens, where Gotama was born, lie in the difficult Nepal Terai, and Kusinara, where the Buddha passed away, has little to show'.

---

[131] M. Shendge, 'The Language of the Harappans, From Akkadian to Sanskrit', New Delhi, 1997.

[132] Ranajit Pal, 'Non-Jonesian Indology and Alexander',[New Delhi, 2002], p. 40. Jones' idea of a Palibothra at Patna was a disaster in world history. Palibothra was in the North-west. No relic of any Nanda or Maurya king is known from Patna. Jones' idea is supported on the basis of the Chinese reports written a thousand years later which are not valid documents for Mauryan history. See also http://bmcr.brynmawr.edu/2007/2007-12-39.html and http://www.classics.und.ac.za/reviews/05-19pal.htm

[133] C. Humphreys 'Buddhism' (Harmondsworth, 1990) 42.

The eminent Buddhist scholar E. Conze also rejects the fanciful text-based accounts[134];

> To the modern historian, Buddhism is a phenomenon which must exasperate him at every point and we can only say in extenuation that this religion was not founded for the benefit of the historians. Not only is there an almost complete absence of hard facts about its history in India; not only is the date, authorship and geographical provenance of the overwhelming majority of the documents almost entirely unknown, ...

The way out of the chaos is shown by T. A. Phelps, who writes that the 'discovery' of Lumbini in Nepal *was a fraud* engineered by A. Führer[135]. This, in one stroke, shifts the centre of early Buddhism from Nepal to Baluchistan-Seistan-Gandhara. Führer's forgeries may have been a part of a larger plan to bolster Jones' false discovery[136]. Vincent Smith[137] rejected Führer and surmised that Gotama may have been a Central Asian. Similar ideas were put forth by J. Fergusson and S. Beal. D. B. Spooner wrote that Gotama and Chandragupta were from Iran but here it has to be noted that parts of Iran were once in 'India'. A. Toynbee and Sir Charles Eliot were aware of the overlap in the history and geography of Indo-Iran. Eliot writes with great insight[138],

> Our geographical and political phraseology about India and Persia obscures the fact that in many periods the frontier between the two countries was uncertain or not drawn as now.

Clearly, Indian history cannot be written on the basis of data from modern India-Pakistan alone. Conversely, many 'Persian' figures were, in fact, half-Indians. Frye notes that the names Kambujiya (Cambyses) and Kurush are non-Iranian. Alexander's *'victory over the Indians'* at Kohnouj[139] near Patali and Jiroft shows that south-east Iran was India in the fourth century B.C.

---

[134] E. Conze, *'A short History of Buddhism'* (London, 1980)15.
[135] T. A. Phelps, "Lumbini On Trial: The Untold Story", http://www.lumkap.org.uk
[136] 'Patna is too far east' writes Prof. N. G. L. Hammond. Private communication.
[137] V. Smith, *The Oxford History of India* (Oxford, 1958) 74.
[138] C. Eliot, *Hinduism and Buddhism,*, part III (London, 1921) 449. Toynbee wrote that the Achaemenian universal state belonged also to the *Hinduis*, the *Pathavis* etc. A. Toynbee, *'A Study of History'*, vol. VII (Oxford, 1954).652 and 654.

Gaumata was Gotama Buddha

Gaumata[140] hangs like a ghost in Persian history but so great was the illusion created by Führer that no one envisaged that he could be Gotama Buddha. His tussle with Darius-I as recorded in stone at Behistun is one of the greatest stories and scandals of history yet little is known about the nature or cause of his revolt. Toynbee and Olmstead doubted Darius' veracity and held that Gaumata was not an imposter. That Darius-I had lied in the Behistun inscription is also noted by M. Dandamayev[141] and W. Culican[142]. Another report of the events is available from Herodotus whose version largely agrees with Darius' story and is seen by historians such as R. N. Frye as an independent confirmation of Darius' version. But T. C. Young Jr.[143] writes that Herodotus' account may in fact have been based on copies of Darius' document which by Darius' own admission were widely distributed. C. Starr[144] also suspects Darius,

> Students of modern history can read many sources, though an abundance of evidence does not mean that they can always establish exactly what happened or explain why it occurred. In ancient history, on the other hand, it is very rare to have two major accounts of the same event... In recreating the history of the past from its sources the historian must ask himself many questions. In this case do the stories agree entirely? Is Darius trying to prove anything in particular about his right to rule? Darius was a devout Zoroastrian and believed in the truth; yet can we trust his official document? As for Herodotus, did he have any reason not to be impartial? How could he have known about the events? Does he make Darius solely responsible for the overthrow of Gaumata?

T. C. Young Jr. comes very close to recognizing the true Gaumata. He boldly goes on to assert that Gaumata may have *preached a new religion,*

> He then specifically tells us that, 'As before, so I made the sanctuaries which Gaumata the Magian destroyed.' Clearly Darius and Gaumata had a difference of opinion about sanctuaries, and, therefore, we may assume about religion or, at least, about ritual forms of

---

[139] Ranajit Pal, [132], p. 40. In sharp contrast to Kanauj in modern India, Kohnouj near Jiroft and Patali is a very ancient city.

[140] P. Briant's account of Gaumata in the *Encyclopedia Iranica* is based mainly on the Greco-Roman and Persian sources and totally ignores the Indian tradition.

[141] M. A. Dandamayev, *A Political History of the Achaemenid Empire* (Leiden, 1989).

[142] W. Culican, 'The Medes and the Persians' (London, 1965) 65.

[143] *The Cambridge Ancient History*, ed. N.G.L. Hammond, et al., vol. 4, (Cambridge 1988) 57.

[144] C. G. Starr, 'Early Man' (New York, 1973) 181.

religious expression. The details of this disagreement escape us. Indeed, we are not even sure who was the innovator; the Achaemenians may have introduced forms of religion which adherents of an older faith reacted against under Gaumata's leadership; or the Magian could have been attempting to introduce a new religion which offended the establishment. What is critical in the present context is that the story of Darius' overthrow of Gaumata probably contains evidence of a religious as well as dynastic, social/economic and political struggle.

This *new religion* is Buddhism and Gaumata was a contemporary and namesake of Gotama.[145]. '*Gut-ama*' in Sumerian means one whose 'mother is a cow' which agrees with '*Gaumata*' in Sanskrit and old Persian. Furthermore, in the Behistun inscription Gaumata's abode is said to be *Sikayauvatish* or *Shakyavati*, abode of *Shakya*, which matches Gotama's title Shakya. Herodotus wrote that Gaumata was widely popular and M. Dandamayev notes that he was a friend of the poor who freed slaves and waived taxes[146].

Another precious clue is offered by Xerexes. In a trilingual inscription, he boasts over his destruction of the Daivas,

> Among these countries (that submitted to him) was (one) where previously daivas were worshipped. Then, by the favour of Ahura Mazda, I destroyed that daiva place, and I had proclaimed, the daivas shall not be worshipped. Where previously the daivas were worshipped, there I worshipped Ahura Mazda properly with the Law (arta).

Who were the Daivas? The identification of the clan is a serious problem in Persian history. R. N. Frye does not recognize the true Gaumata yet writes with clear insight,[147]

> It is generally agreed that the daiva worshippers were not Babylonians or Egyptians but rather Iranians, or at least Aryans. One may ask whether the Indians living within the Achaemenid empire, who worshipped the old gods, may have been regarded as daiva worshippers.

---

[145] Ranajit Pal, *Gotama Buddha in West Asia*, Annals of Bhandarkar Oriental Research Institute, vol. 77 (1995).
[146] M. Dandamaev, [141], p. 113. I. M. Diakonoff held that Gaumata acted against the nobility.

Due to the Nepalese smokescreen, and geographical confusion about the extent of ancient India no one took up Frye's cue. The Indians in the Achaemenian empire were clearly the early Buddhists. Tradition has it that Trapussa and Bhallika, two merchant brothers from Bactria visited the Buddha immediately after his enlightenment, became his disciples and then returned to Balkh to build temples dedicated to him. That this does not fit in with a Kapilavastu in Nepal occurred to none. To study Buddhist art of the 6th century B.C. one has to venture to the North-west. Afghanistan-Seistan-Baluchistan provides the most ancient traces of Buddhism. The most important fact about the Silk route is that it passed through the land of the Buddha.

Darius-I is said to have murdered his father. Curiously this is echoed in the Buddhist sources. Ajātaśatru is said to have murdered his father and in this he is alleged to have been instigated by Devadatta. This may be a garbled echo of Darius' alleged murder. Vincent Smith[148] wrote that Ajātaśatru was succeeded about 467 B.C. by his son Darśaka. If the date is taken back by 19 years, which is not a large margin of error in Indology, one has the accession of Xerxes who may have been mistaken for a Darius[149]. The name Darśaka or Dara-Ŝaka echoes Darius, though he is not known to be a Ŝaka. He is widely suspected to have been close to Zoroaster but there is no direct proof. Gotama is also never called Ŝaka but his title Shakya has such a hint.

The Name Tiśśa of the Persepolis Tablets

The most convincing refutation of a Nepalese Gotama comes from the Persepolis tablets. Thanks to the painstaking work of R. T. Hallock, W. Hinz and others, the tablets have opened up new vistas of research. They provide priceless data about the economic, religious and social life of Iraq, Iran and India, yet much remains unknown. Curiously, although Sanskrit was considered in the study of the tablets, the Buddhist Pali sources were left out which has hampered the study as Pali is closely related to Avestan[150]. Significantly, the name Tiśśa, which has a unique Buddhist imprint, is found in the tablets[151] (PF 781 and PF 1124). Tiśśa is a timeless name in the Buddhist tradition[152] - Tiśśa-kumara was Asoka's brother and Tiśśa was the 17th of the 24 Buddhas. Tiśśantamma or Tiśśa Dharma of PF 48 is another form that stresses his

---

[147] R. N. Frye, *The Heritage of Persia* (London, 1962) 119.

[148] V. Smith, *The Oxford History of India* (Oxford, 1958) 74. This is mentioned in a play by the early dramatist Bhâsa.

[149] It is not impossible that Xerexes may also have been known as a Darius among some sections of the populace. The Old Testament seems to refer to Cyrus by the name Darius.

[150] Prof. Mark Garrison of Trinity University writes, " .... It is good to know that scholars are making use of them. Too often one feels as if one is working in a vacuum. Good luck on your research." Private communication.

[151] R. T. Hallock, *Persepolis Fortification Tablets* (Chicago, 1969) 231 and 327.

[152] Tiśśa may be related to the Babylonian month-name Tisritum and seems to have an astral connotation. Tisri was the seventh month of the Jewish ecclesiastical year.

religious stature. Malalasekera[153] writes that Tiŝŝa was born at Khemaka which may be Kemarukkaŝ.

PF 1970 mentions Śakka the etira whose name echoes Shakya, Gotama's title. Sakka is the ruler of the Trāyastrimśa Heaven. PF 191 names Mariya-baddana which who may be a 6th century B.C. Maurya. Karabba, Śakśaka (PF 1511) and Abbatema (spelled as Ab-ba-da-a-ma) are explicitly declared as Indians. The suffix 'daama' can be a variant of 'Dharma' and 'Abba' meant 'father' in Sumerian (Appa in Tamil). One of the disciples of Gotama's teacher Āḷāra Kālama was Pukkusa and an identical name, Pukŝa, is found in PF 1027 and PF 1049. PF 1138 cites another god-related name Kukamukka which is related to the Puranic Kokamukha[154]. In the Mahabharata, Kokamukha is a pilgrimage centre. Yaŝda or Yaŝudda, the Haturmakŝa of Matezziŝ, (PF 760 and PF 761) reminds one of Yashoda, the foster-mother of Kṛṣṇa, the famous Yadu hero whose namesake was Karaŝna of PF 1959. Śakśaka the Indian of PF 1511 can be Gotama's uncle Sukkho-dana. Nunudda of PF 1946 may have been Gotama's half-brother Nanda. It is possible that Mannanda or Maha Nanda of PF 138 was Gotama's half-brother. Habbamiŝŝa or Sarvamitra of PF 1603 may not have been the learned Sabbamitta[155] who, according to the Buddhist tradition, taught Gotama Buddha, but he may have been a Buddhist namesake.

Ŝudda-Yauda-ŝaramana Was Suddhodana

However, names such as Tiŝŝa, Śakka, Mandumatiś etc. are only curtain-raisers and further study shows the tablets to be a treasure trove in Buddhist and world history. It is well known that the Buddhists were known as *shramanas* but curiously there are numerous occurrences of the term *Śaramana,* some of whom were Buddhists. The *Śaramanas* were officials entrusted with distribution of grain and other commodities and this gave them a very friendly face. One of the most ubiquitous names in the tablets is Ŝudda-yauda-ŝaramana (also called Ŝudda-yauda-damana). Hallock considers him to be a very important supervisor for workers[156] but it is clear that he was in fact Suddodhana, the father of Gotama Buddha. The term Saramana designated officials in charge of the distribution of food-grains and other provisions and it is hasty to consider all the Saramanas cited in the tablets as Buddhists. The term is similar to Damana and corresponds to Bhaga in the Rigveda. Bhaga was a son of Aditi entrusted with

---

[153] G. P. Malalasekera, *Dictionary of Pali Proper Names*, vol. I (New Delhi, 1983) 1018.

[154] The Brahma Purana (Ch. 219, 229) cites Kokamukha Tirtha and places it in the Himalayas.

[155] G. P. Malalasekera [153], vol. II.

[156] H. Koch proposes two officials of that name, one a Kurdabattiŝ or supervisor of workers in her South-eastern Region III and a second who was the Kanzabarra at Persepolis.

distribution. Gotama's title Bhagava may be linked to his role as a distributor. The title Damana reminds one of Rudra-daman and the Damanavadi Sanghas of Panini[157]. In PF 372 Ŝudda-yauda is declared to be a priest. Hallock writes that Ŝudda-yauda was in charge of the Persepolis area but his jurisdiction may have been wider. PFS 32 is the seal of Ŝudda-yauda. The suffix 'yauda' seems to indicate a link with the Yadus or the Jews of Indo-Iran. Names such as Mira-dana and Mira-yauda may indicate that the Danas were linked to the Yaudas. Mira-dana is also called Vira-dana and he (or Irŝena) may be the Maurya king Virasena cited by Taranatha.

Ŝedda-ŝaramana Was Siddhartha Gotama

The name of Suddhodana in the tablets naturally raises the expectation that the name of his son Gotama would also be found in this archive[158]. This is exactly the case. Ŝedda-ŝaramana cited in several tablets appears to be *Ŝedda-arta* or *Siddhartha* Gotama. Apte's Sanskrit dictionary gives the meaning of 'Siddha' as 'Emancipated' or 'Endowed with supernatural powers or faculties'. In Persian language 'Arta' stands for an exalted person. Hallock associates Yamakaŝedda with the Old Persian term Yama-xšaita and renders it as 'majestic Yama' and links it with the modern term Jamshed. Many Iranian theophoric names such as Artaxerexes, Artabanus, Artapata etc. had the prefix 'arta' as a mark of respect for Arta as a divinity but also at times honouring the principle of Arta or ṛta (righteousness). But although the Zoroastrian form is Arta-Ŝedda or Arta-sata (the name of Darius-III), the Indians who wrote in the reverse direction may have transformed it into Ŝedda-arta or Siddhartha. Y. P. Vasil'ev wrote that Gotama was also called Artha-Siddha.

Ŝedda appears with Ŝuddayauda in PF 149, and with Abbateya and Mitrabauddha in PF 1224 where he is called the Hatarmabattis of Persepolis. According to most scholars the title designates a high-priest (Atharva-pati). The name Ŝedda also occurs in PF 148, PF 221, PF 250, PF 376, PF 573, PF 574, PF 587, PF 635, PF 639, PF 786, PF 1215 and in the journal PF 1968.

PFS 79 may have been the Seal of Ŝedda ŝaramana. Courtesy Oriental Institute, Chicago.

---

[157] V. S. Agrawala, *India as Known to Panini* (Lucknow, 1953).
[158] Ranajit Pal, [125], p.82.

The names Arta-Shata (Siddha-artha) and Arta-Gatum which occur in a Babylonian tablet of 504 B.C.[159] may be of Gotama and his step-mother Gotami. Mitrabauddha named in PF 1224 together with Ŝedda and Abbateya may have been Gotama's close associate Ananda. His father was Gotama's uncle who had a Mitra-related name, Amitrodana. Was he the same as Data-Mithra mentioned in the Aramaic ritual texts, who was also a treasurer? There is yet another possibility that Data-Mithra or Mithradata was another name of Parnaka himself.

Although the personal seal of Ŝedda is not known definitely, one of the texts mentioning him (PF 250) was sealed by PFS 79 which makes it likely that it was his seal. Garrison and Root note that PFS 79 always occurs alone in the tablets that it seals which shows that it belonged to a very important functionary[160]. The *five-pointed dentate crown* of the hero of PFS 79 reminds one of the *Panchalas*. It was worn by Darius-I himself and only three other vassal kings. This may indicate a family relationship. Darius-I was related to Kurash and the same may be true of Gaumata who was close to Kambujiya. The bird-headed winged lion creatures that the hero holds may be significant. Garrison and Root note that the birds have their mouths open which may point to an affectionate relation. In a famous Buddhist legend Gotama rescues a fowl which was injured by Devadatta. Whether this is in any way linked to the fact that Bakadada, and Pirtiŝ (PF 1754) are linked to rations for fowls (basbas) is not clear. As will be shown later, Bakadada may have been Zoroaster and the fowls may have been used in rituals. The dove was a symbol of Yama-Shiva and probably of Dharma.

As already stated Gotama's name Buddho-dana places him in the same bracket as Daniel the Jew and indicates a link of Buddhism with the religion of Nebuchadrezzar and the pre-exilic Jews. Nebuchadrezzar's horror of the withering tree reminds one of Siddhartha's horror of withering and decay[161] before his renunciation. The legacy of Nebuchadrezzar appears to have been inherited by Jainism, Buddhism and Manichaeism. Zoroastrianism, on the other hand, appears to have rejected all forms of asceticism and monasticism.

---

[159] A. T. Olmstead, *History of The Persian Empire* (Chicago, 1948) 192.
[160] M. B. Garrison and M. C. Root, *Seals On The Persepolis Fortification Tablets*, vol. 1, (Chicago, 2001)160.
[161] The tree was home to all life and was allegedly cut down later. This reminds one of the Bodhi tree which was said to have been cut down.

Zoroaster was Devadatta of the Pali Texts

Rostam and Zoroaster are the greatest figures of ancient Persia yet due to careless history writing both remain mythical figures. Although there is no real heartache for the historical Rostam, the unremitting confusion in the history of Zoroaster continues to be a blot on Persian history. R. N. Frye candidly admits failure[162] and though W. B. Henning strongly reacted against the studies on Zoroaster by E. Herzfeld and Nyberg, his linguistic approach has not lead to a better reconciliation with archaeological data. G. Gnoli rightly asserts that Zoroaster belonged to Seistan and locates the Avestan homeland[163] *Airyanem Vaejah* in the Hindu Kush, but being unaware of the true identity of Gaumata, overlooks the precious data available from Pali literature. The Zoroaster of M. Boyce, another prominent writer on the subject, is also no more than a textual construct. About the tablets she writes[164],

> Excavations in the 1930's of the Persepolis treasury, and one area of the fortifications, brought to light a remarkable quantity of inscribed material, in Elamite and Aramaic. These discoveries raised great hopes of clear light being shed on the religion of the early Achaemenians, but such hopes were to be disappointed.

Boyce is perhaps referring to the absence of Zoroaster's name in the tablets but her frustration may, in fact, be due to a tilted perspective. For most modern scholars, Zoroastrianism was a Persian phenomenon just as Buddhism was Indian. This contrasts sharply with the holistic view of earlier scholars such as A. Hillebrandt, H. Brunnhofer, Sir Charles Eliot and A. Toynbee. In any study of early Persian or Indian history, religion or culture it has to be borne in mind that at one stage the *Indians and Iranians were one people* and that much of what is now eastern Iran, Afghanistan and Pakistan was once 'India'. Although the religion of Darius-I is said to be Zoroastrianism, he appears to have adopted a tolerant attitude to other religions including Buddhism. It has to be noted that his adversary Gaumata was the same as Gotama Buddha. This policy appears to have been reversed during the reign of Xerexes who conducted a military operation against the Daivas. He may have banished Gaumata.

M. Boyce's surprise over the absence of Zoroaster's name in the tablets is reminiscent of the claim of R. Thapar that the name of the great Asoka is absent in ancient Greco-Roman

---

[162] "Zarathustra, or Zoroaster as the Greeks called him, presents many problems, and it is discouraging that after so many years of research we do not know when or where he lived or even precisely his teachings." R. N. Frye [147],

[163] The homeland of the Avesta has to be the same as the Vedic homeland and this may have been the Turkmenistan area from where Rama probably came.

[164] M. Boyce, 'A History of Zoroastrianism', vol. II, (Leiden, 1982), p. 132.

literature[165]. It is interesting to note that the name Devadatta (Diodotus) by which Asoka was known in the West[166] was also the name by which Zoroaster was known to the Indians and Elamites. It has already been suggested that Devadatta, the adversary of Gotama in the Buddhist texts, was Zoroaster himself[167]. Herzfeld[168] correctly recognized that Grehma, the adversary of Zoroaster was Gaumata. Most significant is the information that Devadatta broke away from the Buddhist Sangha and founded a rival sect which existed even in the time of the Guptas in the fourth century A.D.

Like the name Tiŝŝa, the name Supra in the tablets also indicate a link with Buddhist history. Devadatta, was a son of a maternal uncle of the Buddha, who is said to have been converted by the Buddha himself. After years in which he had become a respected member of the Sangha, Devadatta is said to have started a series of plots including three attempted murders, in order to take control of the Sangha from the Buddha. Devadatta confronted the Buddha over a number of ascetic practices (dhutanga) which he sought to have made compulsory, but which the Buddha decided should be optional. The Jataka stories speak of an enmity between the two that was not limited to this life, but each of Devadatta's efforts to overthrow the Buddha is said to have resulted in failure.

Zoroaster's father is named as Pourushaspa Spitāma, and his mother was Dughdova. His wife was Hvōvi. In the Indian texts, on the other hand, Devadatta was a son of Suprabuddha, a maternal uncle of Gotama. It is just possible that the name Supra may be a variant of Su-Pouru. Suprabuddha, should have been dead when the tablets were written, but surprisingly there are about eight references to Supra in the tablets who may be close relatives. Gopa, (also called Bhaddakacchana) the wife of Gotama, was the daughter of Supra-buddha. Zoroaster's wife was Hvôvi. In some texts Gotama's close associate Ananda is a brother of Devadatta. In the 13th year after his enlightenment Gotama is reported to have been insulted by his father-in-law Suprabuddha. The reason for this is unknown but it could be due to Gotama's deserting of his wife and family and becoming a wandering monk but there could be other reasons.

---

[165] R. Thapar, *Ashoka and the Decline of the Mauryas*.

[166] Ranajit Pal [125] 90.

[167] ibid., p. 190.

[168] E. Herzfeld, *Zoroaster and his Men* (Princeton, 1948). The name may have been used by many religious heads before the last Zoroaster who was a contemporary of Gaumata. It is likely that many of the pre-Gotama Buddhas were also known as

Damidadda of the Persepolis Tablets May Be Zoroaster

The fact that the tablets do not contain the name Zoroaster need not be taken too literally; the Elamite scribes probably used a different name. Only one tablet (PF 1752) mentions Damidadda who seems to be Devadatta or Zoroaster. About Damidadda, a functionary at Susa, M. Boyce writes[169],

Another name attested on the Elamite tablets, and elsewhere in Aramaic script, is Dāmidāta. There is no dispute that this means 'Created (or given) by the Creator', but it is uncertain to which divinity it refers. It seems probable that in ancient times it meant Varuna, and so this may well be yet another traditional name in honour of 'the Baga' - the god who in Iran was never named. In later times, however, the adjective was understood to refer to Ahuramazda.

The undisputed meaning of the name Dāmidāta may not be 'Created (or given) by the Creator', as claimed by Boyce for 'dat' in Persian also means 'law'. Spooner wrote that Chandragupta was a Zoroastrian which created a furore among Indian historians but may still be correct. In line with Spooner, A. Coomaraswamy also wrote that Asoka may have been a Magian before his conversion to Buddhism which can only imply that he was a Zoroastrian[170]. The line "ldmy dty `l" in Asoka's famous Taxila Aramaic inscription,[171] which Marshall and Andreas translated as `for Romedatta', refers to Damidatta or Devadatta. This has been translated as 'for the creation of law" but a better rendering may be 'ordainer of Law'. "ldmy dty `l" may either be an invocation of Zoroaster as a patron or more likely, a reference to Asoka's own name Devadatta or Diodotus-I[172].

Closely linked to the name Damidata is Bagadates or Bagadatta which was often adopted by Zoroastrians. Bhagadatta is an ancient name in the Puranas. As 'Baga' had the sense of 'Deva' the name Bakadada cited in many tablets may be linked to Zoroaster. The fact that Pirtiŝ appears together with Bakadada (PF 1754) and Damidadda (PF 1752) and in both cases in connection with rations for fowls, is a significant piece of information that implies that they may have been the same person. There were perhaps several persons having the name Bakadada and one of

---

Zoroasters. The same may be true of the name Darius. In fact Buddhism and Zoroastrianism may have the same before the schism of the last Zoroaster.

[169] M. Boyce, [164], p. 143.

[170] A. Coomaraswamy, *History of Indian and Indonesian Art* (London, 1929) 15.

[171] B. N. Mukherjee. 'The Aramaic Edicts of Asoka', Indian Museum, p. 26.

[172] Ranajit Pal [132], p. 53.

them is qualified as an Anshanite (PF 777) but it is highly likely that the owner of the seal PFS 1243 whom Garrison and Root[173] identify as Bakadada may be Devadatta or Zoroaster himself. H. Koch identifies one Bakadada as a high-ranking official in the Shiraz area.

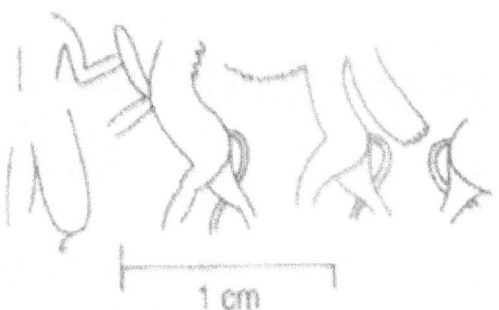

PFS 1243 may be the seal of Zoroaster. Picture courtesy Oriental Institute, Chicago

Incidentally PF 732, which is sealed by PFS 38, the personal seal of Irtasduna (Artystone), names Ŝedda, Artystone, and Bakadadda together which may be very significant. Being the wife of both Darius and Bardiya, Artystone surely knew Gaumata very well. This priceless seal may indicate that Zoroaster was alive in the 25th year and that Bakadada was not a namesake.

Bagadates also appears to have been the name of Asoka's father Bindusara who was called Amitrachates. This seems to be an error for Amitradates or Mithradates. As the term Baga was often substituted for Mithra, Bagadates may have been the same as Mithradates. Bagadates was the first Seleucid satrap whose coins have been found from the Istakhr area. His date coincides with that of Bindusara who is said to have been a great lover of Hellenic culture - a trait which agrees with the fact that during Bagadates' rule there were many Greco-Macedonians in the higher administrative posts.

The Many Faces of Mitra

Mithraism/Mitraism, which was a world-religion that swayed people from the British Isles to India and Central Asia, holds the key to a deeper understanding of ancient religions. Much has been written about the *Indian* Mitra[174] and the *Persian* Mithra[175] but the Persepolis tablets call for a unified approach. Significantly, the symbol of Mithra ✕ also occurs in the

---

[173] M. Garrison and M. C. Root [160] 106.

[174] J. Honda, *The Indian Mitra*, in *Mithraic Studies* ed. J. R. Hinnells, (Manchester, 1975) 40.

[175] Many ideas on Mithraism are derived from second hand sources such as Plutarch and Porphyry. F. Cumont traced the roots of western Mithraism to Iran but this has been disputed by others. The bull-slayer Mithra is not found in Persian art. A. Momigliano considers Mithra from a narrow perspective. A. Momigliano, "Alien Wisdom", Cambridge, 1975, p. 148.

Harappan seals. Mitra is cited in a 15th century B.C. treaty between the Hittites and Mitanni found at Boghazkoy. The Avestan hymn to Mitra is well-known and Mitra was also a Vedic god, but theophoric names such as Mitrabada (PF 333, PF 1295) or Mitrabaudda (Miŝŝabaudda, PF 1553) reveal an unknown face of Mithra. Herodotus describes Mithra as a feminine god which may not be a mistake as is generally thought, but a reference to Ushas who was related to Mitra. The Persian Mithra is also grouped together with Anahita, goddess of the fertilizing waters. In the Zoroastrian texts Mithra is a Sun-god of justice and contract who apparently had little to do with monasticism or asceticism but there seems to be more. Frye writes[176] with insight that Mithra can be seen as a Daiva god and that the Magians of Mithra differed from Mazdayasnian Magians but misses that the former were the Buddhists. The Chehelkhaneh and Haidari caves are probably very ancient and may have belonged to both the Buddhists and Mitraists. The Vedic Mitra was a son of Aditi and a brother of Bhaga entrusted with distribution who may have been less concerned with war. Gudea or Budea of Sumer may have been a Mitra on earth. B. Kuznetsov[177] holds that Bon-po, the pre-Buddhist religion of Tibet was Mithraic and originated from Pasargada. In his view the Buddhist Kalachakra is influenced by Mithraism.

Mitra may have been linked to the mysterious god Shiva[178] who was a world deity. King-names such as Kak-siwe Tempti, Kaksivant, Siwe-Palar-Khuppak, Queen of Sheba and place-names such as Seistan, Sippar, Borsippa etc. show the role of Śiva in the world. *Amon of Siwa* may have been a Mitraic deity for Shiva, whose consort was the goddess Minakshi, was probably called Minuksha[179] (Min = fish, Uksha = Bull) in India and Min in Egypt. The RgVeda mentions caturashri, the 4-pointed (or 4-cornered) weapon of Mitra and Varuna.

Shiva was an ancient Mitraic deity

---

[176] R. N. Frye, [144], p. 120

[177] J. R. Hinnells, *Mithraic Studies*, [174], 134.

[178] R. C. Zaehner points out that Mithra is a counterpart of Indra. W. Doniger is not aware of the antiquity of Shiva, but points to many similarities between him and Indra. The Proto-Shiva in a Harappan seal has been seen as an overlord of the four quarters and may be an early form of Mitra.

[179] All the scholars hold that the fish-sign in the Indus scripts reads as 'Min'. Thus from the 'Proto-Shiva' seal in which the last but one symbol is the fish, the Indian name of Shiva can be seen to contain 'Min'.

Names such as Mithradates and Bagadates are Zoroastrian but Mitrabaudda links Mitra with Buddhism. Compassion or 'Maitri' is a central theme in Buddhism which is linked to Mitra. As the symbol of Mithra ⋈ at Sanchi[180] shows, early Buddhist Sanghas may have evolved from Mitraic communes. Sanchi or Ajanta cannot be fully understood without the Chehelkhaneh and Haidari caves which are wrongly dated to the early Islamic era. The monk Sanghamitra probably belonged to a Mitraic Sangha. The Pali texts indicate that he was not a Buddhist. From Parnaka's remarks in PF 2067 and PF 2068 *Kemarukkaś* appears to be a very ancient religious centre which may be the ancient *Khema-migadava* of the Pali texts[181]. Was it near the Chehelkhaneh-Haidari area?

The Dawn of Religions in the Land of Prophets

The Bamiyan Buddha statue (now destroyed) ranks as one of the greatest religious monuments of humankind[182]. But the greatest religious monument may conceivably be close to the greatest religious centre of the world. Nearby Seistan was not only the locale of the Shahnama and all ancient Persian lore, it was also the *Land of Prophets*. Zabulistan was known to the early Islamic geographers as Darmashan or *Dharmasthan*, abode of religions[183]. Significantly, the name *Alexandria Prophthasia* of Kuh-e Khwaja in Seistan shows that even during Alexander's day this area was known as the Land of Prophets[184]. One of the Prophets was Zoroaster. I. M. Diakonoff and G. Gnoli[185] place Zoroaster in Seistan. Significantly Sir Aurel Stein found an ancient Buddhist shrine at Kuh-e Khwaja[186] and R. Ghirshman wrote that the murals here were the *precursors* of Gandhara art. This is near Dahan-e Gholaman which echoes Gotama's name. Also, nearby place-names such as Zabulistan, Zabol, Vasht etc. imply that this was Gotama's birth-place Kapilavastu[187]. A thorough study reveals that Seistan-Baluchistan was the homeland

---

[180] J. Fergusson, *Tree and Serpent Worship*, (London, 1868) Plate XXX.

[181] Malalasekera, Dictionary of Pali Proper Names,

[182] W. Ball, "How Far Did Buddhism Spread West?", al-Rāfidān, X, 1989: 1-11

[183] See the Map in the *Encyclopedia of Islam*.

[184] That even such a learned scholar as Sir William Tarn had to fall back on 'intuition' to explain the name Prophthasia, shows the damage done by the rogue Dr. Fuhrer.

[185] G. Gnoli, *Zoroaster's Time and Homeland* (Naples, 1980). Gnoli holds that the place-names of the Avesta belong to eastern Iran. The oldest areas known to the Iranians were Afghanistan and areas to its east. The western and the northern regions being either totally unknown, or else they were newly known. The recent archaeological discoveries in the Jiroft area call for a refinement of Gnoli's ideas.

[186] See http://www.cais-soas.com/CAIS/Archaeology/Ashkanian/khuh_e_khwajeh.htm

[187] Ranajit Pal, [132], p. 57. This is only a few kilometers from the Baluchistan border. Seistan is called India in the early Christian sources.

of not only Zoroastrianism and Buddhism but also early *Judaism*[188]. The name Sarā I Ibrahim at Kuh-e Khwaja links Abraham with Alexandria Prophthasia[189] but this has been misjudged. E. Herzfeld writes[190],

> .... Kuh-i-Khwāja, an isolated table rock of Basalt, which rises from the shallow Hamun lake in Sistan, the region where modern Iran, Afghanistan and Baluchistan meet. That strange and deeply impressive rock (cf. Pl. XCVI), the only eminence in the immense plain, is a place, doubly holy. The modern name means 'mount of the Lord', and popular tradition remembers him as Sarā I Ibrahim, a name belonging to the strange assimilations of old Iranian figures to the Biblical ones; the pre-Mohammedan prophet Abraham was identified with Zoroaster. It is the mount Ushida of the Avesta, where under the protection of the king Vistāspa, Hystaspes, father of Darius, the prophet Zoroaster had taken refuge. The pilgrimages during the first fortnight of the Zoroastrian year still testify to its sanctity.

Sadly Herzfeld overlooks the message contained in the name *Alexandria Prophthasia* and is misled by Führer, Tacitus and Woolley. The eminent scholar André Parrot[191] also takes a similar view but his cynicism is unwarranted and stems from Führer's fraud and Woolley's 'discovery' of Abraham's homeland Ur Kashdim. The name is freely rendered as Ur of the Chaldees but this is doubtful as 'Kashi' is a famous ethnicon that belongs to Indo-Iran. The Assyrians referred to Kar-Kassi which was in the East. At any rate there is no good reason for associating Ur in Sumer with the Chaldaeans or Kaldus[192]. Both C. H. Gordon[193] and E. A. Speiser doubted Woolley's idea and the latter gave the clue that many Sumerian city-names echo older Elamite city-names. Ur may have been in Urva, one of the 16 good regions of the Dinkard. After enlightenment Gotama is said to have preached at Uruvela which echoes Ur. Cutha, near Babylon, was known as Tell Ibrahim and may have been linked to Abraham's trek. But there were other Cuthas

---

[188] Rev. M. Black states in the Peake's Commentary of the Bible, "What we know as Judaism, as distinct from the ancient religion of Israel, is a post-exilic phenomenon."

[189] Tarn placed Alexandria Prophthasia at Kuh-e Khwaja.

[190] E. Herzfeld, 'Iran in the Ancient East', p. 29.

[191] There can be no biography of Abraham in the ordinary sense. The most that can be done is to apply the interpretation of modern historical finds to biblical materials so as to arrive at a probable judgment as to the background and patterns of events in his life. Encyclopedia Britannica, 2007.

[192] It is likely that the sign-pair ⊞ ⊞ in the Harappan seals reads as Kala-Kala or Kal2. Ranajit Pal, op cit., p. 170. This shows that India was also a part of Chaldea

[193] T. L. Thompson, 'The Historicity of the Patriarchal Narratives', Harrisburg, 2002, p. 303. See also V. P. Hamilton, 'The Book of Genesis', Michigan, 1990, p. 363.

(Sumerian Gudua); Josephus ("Ant." ix. 14, § 1, 3) places Cutha in Persia.[194] Hansman writes about a Mari in Elam[195]. There may have been another Harran in Arachosia which was Haraiva. Herat may be related to Haraiva. Haranpur near Lahore has a similar name although it is not related to Abraham. There are many towns named Haran or Hairan in this area.

More important are the clues hidden in the name Alexandria Prophthasia which was Kapil (avastu) or Babil. I. J. Gelb suggests that the name Babylon or Babil does not mean 'gate of God' as is usually supposed[196] but echoes an earlier city-name. E. Herzfeld wrote about the city 'Bawer' in Iran, allegedly founded by Jamshid. Bawer is clearly an echo of Babil. That Abraham could have been related to Babil, which echoes the name Bible, seems natural. Babil is cognate with Kapil. Many city-names in Palestine such as Byblos, Karkuia and cities with Ram-names echo earlier city-names near Afghanistan-Seistan and the Indus region.

That the early Jews were Indo-Iranians is shown by the close links between Judaism and Zoroastrianism[197]. Judaic angelology, demonology, the doctrine of resurrection, the eschatological doctrines, and the monotheism of Yahweh bear strong resemblances to Persian religion but as the ancestors of the Jews were Indo-Iranians, this was not a one-way traffic. Similar statements have been made regarding Zoroastrianism and Buddhism which require more careful analysis.

D. P. Mishra linked the Jews with Indian history[198]. In his view Yadu and Turvasu, sons of Devayani, came from eastern Iran. However, the Yadus may have been in the Indus-Saraswati valley from a very early period. In fact Abraham's father Tera may have been Yadus-Tera or Yudhisthira.[199] Abraham's trek is usually dated to the mid-eighteenth century B.C. which coincides with the fall of the Indus-Saraswati and the Sumerian cultures. After the Bharata War, which may be coincident with the fall of the Indus-Saraswati, Yudhisthira undertook a westward journey to Meru which may have been continued by Abraham. The name of one of Yudhisthira's sons was Yaudheya which echoes Jadu.

---

[194] Thousands of tablets found at the palace of Mari have greatly impressed Biblical scholars. These mention the 'Hapiru' which echoes the term 'Hebrew' but also seems to be cognate with Babiru. There is also mention of the 'Banu Yamina' or the Benjaminites who are placed in an area north of Mari, i.e. Harran which was famous for the temple of Sin. Incidentally the Amorite homeland is also indicated in the same area in some sources but there are other possibilities. There was another Sippar in the East. Harappan writing was from right to the left like Hebrew and there may have been other points of contact. It is very likely that the name Ben Yamin or Min Yamin also occurs in the Harappan seals.

[195] J. Hansman, "A "Periplus" of Magan and Meluhha". Bulletin of the School of Oriental and African Studies, 36 (3): 554–587. 1973.

[196] See J. Oates, 'Babylon', (London, 1979, p.60)

[197] "Now it was from this very creed of Zoroaster that the Jews derived all the angelology of their religion...the belief in a future state; of rewards and punishments, ...the soul's immortality, and the Last Judgment - all of them essential parts of the Zoroastrian scheme." King and Moore, "The Gnostics and Their Remains", London, 1887.

[198] D. P. Mishra, [123] p. 123.

Kabbala and the Religion of the Yadus

The link of Abraham's forefathers with Iran, Afghanistan and India can be seen from the Jewish Kabbala, the central plank of which is the startling doctrine of the deity. S. Radhakrishnan writes[200] that many of its features like the potency assigned to letters, the use of charms and amulets, the theory of emanation as opposed to creation ex nihilio, the doctrine of the correspondence between the macrocosm and microcosm, belief in rebirth and a definite pantheistic tendency, are alien to the spirit of Rabbinic Judaism and akin to that of the Indian Upanishads and Tantrism. The roots of Tantrism are ancient. R. J. Zwi Werblowsky writes[201]

> Of course Kabbalah is not the same as Jewish mysticism, of which it is merely one phase, though the most important and far-reaching in its effects. In spite of its name which means '[esoteric] tradition' and in spite of the Kabbalist's sincere belief that they only revived the old mystical teachings of Moses and earlier sages, there can be no reasonable doubt that the system as such evolved in the thirteenth century in Southern France and Spain.

This view is clearly short-sighted but it is shared by many scholars for whom Judaism begins with Abraham the wanderer. Werblowsky wonders in vain,

> How must one explain the resurgence of myth in the midst of what is usually considered to be the moral enemy of mythical religion? By what channels or mechanisms did mythical and Gnostic symbols reassert themselves in medieval Jewry? What is the relation of the old, Oriental Gnosticism and the almost explosive reappearance of similar ideas .... For our present purpose we can ignore these questions .... .

Sadly Werblowsky's equipment allows for no other alternative. The answer has to be sought in the Eastern Judaism of Terah. A. Edrei and D. Mendels write about the split between the eastern

---

[199] Ranajit Pal, *Non-Jonesian Indology and Alexander,* (New Delhi, 2002), p. 175. Yudhisthira was closely related to the famous Yadu hero Krishna and one of his sons was Yaudheya.

[200] S. Radhakrishnan, 'Eastern Religions and Western Thought', [Oxford, 1939], p.197.

[201] The Concise Encyclopedia of Living Faiths, p. 26.

and Western Diaspora[202] but are not aware of the true nature of the split. Eastern Judaism appears to have been less absolutist and closer to Buddhism. Also their Eastern Jews are only from Babylonia and Russia. Kabbala is akin to 'Kephalia' of Mani, 'Kaivalya' of the Jainas, 'Nirvana' of the Buddhists and Moksha of the Hindus.

Daniel, Haman, Shethar and Boznai

The suffix 'yauda' in the name of Ŝudda-yauda (Gotama's father) strongly implies that Buddhism may have evolved from Judaism. This is supported by Al-beruni's data that Gotama's name was Buddho-Dana which agrees with the fact the names of his father, and all his uncles had the suffix 'dana'. Gotama, therefore, belonged to the same clan as *Daniel the Jew* who was older.

The Book of Esther of the Old Testament, together with the Book of Ezra[203], provides evidence of contact between the Jews and Buddhists in the sixth century B.C.. The book is a secular and strongly sectarian document the historical background of which has perplexed scholars. R. de Vaux wrote that it refers to the intrigues in the Achaemenian court and this is usually taken to be the reign of Xerexes. According to some scholars the book may have been composed as late as the first half of the 2nd century B.C., though the Purim festival could belong to the earlier Babylonian exile of the 6th century B.C..

The name of the seven princes of Persia and Media, who saw the king's face, and sat first in the kingdom are given in the Book of Esther as Carshena, Shethar, Admatha, Tarshish, Meres, Marsena, and Memucan. Carshena appears to be a namesake of the Yadu hero Krishna and may in fact be Karaŝna of PF 1959 who is called hazatap. Marsena may be Virasena who may be Mira-dana or Mirayauda of the tablets. Finally, Sether is clearly Siddhartha Gotama who is Ŝedda-ŝaramana of the tablets. Haman appears to be Ŝaman of PF 1537.

A. Kuhrt[204] refers to the 'good Iranian name' of Bagapa, the satrap of Babylon and 'eber nari' during Darius' reign and even considers the link with Tattanu but misses that Bagapa and Tattanu correspond to Gotama's titles Bhagava and Tathagata. The Book of Ezra also refers to Shether (Shiddhartha) and Boznai (Buddha). The latter can also be a close associate such as Ananda who could have been Mitrabauddha. The name Shethar occurs in the Book of Esther.

---

[202] Journal for the Study of the Pseudepigrapha, Vol. 16, No. 2, 91-137 (2007)

[203] Ezra was a Persianized Jew(4th cent. B.C.) who was a member of the Persian court. He read from a book of Law which was illegible to both Hebrew and Aramaic speakers (Nehemiah Ch.VIII) which indicates that the language was either Avestan or Pali which is similar.

[204] Cambridge Ancient History, vol. IV, 1988.

The name Buddho-Dana puts Gotama in the same bracket as Daniel the Jew, a contemporary of Nebuchadrezzar-II and shows that Gotama himself was a Yadu, an Eastern Jew.

The Amorites, Indo-Europeans and Early Jews in Indo-Iran

The history of the Amorites reveals the intimate bonds between the Jews and India-Iran-Afghanistan[205]. They are usually given the blanket label 'Semite', but this is hasty[206]. It has escaped the notice of all that they were one of the *ancient inhabitants of Indus-Saraswati civilization*[207]. The Amorites are shown as tall and fair in ancient Egyptian art, and can also be seen as *half-Indo-Europeans*. They shared many features with the Vedic people. The Sumerians called them nomads, a well known characteristic of the Vedic people. They were not buried after death which also fits with Indian customs. Their homeland *Mar-tu* closely corresponds to the Sanskrit *Martya*, the abode of the mortals. Indra's palace was Amaravati (vati='house') which echoes the name 'Amar' of the Amorites. The name Maurya also appears to be linked to the Amorites (Heb. ᶜmori).

Despite occasional references to clashes with them it is clear that the Amorites were the next of kin of the Jews; 'Thy father was an Amorite', wrote Ezekiel. The Israelites are referred to as Aziru in the Amarna tablets which may correspond to Aja, the mythical progenitor in the Indian texts. They are usually equated with the Phoenicians/Canaanites but this is only partly true. The Phoenicians, according to Herodotus, came from the 'Red Sea' which can be seen to be the Persian Gulf. C. H. Gordon and L. Srinivasan point to the link of *Canaanite language*[208] with *Bengali* which is generally thought to be an *Indo-European language*. A. Haldar writes[209] that an Amorite person had the title *'Lapputtum'* which has a straightforward rendering in Sanskrit-like languages as 'Son of Lava'. This is reminiscent of the phrase *'He Lavo'* quoted in the Satapatha Brahmana[210] as an example of alien speech. Lapputtum may have been a very early Levite. 'Laban' in Hebrew means 'white' whereas in Akkadian 'Laba' meant 'lion'.

---

[205] The location of the original Amorite homeland is not definitely known. One extreme view that emerges from the Sumerian and Akkadian inscriptions is that kur mar.tu/māt amurrim covered the whole area between the Euphrates and the Mediterranean, Arabia included. Another radical notion is that the "homeland" of the Amorites was a limited area in Syria (Jebel Bishri). One theory refers to Arabia in general as the area from where the Amorites once came. Another refers to a limited area (unknown) in Arabia, the mountain district of Martu. A. Halder, 'Who Were The Amorites?', (Leiden, 1971), p. 7.

[206] See http://www.historyfiles.co.uk/KingListsMiddEast/MesopotamiaAmorites.htm

[207] All the scholars agree that the fish-sign in the Indus scripts has to be read as 'Min'. Thus from the 'Proto-Shiva' seal in which the last but one symbol is the fish-sign, an Indian name of Shiva can be seen to contain 'Min'. While 'Min' stood for the procreative aspect of Shiva his destructive aspect was typified by Mahakal who closely matches the Amorite god Mekal. The name Mahakal seems to be in the Harappan seals. See Ranajit Pal [132], p. 169.

[208] C. H. Gordon and L. Srinivasan, 'Mother Tongue': Issue 1, Dec. 1995, pp. 202-206,

[209] A. Haldar, [205], p. 5.

[210] "The Asuras, deprived of speech, saying 'he lavo', 'he lavah', were defeated". 'Śatapatha Brâhmana' 3.2.1.23-24.

As the links of Bengali with Canaanite shows, many of the problems can be traced to the much-abused blanket term 'Semitic'[211] which is the cornerstone of Judaic scholarship. S. N. Kramer's statement that the Semites were present in Iraq in the fourth millennium B.C. even before the Sumerians[212] may be due to the arrival of the Amorites who were a mix of Semites and Indo-Europeans. The Jews are seen as Semites but the Sanskritist John Brough pointed to the existence of Dumězilian tripartite ideology characteristic of the Indo-Europeans in the Old Testament[213]. This is also demonstrated by the fact that *Rishava* of the Sanskrit texts corresponds to *Resheph*, a so-called Semitic god. Rama was an 'Aryan' par excellence of the Ikshvaku line who seems to be related to the so-called 'Semite' King Lamgi Mari who calls himself an Issakv. The links between Anatolia, in particular the Mari area, and India and Iran seems unfathomable. Mari was located near ancient 'Barata'[214] which echoes the elusive toponym Bharata (India) and ancient Hinduism. Mithridates-I (same as Chandragupta and Orontobates), who had Amorite links, was the[215] Satrap of Pontus and ruled India. The same may have been true of Parnaka who may have been an early Mithradata. There are numerous other evidences including the symbolism of the *three hares* which link early Judaism[216] with Buddhism and the East.

Acknowledgments

The author gratefully remembers the kind encouragement of the late Prof. T. C. Young Jr. of the Royal Ontario Museum, Toronto, from an early stage of the present work.

---

[211] Colin Renfrew, 'Archaeology and Langage'(Cambridge, 1987), p.13. The Russian linguist N. S. Trubetskoy denied any family-tree relationships among the I-E languages. In his view the ancestors of the Indogerman language groups could have been quite dissimilar but through continued contact, mutual influence and word borrowing became similar.

[212] S. N. Kramer, American Journal of Archaeology, 52 (1948), pp. 159 ff.

[213] C. Scott Littleton, 'Indo-European Religions', in 'Encyclopedia of Religion', ed. Mircea Eliade, p. 211.

[214] Bit Buruttash, Mygdonia, Barata, Ambarish R.D. Barnett Cambridge Ancient History Animal fables p. 434 The Phrygians have been linked to the Vrigus of the Indian texts

[215] See the online resource Http://www.ranajitpal.com

[216] The 'three-hares' motif was used by both the Buddhists and the Jews and point to a common heritage. The earliest occurrence of the symbolism is in the Buddhist Dun Huang caves. It was also adopted by Islam and Christianity. In Britain the motif is most common at Devon where 17 parish churches contain roof bosses depicting the three hares.

Dacia and the cult of Mithras by Csaba T. Szabó

Introduction

The paper's main goal is to affix to a proper place the province of Dacia, a rarely researched or misinterpreted topic in international scientific literature. Furthermore, our study presents the cult of Mithras in Dacia, one of the most recognizable and most popular spiritual phenomena in the province, which was an integral part of the Roman Empire for more than one and a half century.

Dacia- a province of variety

The territory of Dacia –today Romania's central part, the major political, cultural and economical zone of this area- became a part of the Roman Empire in the time of Trajan (*Cizek, E.,pp.258-264*), after two bloody wars between the Roman Army and the Dacian Kingdom (*Petolescu, C.C pp. 1-2*). This territory was important for a developing and growing empire not only for its rich and essential natural resources, but also because Trajan's aim and the object of the First and Second Dacian War (101-102 and 105-106 AD) was a geopolitical one: to create a buffer-state, an assurance for the military and political stability of the empire. Dacia's favorable geopolitical location served to protect the limes of the Roman Empire and to divide the Barrbaricum, world of unknown and danger for the Romans. For this reason Dacia, one of the last provinces created, had the longest direct border with the Barrbaricum. The Dacian limes became one of the most highly protected and militarized area in the Danubian territories. The province became a propugnaculum Imperii, a natural fortress in a dynamic zone of the Empire.

The great and diverse dynamism of military and commercial groups had created a multicultural and multiethnic atmosphere perfectly fit in the Roman world and mentality.

The first city of Dacia became Colonia Ulpia Traiana Augusta Sarmizegetusa, the only city founded by *deductio*. Sarmizegetusa–named after the previous capital of Dacian Kingdom- became the political, economical and spiritual capital of the province. Later, in the 3rd century AD the city got the honorific title of *"metropolis"*. There were ten other cities in roman Dacia: Apulum- which became later the seat of the legatus Augusti pro praetore, governor of the province-Potaissa, Napoca, Drobeta, Romula, Dierna, Tibiscum, Ampelum, Porolissum and Apulum Severiana. 48 Roman settlements are mentioned in the Tabula Peutingeriana appear, which indicates a great urban life, a dynamic and prosperour economy and also a powerful roman layer of bureaucracy.

The religious composition of the province reflects this variety. The multiethnicity of the region was reflected in the religious and spiritual palette by the phenomena of syncretism. The *interpretatio romana* changed the spiritual spectrum of the region: Roman gods appeared in Dacia in a new form, reflecting a changing world, the reborn and the fundamental reform of the ancient spirit (*Nemeti, S. 2005, pp.39-79.*). "Orientalism" – word dignified by Cumont in scientific literature – created new "gods", a strict spiritual pantheon, where spirit, redemption, after-life and sacrament obtained new interpretations and meanings (*Cumont, F. 1956, pp.10-21.*).When Dacia appeared on the map of the Roman Empire, suddenly as a *"night miracle"*, oriental cults were already spread in Roman Empire and the process of a spiritual revolution predicted by ancient authors (Cicero, Iuvenalis and others) became a real phenomenon in almost every segment of this dynamic political entity: old gods were changed with new ones in the everyday life of the people. The structure and " *libens voto et merito- system*" remained unchanged as the official facade of the imperial religion too, but the casual and ordinary spiritual life of people changed deeply not only formally by it's traditions and externals, but also theologically, substantively. Isis, Cybele, Attis, Mithras and the other Oriental gods took a more human form by their principle of redemption and greater mysticism which opened undiscovered segments of the human soul.

This syncretic variety was present in Dacia too, with local features, reflected especially in Oriental cults, including the cult of Mithras.

The cults of Dacia

A complete and up to date monography about the spiritual life and cults of roman Dacia is painfully missing from Romanian historiography and bibliography. The existing works are methodologically imperfect and professionally objectionable, or their actuality is played out by the new archaeological and philological discoveries. There was always a main problem –especially in the age of communism- to escape the religious topics from the influence and harmful effects of some dogmatic ideologies. The first scientific works about ancient religion and the cults of the region appeared in the 20th century, all of them influenced by the main German currents, such as of Wissowa and Domaszewski. The first – and still the only available- monography was that of an English author, Leslie Webber Jones, whose work *"The cults of Dacia"* from 1929 became a highly quoted and a reference book in the history of religion (even the great historian, Mircea Eliade quoted Jones with some critical notes) but later its unique status transformed into a heavily criticized one. The research of Romanian ancient historians at the beginning of the 20th century focused especially on archaeology and topography, the political and administrative history of Dacia and the creation of the province. There are few articles from this period, most significant are the works of Octavian Floca, Constantin Daicoviciu , Mihail Macrea and Emil Condurachi.

> In the 80's and most significantly, in the 90' when important excavations began, religious studies got a higher popularity in the field of research. New monographies appeared about some popular cult such as the cult of Iupiter Dolichenus, the "Trachian rider", or about Sol Invictus. Works by Silviu Sanie, Mihai Barbulescu and others opened a new perspective in the Romanian Roman studies integrated these currents in the international circulation (for further reading: Sanie, S.: *Cultele orientale in Dacia romana*. 1981, Barbulescu, M, *Interferente spirituale in Dacia romana*. 1984., Felix Marcu, *Places for worship in forts*. In: AMN 41-42. I. 2004-2005).

The last significant work in this topic is the monography of Sorin Nemeti about the religious syncretism in Roman Dacia, appeared in 2005.

The book summarizes the last results of religious and archaeological studies, and as a reason, we can get a great kaleidoscope of ancient gods and their syncretistic, in a new and locally interpreted form. The pantheon of Dacia, formed as a result of *interpratatio romana* and - possibly- "*interpretatio dacica*" is created by the following archaeologically or epigraphically attested gods : Iuno Regina, Venus Genetrix, Semlia, Fortuna, Neptunus, Nymphae, Ianus Geminus, Silvanus, Diana, Apollo, Castores, Saturnus, Caelestis, Aesculapius- Eshmoun, Liber Pater, Libera, Nemesis, Hercules, Dii Penates, Dii patrii, Dii Mauri, Hecate, Vulcanus, Mercurius, Mars, Lares militares, Terra Mater, Venus, Ceres, Luna, Sol, Priapus, Dis Pater, Minerva, Sucellus and Nantosuelta, Aeracura, Epona, Bel, Iarhibol, Aglibol, Malakbel, Bene Agrud, Azizos, Iupiter Optimus Maximus, Iupiter Dolichenus, Iupiter Turmazgades, Iupiter Heliopolitanus, Iupiter Hierapolitanus, Iupiter Balmarcodes, Iupiter Cimistenus, Zeus Syrgastos, Iupiter Erusenus, Iupiter Bussumarus, Iupiter Bussurigius, Zeus Narenos, Sarnendenus, Zeus Sittakomicos, Iupiter Cernenus, Iupiter Sabazius, Iupiter Zbelsurdos, Iupiter Depulsor, Iupiter Taranis, Theos Hypsistos, Abraxas, Deus Aeternus, Ipiter Summus Exsuperantissimus, Magna Mater, Sol Invictus, Isis, Osiris, Apis, Attis, Atargatis, Baltis, Mater Troclimena and most specially Mithras the Invincible, whose cult is one of the most highly attested by material sources and evidences.

This short overview is just a little taste from the spiritual and religious life of this multiethnic and multicultural province, where dozens of nations circulated for more than one and a half century.

One of the main gods of this crowded pantheon was Mithras.

Mithras in Dacia

The origins and the exact itinerary of the Roman Mithras is still a black spot in historiography even after a hundred years of intense research. Being a mystery cult, the sources of Mithraism are poor and incomplete, insufficient for a detailed research and to reveal the everyday life and the historical movements of this phenomenon. With more than two and a half thousand of mithraic monuments from all around the Empire, this cult has the largest archaeological and epigrafical evidence of his large and wide-spread existence. Despite all of this evidence, the circumstances of the formation of the cult and the exact itinerary and historical backround are unknown or full with unaccountable details. The main cause of these proliferating questions and problems is the unrevealed theology, the spiritual essence of Mithraism, which made from this syncretic process a mystery cult based on seven-grade initiation and secret procedures *(Clauss, M. 2000, pp.21-26.)*

Wherever and howsoever formed the roman – or so called "western" –Mithras *(Beck, R. 2006, pp.1-15.)* it is certain, that in the 1st century, when the earliest datable sources appeared, we observe an original, new God, with specific oriental features. The question is- which became a highly debated sctientific and historiographical topic, the basis of the mithraic studies- whether these oriental features of Roman Mithras are just some historical-traditional fossils, remains of a long culture-spiritual process, or the creations of an unknown founder, a spiritual leader, whose work and activity fit comfortably in the religious zeitgeist of the 1st century AD. *(Merkelbach, R. 1984, p.25.)*

The Roman Mithras – radically different from its onomastic predecessors- appears in the first sources with a complete theology, cosmogony, mythology where every small symbol, every word and movment represent an integral part of a highly conceptualized theology of redemption and salvation. In Mithraism the sanctuary gets a new sense of interpretation: it became a "miniuniverse", an image of the universe, where the architectural exteriority fit perfectly with the theological essence of the cult. Every main element of this universe- the pronaos, the steps, the naos, the two benches, the zodiac elements, the symbolic sacrificial holes on the ground, the statues of the two torchbearers Cautes and Cautopates and the main altar – are brought together by a spiritual force. This new context, that a mithraeum is a small recreation of the Mithraic world and theology *(Beck, R. 2006, pp.102-152)* gives a new perspective in researching and analyzing the Dacian sources.

The research of the cult of Mithras in the territory of ancient Dacia begun in the 19th century with the systematic excavation of the Sarmizegetusa mithraeum. The excavations between 1882 and 1884 revealed a very rich sanctuary *extra muros* of the Roman city, near a small brook. The Sarmizegetusa mithraeum- still the only scientifically analyzed- was discovered by the Hungarian

Király Pál and his team, who worked as a member of the History and Archaeology Association of Hunyad County. He has published the artifacts in a very adequate, positivist and extremely detailed monography in 1886, which became the only monographic work in the Dacian mithraic research still today (*Király P., 1886*) In the 20th century after Transylvania became part of Romania, the archaeological excavations multiplied, but their professional quality was less reliable. Excepting a few articles about Mithras and the occasional discoveries, the next great catalog and monography about mithraic artifacts and the whole cult was the monumental work of Vermaseren, the Corpus Inscriptionum et Monumetorum Religionis Mithriacae, where more than 270 elements from Dacia are included.

After the CIMRM, some new discoveries appeared in Dacia (the Pojejena artifacts, Porolissum artifacts, new excavations in Apulum by Alexandru Diaconescu between 1986-2005). These new objects were generally published in local Romanian articles and journals, with few international connotations (*Gudea, N.- Bozu,1976*).

The summary of this centenarian research is a great perspective of Mithraism in Dacia. Almost 10% of the total religious sources belong to Mithras.

It is hard to reconstruct the itinerary of Mithras in Dacia, but there is some nuanced evidence that shows how this popular god spread in the new Danubian province, which became- after the theory of Merkelbach and Tóth- one of the main playgrounds of Mithras, the Invincible God.

One useful tool is the onomastic of Mithras. There are thirteen forms in which this God appear in Dacia. This can help us to categorize the mithraic material in some chronological intervals: the name "Nabarze (Persian word for "victorious" or "invincible") and Sol Invictus Nabarze Mithras are probably the earliest examples of the presence of this cult in Dacia. After the analogies from the other Danubian provinces, it's seems arguable that after 106 AD, Mithras was brought in Dacia by the multiethnic groups "*ex toto urbe romano*" as Cassius Dio mentioned.

It is sure that in the first part of the 2nd century AD Mithras was already an important part of the Dacian pantheon. The seventy names of the followers reflect an interesting social perspective about the Mithras community: we can find priests, actors, soldiers (the vast majority of the cultivators) and urban officials too. The moment of the apparition is probably the occupation of the province.

We don't know how the cult spread in Dacia: who were its spreaders, chief-distributors of this new, and uncommon cult in the region and what was theirs itinerary, tool and method to spread this new cult. The oddity of the cult may reflect the followers' social and ethnic composition: there is no evidence that Mithras was popularized in the circle of Dacian people. The first half of the second century was probably characterized by the slow propagation of the cult in urban and powerfully militarized areas of the province (especially in Apulum and Sarmizegetusa, where sanctuaries are attested epigraphically or archaeologically).

In the second half of the 2nd century AD the process accelerated. This fact is argued by the great number of altars, the variety of the Mithras onomastics (twelve epithets are known from Dacia for Mithras) and the geographical extension of artifacts. There are 26 settlements in Dacia where mithraic monuments were found.

The golden age of the cult in Dacia was in the first half of the 3rd century, when possibly twelve (Sarmizegetusa, Apulum, Slăveni, Potaissa, Dostat, Decea Mureșului, Vințu de Jos, Cincșor, Pojejena, Porolissum, Romula, Peștera Veterani) sanctuaries existed here. It is difficult to locate and to define a mithraeum in Dacia (there is no definition for a mithraeum, but such a a sanctuary has many architectural specificites and as such requires a real definition in scientific literature), because there is little archaeological evidence for sanctuaries. The only sanctuary excavated is the Sarmizegetusa mithraeum, but even its reconstruction is too superficial and schematic. Király Pál, the discoverer, made the reconstruction after German analogies (Heddernheim Mithraeum and some sanctuaries from Ostia). In the 19th century, when mithraic studies were in their infancy, these analogies were the only possibilities available. The other sanctuaries are known only from epigraphic inscriptions or from 19th century excavations, which location and data vanished by time.

The Sarmizegetusa mithraeum was one of the largest in the Roman Empire: its length was more than forty meters and after the calculations of Király, it had more than a hundred worshippers. Even if it was proved that the initial calculations were wrong in some aspects, what is certain is that this sanctuary was the biggest in Dacia and with the largest civilian community. There were found more than a hundred pieces from votive altars.

Apulum had a special situation. As the seat of the governor, the two cities formed there had at least four sanctuaries, only two being attested archaeologically.

The other sanctuaries- or possible mithraeums- were small chambers, where a moderate community got together, especially in a military or commercial zone (castrum, near a mansion or even in a vicus).

Dacia remained a part of the Empire until the end of the 3rd century, when Roman troops were withdrawn from the main part of the province. Probably the cult of Mithras flourished after this political and military act as well, as the Pannonian analogies suggest this. The lethal blow came from the arriving and spreading of Christianity, which probably represented the end of the most popular mystery cult in Dacia. Mithras' altars and prayers were silenced for thousands of years in the Carpathian Basin, until human curiosity rediscovered its mighty altarpieces.

Bibliography

- Alicu, D., *Le temple de Mithras de Pojejena*. In: *Sargeția*, 1999-2000, 28-29, nr. 1.
- Beck, R.,*Beck on Mithraism- collected works with new essays*. Cromwell Press, 2004.
- Beck, R. *The religion of the Mithras cult in the Roman Empire*. Oxford University Press, 2006.
- Benett, J. *Trajan Optimus Princeps*, London,1997.
- Cizek, E.,*L' Époque de Trajan*, Paris, 1983.
- Clauss, M., *The roman cult of Mithras*, Edinburgh University Press, 2000.
- Cumont, Franz: *The mysteries of Mithra*. Dover Pub. NY. 1956.
- Király P., *A sarmizegetusai mithraeum*. In: Archeológiai Közlemények, Budapest, 1886.
- Nemeti, S.. *Sincretismul religios în Dacia romană*, Cluj, 2005.
- Nemeti, S.-Nemeti, I., *Plantes, grades and soteriology in Dacian Mithraism*. In: Acta Musei Napocensis 41-22/I. pp.107-124.
- Paribeni, R. *Optimus Princeps I-II.*, Messina, 1926-27
- Petolescu, C.C., *L'organisation de la Dacie sous Trajan et Hadrien*. In: Dacia NS 29,1985.
- Vermaseren, M., *Corpus Inscriptionum et Monumentorum Religionis Mithriacae* I-II (CIMRM). Hagae, 1956-60.

Appendix

The plan of the Sarmizegetusa Mithraeum (from: Pál Király, A Sarmizegetusai Mithraeum. Budapest, 1886).

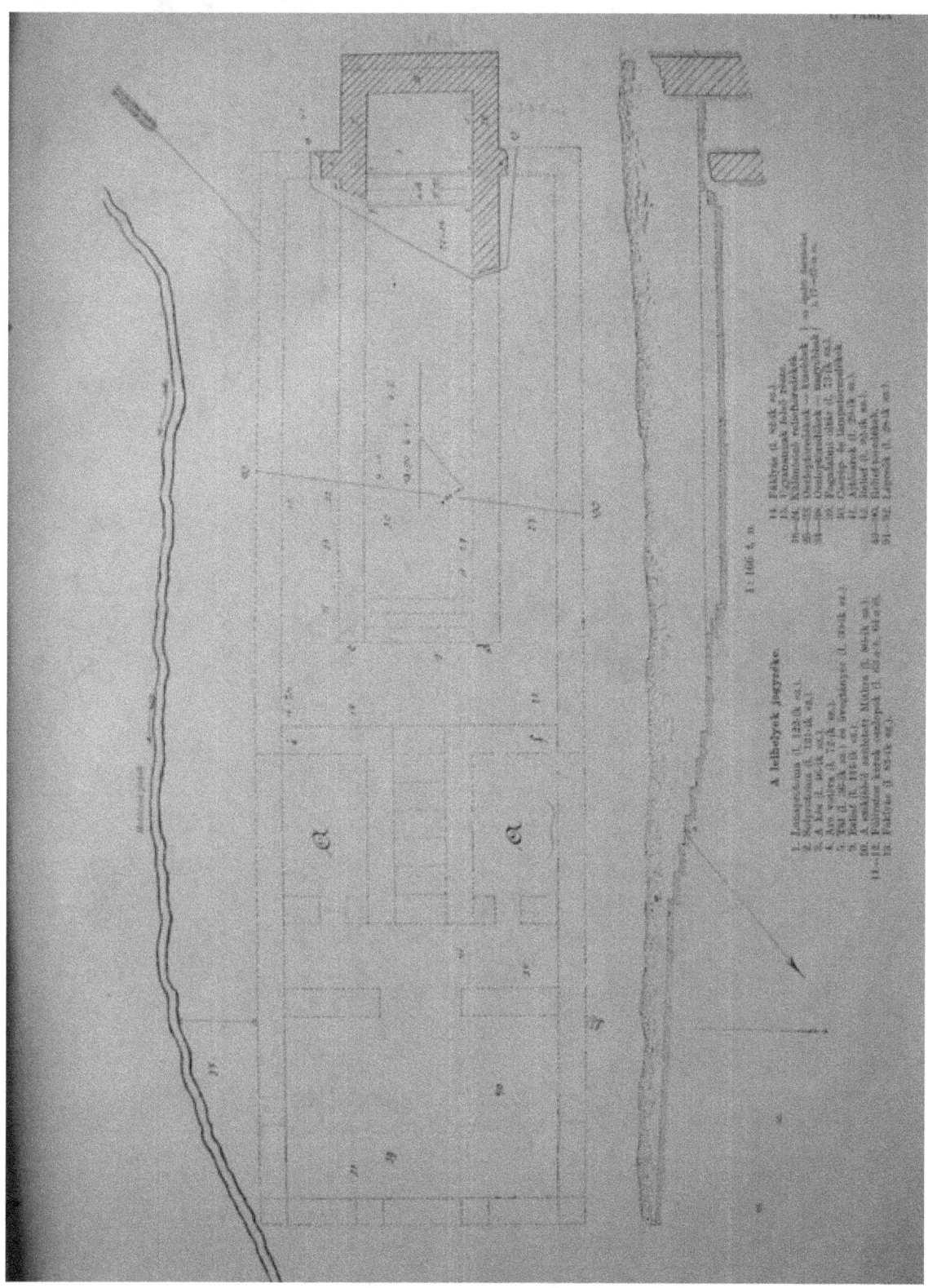

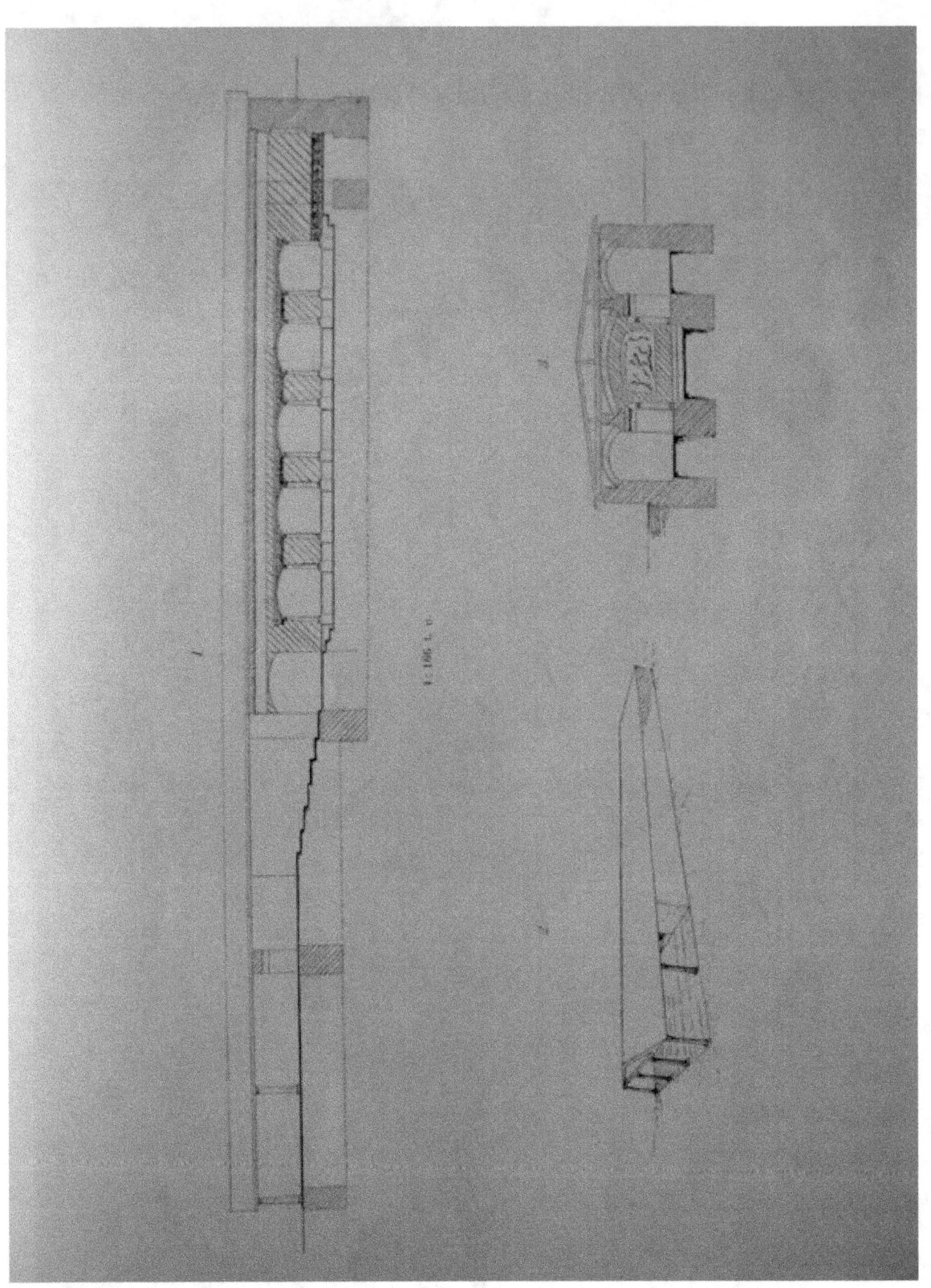

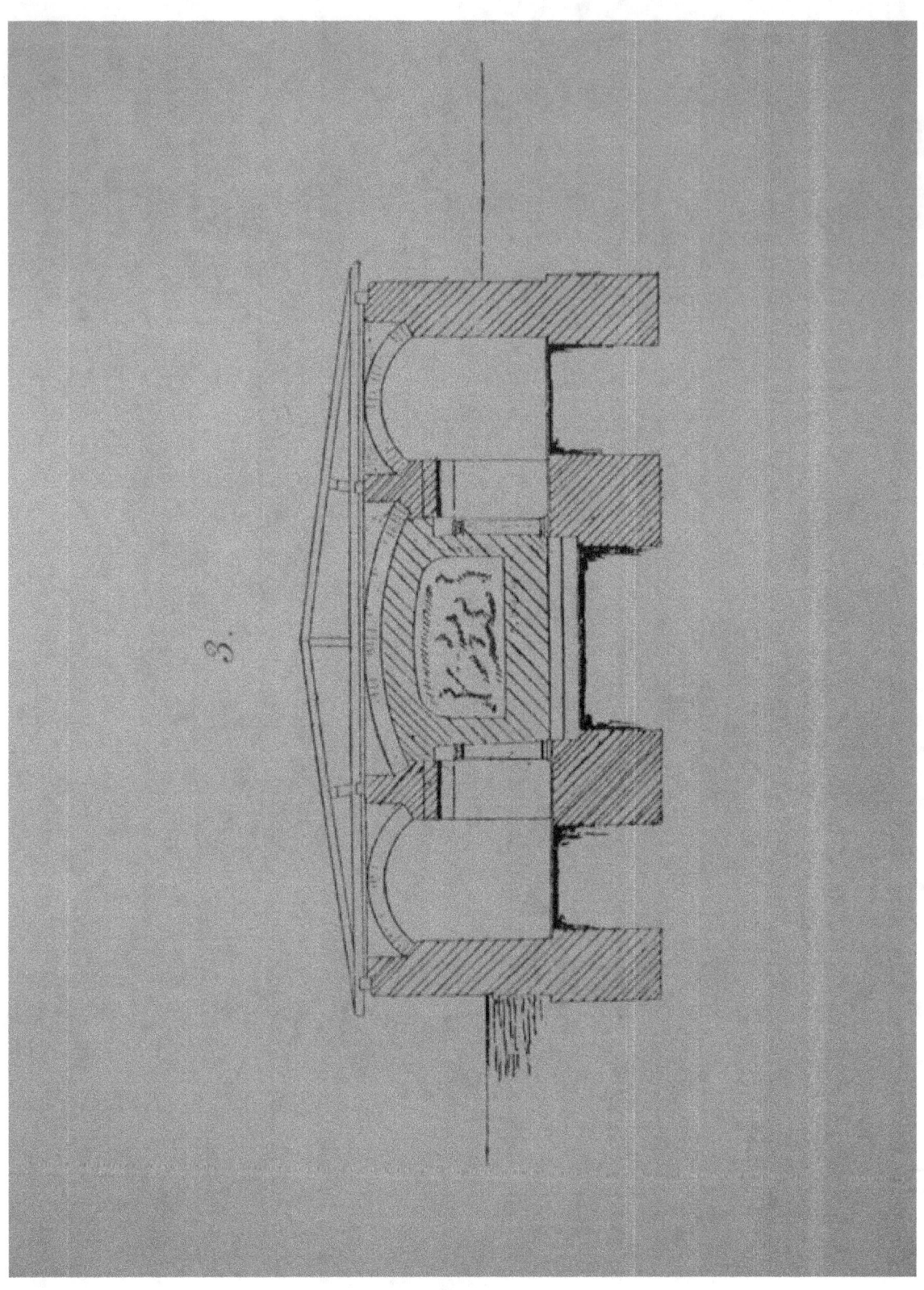

Figura I. The itinerary of Mithras

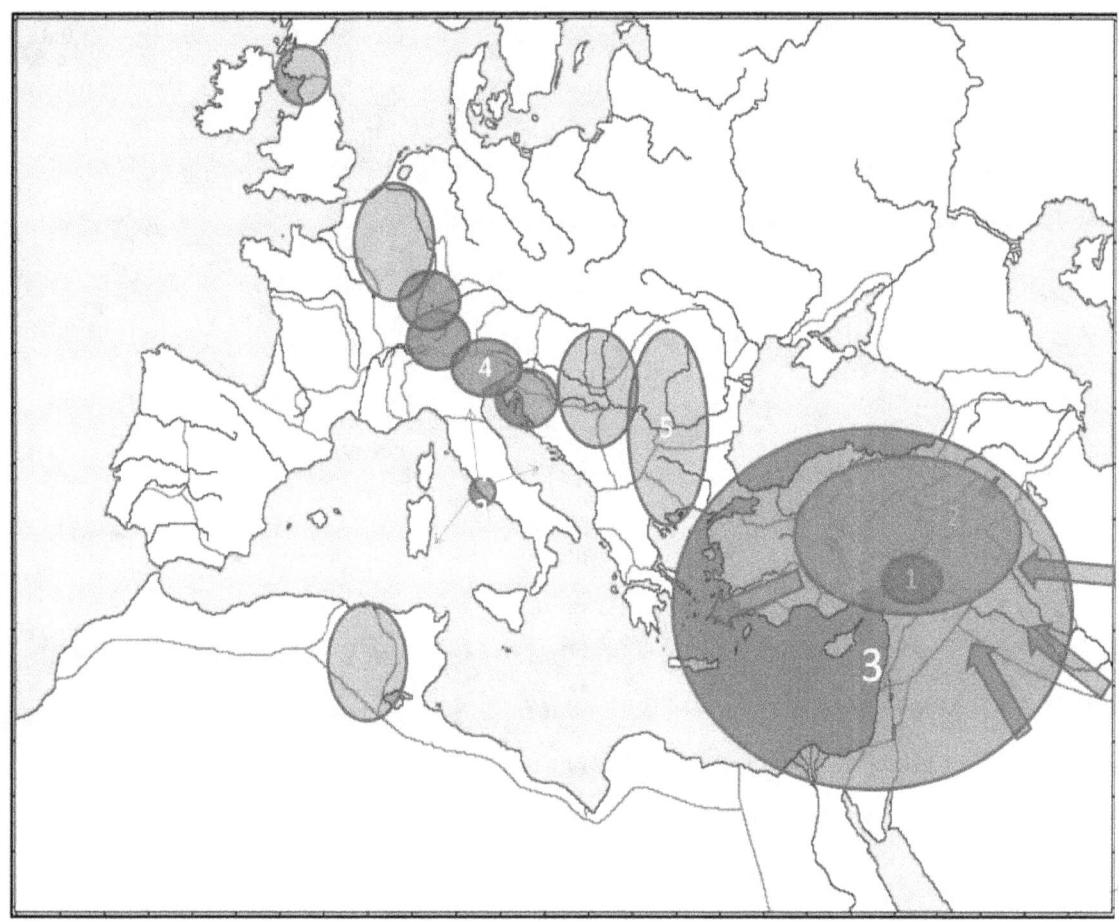

    1- Kingdom of Commagene (II-I centuries BC.)

    2- Kingdoms Pontus, Armenia, Cilicia (III-I. centuries BC.)

    3- Μιθρας becames "Mithras", the Roman god- the origins of the roman cult (I. century BC.-I.century AD.)

    4- Mithras appears in the Roman Empire (I. century AD.)

    5- Mithras appears in the Danubian provinces (II. century AD.)

Figura II. – Cultores Mithrae in Dacia

Name	Location	Function
M. Cocceius Genialis	Napoca	vir egregius procurator Augusti
Manius Cretinus	Gherla	praefectus alae II. Pannoniorum
Aelius Maximus	Potaissa	miles legionis V. Macedonicae
Iulius Iulianus	Potaissa	-
Aurelius Dolens	Potaissa	miles legionis
Aurelius Victorinus	Potaissa	
Flavius Marcellinus	Potaissa	tesserarius
Aurelius Montanus	Potaissa	miles legionis V. Macedonicae
Iulius (?) Quintus	Bruckla	centurio
Marcus Aurelius Thimotheus	Apulum	
Aurelius Maximus	Apulum	
Sextus Syntrofus	Apulum	
Lucanus	Apulum	
Dioscorus Marcus	Apulum	servus
Lucius Valerius Felix	Apulum	
Marcus Valerius Maximianus	Apulum	Legatus Augusti
Caius Nummius Amandus	Apulum	
Q. M.Victor Felix Maximillianus	Apulum	legatus Augusti legionis XIII. Gemina
Publius Marcius Victor Maximillianus	Apulum	
Marcus Ulpius Linus	Apulum	imaginifer
Titus Aurelius Fabia tribu Marcus	Apulum	veteranus legionis XIII. Gemina
Caius Iulius Marcianus	Apulum	signifer legionis XIII. Gemina
Valerius (?) CIMRM 1963	Apulum	
Aelius Mestrius	Apulum	
Aelius Gordianus	Apulum	
Claudius Niger	Apulum	
Caius Carellius Sabinus	Apulum	legatus Augusti legionis XIII. Gemina
Quintus Caecilius Laetus	Apulum	legatus Augusti legionis XIII. Gemina
Ulpius Proculinus	Apulum	speculator legionis XIII. Gemina
Suaedemus	Apulum	
Turranius Marcellinus	Apulum	conductores armamentares

Antonius Senecio Iunior	Apulum	conductores armamentes
Aurelius Chrestus	Apulum	
Posphoro (?)	Apulum	
Caius Iulius Valens	Apulum	haruspex coloniae Apuli
Lucius Octavius Gratus	Apulum	
Potinus	Apulum	
Lucius Aelius Hylas	Doștat	
Publius Aelius Artemidorus	Doștat	decurio sacerdos
Caius Iulius Valentinus	Păuleni	conductoris salinarum
Caius Iulius Omucio	Păuleni	
Aurelius (?) CIMRM 2021		
Rutus	Micia	
Protas	Sarmizegetusa	vicarius
Flavius Trofimus	Sarmizegetusa	
Marcus Ulpius Victorinus	Sarmizegetusa	decuriones coloniae Sarmizegetusae
Carpion Augustus	Sarmizegetusa	libertus
S. Spedius Valerianus	Sarmizegetusa	Augustalis coloniae Sarmizegetusae
Priscus	Sarmizegetusa	
Iulius CIMRM 2041	Sarmizegetusa	
Gaius CIMRM 2045	Sarmizegetusa	
Terentianus CIMRM. 2065	Sarmizegetusa	
Cassius Maximus	Sarmizegetusa	augur coloniae Sarmizegetusae
Marcus Ulpius Gaius	Sarmizegetusa	
Aelius Nepos	Sarmizegetusa	
Aurelius Theofilus	Sarmizegetusa	
Longus	Sarmizegetusa	salariarius
Severus Augustus	Sarmizegetusa	liberti
Aurelius Valentinus	Sarmizegetusa	
Hermadius	Sarmizegetusa	
Lucius Domitius Primanus	Sarmizegetusa	
Marcus Luccius Felix	Sarmizegetusa	Procurator Augusti
Publius Aelius Mars Hermadio	Tibiscum	Actor Turrani
Valerius	Drobetae	
A. Phoebus	Romula	
Antonius Zoilo	Romula	actor
Total: 66		

Sun Tzu and the Achaemenid Grand Strategy by Sheda Vasseghi

Introduction

Although between the rise and fall of the Achaemenid Persian Empire (550-330 BCE) military weapons, techniques, and recruitment evolved to meet the empire's needs, the key components of its military strategy remained intact. Some of those key components are interestingly echoed in *The Art of War*, a manual attributed to Sun Tzu (5th c. BCE), a Chinese philosopher-general. This paper will examine notable similarities between the teachings in *The Art of* War and the Achaemenid military warfare.

Competition and the need for excellence are natural human desires. Competition and desire to excel bring progress to mankind. It is the fuel for human social evolution. The reasons as to why a group conquers another vary, but the end result is the same rendering the catalyst insignificant. In modern era, old fashioned territorial conquests have been replaced with technological and scientific warfare as nations compete for limited resources to gain the upper hand in economic advantages which directly affect social advancement. What is important is how these conquests are made to minimize trauma and chaos while establishing order as quickly as possible.

The Art of War is a revered manual mastering strategy during conflict. Its lessons on how to remain victorious or survive at best is timeless. Its lessons are directed to leaders both in military and civilian capacities, and to citizens, who should not underestimate the importance of a strong and competent military for the survival of their society.

The Achaemenid Persian Empire was the first world empire covering 23 nations spread across approximately 3,000,000 square miles stretching from North Africa to Indus Valley.[217] This world empire was based on law and order. It was the first time tolerance and benevolence towards different cultures was to be standard practice. The Persians viewed military service as a supreme duty and were expected to serve unconditionally. Law and order applied to everyone including military leaders and rulers. This military strategy created the proper conditions for relative peace across an immense territory and greater cultural and economic exchanges.[218]

Figure 1: Achaemenid Army in Plaza, Persepolis. ©persepolis3d.com - K. Afhami & W. Gambke.

The Art of War covers military strategy and leadership. Despite its age, it is very applicable to modern day issues. The central theme in *The Art of War* teaches that it is most ideal to win without fighting, and to gain the most by doing the least. The Achaemenid military grand strategy favored diplomacy over battle. It is at this point that an interesting connection is noted between *The Art of War* and the military strategy of the Achaemenids.

The first known official diplomacy between Iranians and the Chinese was around 121 BCE -- some 200 years after the fall of the Achaemenids. But the Achaemenids' needs for more

---

[217] The British Museum 2005-06. *The Forgotten Empire* Exhibition, London, UK, (http://www.thebritishmuseum.ac.uk/persia/home.htm).

horses and pasture lands, and the expansion of China during the Warring States Period (476-221 BCE), led various Central Asian Iranian nomads to greater contact with the Chinese. Given the similarities between the essence of *The Art of War* and the grand strategy of the Achaemenid military warfare, a question arises: Was Sun Tzu familiar with Achaemenid (Iranian) warfare?

Conflict Resolution Strategies

> **According to Sun Tzu, the most important strategy is to win without fighting. It is best to encourage a people to surrender by political means and events rather than use of force.**[219]

The Achaemenids preferred diplomacy and bribery to subject people and gain the upper hand. As a general rule, the Achaemenids sent word in advance for a nation to voluntarily submit and avoid conflict. They often tried to gain influence from local supporters to facilitate submission even before embarking on a campaign. In other words, the Achaemenid grand strategy was to gain the most by doing the least with minimal bloodshed.

As for subjecting nations, the Achaemenid founder Cyrus the Great (559-530 BCE) declared if people surrendered, they would be able to lead their normal lives as usual. If others were unjust to them, the Persian army would defend them. If people were friendly, then they were treated as friends.[220] The Persians typically preferred achieving their goals through diplomatic means than use of military force. It is this military and political strategy that set the Achaemenids apart from their contemporaries.

In the first known bill of human rights or the *Cyrus Cylinder* dated 539 BCE, Cyrus ordered the captives in Babylonia to be set free to return to their native lands. Under this decree, the captive Jews also returned to their homeland. A Persian-friendly Jerusalem played a role in

---

[218] Dandamaev, M. A. et al. 2004. *The Culture and Social Institutions of Ancient Iran*, Cambridge, UK: Cambridge Univ. Press, p. 367.
[219] Sun Tzu, 1988. *The Art of War*, Thomas Cleary (transl.), Boston, MA: Shambhala Publications, Inc., pp. 66-67.
[220] Xenophon 2001. *The Education of Cyrus*, W. Ambler (trans.), Ithaca, NY: Cornell Univ. Press, pp. IV(5)129.

Achaemenid policies concerning Egypt.[221] As the Achaemenids established their empire, the first step in Persian control over an area was to demand the symbolic "earth and water" offering representing surrender. This gave the Persians an idea as to which cities could be counted on before they moved into a territory.[222]

Greek sources accuse the Persians of having installed tyrants, but there is no evidence of that. Rather, the ruling tyrants formed alliances with the Persians.[223] In the extreme western parts of Greece which was harder to control, the Persian policy involved compromise. Native despots were used to maintain order with garrisons of Greek mercenaries. Down the coast, influential Greek families held fiefs in the plains and fruitful valleys alongside Persian landowners. These landowners created the basis for Persian control in western Asia Minor.[224] In 494 BCE, during the Ionian revolt, the Persians did not use their naval superiority. Instead they resorted to political warfare by asking exiled tyrants to contact their respective cities letting them know a voluntarily surrender would avoid conflict.[225] At Marathon in 490 BCE, the Athenians hoped for Spartan support to arrive, and the Persians were counting on diplomatic overtures from pro-Persian Athenians.[226]

Greek warfare was a no-nonsense, head-to-head confrontation that was decisive. The Greeks, who set the tone for Western warfare, fought for an idea. Those who joined to fight for the community, owned a piece of property and fought to protect their homeland willing to kill or to be killed.[227] The Greeks engaged in frontal attacks and no envelopment or special

---

[221] Briant, P. 2002. *From Cyrus to Alexander: A History of the Persian Empire*, trans. P. T. Daniels, Winona Lake, IN: Eisenbrauns, pp. 48-49.

[222] Cawkwell, G. 2005. *The Greek Wars: The Failure of Persia*, Oxford, UK: Oxford Univ. Press, p. 52.

[223] Cawkwell, pp. 33-34.

[224] Cook, J. M. 1985. The Rise of the Achaemenids and Establishment of Their Empire in *The Cambridge History of Iran, Vol. 2: The Median and Achaemenian Periods*, I. Gershevitch (ed.), Cambridge, UK: Cambridge Univ. Press, pp. 274-275.

[225] Burn, A. R. 1985. Persia and the Greeks in *The Cambridge History of Iran, Vol. 2: The Median and Achaemenian Periods*, I. Gershevitch (ed.), Cambridge, UK: Cambridge Univ. Press, pp. 309-310.

[226] Burn, p. 317.

[227] Hanson, V. D. 1989. *The Western Way of War: Infantry Battle in Classical Greece*, 2d ed., Berkeley, CA: Univ. of California Press, p. xv.

maneuvers.[228] To the Greeks, this was the only type of warfare that was "fair." They viewed the use of archers as cheating which caused the death of brave soldiers in vain. The Greeks wanted to die while engaged in a "manly way" of fighting or one-on-one, hand-to-hand engagements.[229]

The Persians, on the other hand, did not necessarily wish to kill or be killed during a campaign. They were more interested in figuring out how to achieve their goals with low mortality rates. The Greeks met in the middle of an ideal battlefield and engaged hand-to-hand with the outcome of the battle totally relying on the strength and courage of the hoplites. The Persians viewed this as rather irrational.[230] They had no desire for this "methodical killing" and clash of arms.[231]

The Persians could not understand why the Greeks had never agreed to a general peace among themselves. In 492 BCE, the Persian general Artaphernes ordered the Greek cities to make treaties with each other and provide judicial settlement of disputes instead of pillaging. He also set up an equitable tribute system. Further, Darius the Great (522-486 BCE) sent a large army and fleet with another remarkable reform -- Ionian tyrants were to be replaced with democracies.[232] These diplomatic overtures were part of a military strategy of subjecting without use of force.

Early on the Persians learned how to use the Greek internal conflicts to their own benefit. The central Greek cities agreed to submit, and many such as the Thessalians joined the Persians. Xerxes (486-465 BCE) had many noble Greek family members such as Demaratus of Sparta and the Pisistratids in his entourage. One of his strategies was to install client

---

[228] Hanson, p. 10.
[229] Hanson, p. 14.
[230] Hanson, pp. 9-10.
[231] Hanson, p. 16.
[232] Burn, pp. 311-312.

governments in some of the cities. The Persian diplomacy paid off. Their agents had penetrated northern Greece for several years securing west of Olympos.[233]

During the Peloponnesian War (431-404 BCE), it was Persia that tipped the balance of power. Persia had the resources to help whichever side was willing to meet its conditions later.[234] The Persians knew enough about internal Greek politics to be able to play one state against another, and make cunning use of their gold in bribery and corruption. The Persians promised Sparta unlimited financial and military assistance in exchange for control of the Aegean and Ionia.[235] In fourth and third centuries BCE, all Greek powers sought Persian endorsement or consent for one reason or another and even Athens was very careful not to infringe openly on Persian naval or land power in Asia Minor.[236]

In 395 BCE, Sparta confronted the Persians in Asia Minor, who were reestablishing their authority after the battle of Cunaxa. The Persian general Tithraustes sent word to the Spartans that the cities would be left autonomous, if they paid their old tribute and the Spartans left Asia. The Persians wanted to keep Sardis and Lydia safe from war and shift operations to Phrygia. Tithraustes provided the Spartans with money and supplies so they could reach Hellespontine Phrygia.[237]

If diplomacy and bribery fails, Sun Tzu advises attacking enemy alliances.[238]

The Achaemenids influenced Greek affairs for over two centuries simply by dividing them and breaking up alliances. In many cases, this also minimized the need for force while obtaining victory. This strategy was not exclusive to Achaemenid policies concerning Greeks. In 525 BCE, the Egyptian ruler Amasis died and his son Psammetichus III succeeded him. This

---

[233] Burn, pp. 321-322.
[234] Freeman, C. 1999. *The Greek Achievement: the Foundation of the Western World*, Penguin Group, p. 212.
[235] Ferrill, A. 1997. *The Origins of War: From the Stone Age to Alexander the Great*, rev. ed., Boulder, CO: Westview Press, p. 141.
[236] Starr, C. G. 1965. *The History of the Ancient World*, Oxford, UK: Oxford University Press Inc., p. 65.
[237] Burn, p.361.

ended the alliance between Egypt and Samos as the odds now were in favor of the Achaemenid invaders. The tyrant of Samos Polycrates secretly contacted the Persians, and provided them with 40 triremes and crews. The second blow to Egypt was the defection of Phanes of Halicarnassus, who was close to Amasis, and knowledgeable about the Egyptian military and access routes to the Delta. Also a treaty with the desert Arabs gave access to water so Cambyses (530-522 BCE) and his troops could reach the Nile Valley.[239]

In 479, during the Greco-Persian Wars, the Achaemenids sent their Macedonian allies to the Athenians with a proposal whereby their injuries would be forgiven while their land and self government restored in exchange for submission to the Persians.[240] The Persian strategy was to divide the Greeks and prevent military cooperation between the Athenians and the Spartans. The Persians noted signs of diplomatic overtures from among the Athenians. The Spartans fearful of a Persian-Athenian alliance sent representatives to persuade the Athenians to reject a Persian proposal.[241]

When the Persians marched from Thessaly to Athens, the Great King gave the Athenians another opportunity to maintain their autonomy in exchange for accepting Persian dominion.[242] Another message was sent to the Athenians at Salamis with this proposal. Athenians were upset that the Spartans broke their promise by not sending any support while the Persians invaded Attica. They sent an ultimatum to the Spartans that if they continued this behavior, the Athenians would be forced to consider an agreement with the Persians. The Spartans finally sent 5000 hoplites against the Persians to prevent a Persian victory and potential threat to the Peloponnese.[243]

---

[238] Sun Tzu, p. 69.

[239] Briant, pp. 52-53.

[240] Herodotus, rev. 1996. *The Histories*, A. De Selincourt (transl.), London, UK: Penguin Books, p. VIII(140).

[241] Herodotus, pp. VIII(141-142).

[242] Briant, pp. 532-533.

[243] Herodotus, pp. IX(9-10).

By the 460s, there was a gradual shift among the Delian League members with some no longer interested in providing ships and crew while others wanted to sever ties in response to Athens' ambitions. The Persians were aware of the internal conflicts among the Greeks and led various counteroffensive acts to profit from it.[244] The Great King maintained an army at Sardis to continue its wars against the Greeks. The Achaemenids also stepped up their influence in Hellespontine Phrygia in order to maintain their control of Asia Minor. Diplomatic overtures were made with various influential Greeks to gain their support.[245] Royal land concessions were made to influential Greeks from the island cities close to the coast, so the Persians could intervene with Greek affairs even during the period of Athenian dominance.[246]

Around 462/461 BCE, internal conflicts forced the Athenians to rethink their position. When Persia sent ambassadors for peace talks, Athenians dispatched an embassy to discuss ending of hostilities.[247] The Athenians withdrew their forces from Cyprus and Egypt, and for four decades there was peace between the Persians and the Athenians. The Greek cities in Asia Minor may have been granted autonomy, but by 431 they were all without protective walls. The Persians were going to rule all of Asia unconditionally.[248]

Artaxerxes I (465-424 BCE) was not going to accept conditions in which Athens would be the deciding factor. There is no evidence the Achaemenids experienced any diplomatic or military disasters in Greece at this time. Artaxerxes I did not give up his rights to Asia Minor, and directed his satraps at Sardis to continue their attempts to regain lost territories. It is unknown why a mass mobilization never took place for a reconquest of Greece, but perhaps the Great King believed disunity among the Greeks would eventually lead to the same result. As a matter of fact, the Achaemenids rarely mobilized a royal army.[249]

---

[244] Briant, p. 557.
[245] Briant, pp. 559-560.
[246] Briant, pp. 562-563.
[247] Cawkwell, pp. 135-136.
[248] Cawkwell, p. 139.
[249] Briant, p. 582.

In 396 BCE, the Persian navy successfully incited a Rhodian party to rise up against Sparta. After defeating the Spartan navy, a victorious Persian fleet sailed the coast and expelled Spartan military governors from the cities. In spring 393, the Persian fleet sailed through Cyclades without opposition and raided Lakonia itself while occupying Kythera. They left a garrison there under an Athenian governor. The Persian general Pharnabazos then sailed to Corinth, and met with allies at a war council where he gave them money, and urged them to fight Sparta vigorously and show their loyalty to the Great King. For a Persian, Pharnabazos' influence among the Greeks was unprecedented.[250]

According to Sun Tzu, a good leader should exhaust enemy soldiers to weaken them before an actual engagement.[251]

In 513 BCE, Darius the Great left his army in Europe under the command of Megabazos, who marched west and subdued Macedonia. Megabazos did not have the time or resources to conquer mountain tribes and occupy the region, so he followed the policy of weakening "trouble-makers outside the occupied zone." Megabazos gathered the Paiones and resettled them in Phrygia.[252] In 494, the Persians blockaded Miletos by sea. The Ionians on ships cornered at the islet of Lade began to crack as they ran out of drinking water.[253]

Achaemenids used their superior cavalry for "shock-n-awe" to wear out enemy soldiers and keep them weary. In 479 BCE at Plataea, the Greek forces took position at the high ground of Cithaeron. When it became apparent the Greeks were not going to make a move, the Persian cavalry began assaulting them and inflicting heavy losses on them. For eight days the two sides faced each other in battle formation. The Persians sent a cavalry contingent to the pass over Cithaeron to block the daily arrival of men joining the Greek army. The blockage was successful as the Persians captured a long train of food and provisions from the Peloponnese. Two more

---

[250] Burn, p. 365.
[251] Sun Tzu, p. 53.
[252] Burn, p. 303.

days passed without battle. The Persian cavalry continuously harassed the Greeks by riding within striking distance just to intimidate them.[254] Later the Persian cavalry charged and pushed the Greeks away from their water source.[255] Eventually, the exhausted Greek armies were forced to change their position to avoid daily harassing tactics by the Persian cavalry.

At the battle of Cunaxa in 401 BCE, part of Artaxerxes II's (435/445-358 BCE) tactical strategy was to isolate and neutralize the Greek mercenaries by blocking them from food and supplies to force a truce and eventual retreat.[256] In 333 BCE, during their march to Syria-Palestine, Alexander III (356-323 BCE) and the Macedonian army hugged the coast hoping to draw the Persians to battle at constricted grounds. Instead, they received word that Darius III (380-330 BCE) was at Issus blocking Alexander's retreat back to Asia Minor as well as his supply line. This was an attempt at weakening the invaders by cornering them in hostile territory without food and supplies.[257]

Sun Tzu advises to treat enemy captives well so they would cooperate.[258]

Under the Achaemenid standard practice, the defeated foreign leaders often ended up in Persian courts as respected advisors, or returned to their role as local rulers under Persian suzerainty. Even in their treatment of subject people and local kings the Persians abided by law and order, and molded their military tactics to fit this scheme. Herodotus tells of the relationship between Cyrus and the king of Lydia Croesus (560-547 BCE), who was defeated by Cyrus in 547 BCE. After his capture Cyrus freed Croesus from chains and eventually treated him as a respected and close advisor.[259] Babylon was captured on October 12, 539 BCE. Nabonidus was arrested shortly thereafter as he attempted to leave the city, but following Persian

---

[253] Burn, pp. 309-310.
[254] Herodotus, pp. IX(39-40).
[255] Herodotus, pp. IX(48-49).
[256] Vasseghi, S. December 2009. The battle of Cunaxa in *Ancient Warfare* III(6), the Netherlands, p. 33.
[257] Ferrill, pp. 199-200.
[258] Sun Tzu, p. 64.

policy, his life was spared.[260] Cambyses also allowed the deposed Egyptian King Psammenitus to live at the royal court for a long time as a well-treated guest. Psammenitus may have even served as Egypt's governor under Persian control.[261] Generally, the Achaemenid policy towards foreign royalty was to treat them with respect and honor. Some local royalties were even restored to their thrones under Persian dominance and served as military advisors.

The Achaemenids made an effort not to rule by force. They sometimes forgave rebels or deported them to new lands and enrolled them as ordinary subjects. Part of their strategy in minimizing restless and unhappiness was to allow foreigners the chance at accumulating wealth. The Achaemenids used peace and order to promote and protect agriculture, trade, and economic growth. The Persians were unique among their contemporaries, because they did not use terror as a tool for conquest.

Even during the Great Satrapal revolt of 366 BCE, the Great King's agents contacted the rebel Orontes and offered him his old position if he abandoned the other rebels. Orontes took the offer and delivered his war chest and troops to the Persians. The rebel Autophradates sued for peace and was able to keep his satrapy. As of 360 BCE, the rebel Artabazos too was able to keep his post as satrap of Phrygia.[262]

In 362, Tachos of Egypt planned to take Syria and Palestine from Persian control and gained support from Sparta and Athens for his campaign. Tachos placed heavy tax burden on all citizens and the temples to raise a sizeable army. He secured Palestine, but a general he had left in charge of Egypt seized the throne. Having been deposed, Tachos sought refuge at the Persian court.[263]

---

[259] Herodotus, pp. I(88-90).
[260] Oppenheim, A. L. 1985. The Babylonian Evidence of Achaemenian Rule in Mesopotamia in *The Cambridge History of Iran, Vol. 2: The Median and Achaemenian Periods*, I. Gershevitch (ed.), Cambridge, UK: Cambridge Univ. Press, pp. 542-543.
[261] Herodotus, p. III(15-16).
[262] Burn, pp. 380-381.

In dealing with a surrendered army, Sun Tzu advises giving a way out. Desperate soldiers will fight to the death causing more bloodshed.[264]

Achaemenids gave defeated armies a way out. In 401 BCE, after the battle of Cunaxa, the Greek mercenaries, who had accompanied Cyrus the Younger (424?-401 BCE) on his failed mission to fight his brother Artaxerxes II for the crown, were shown a way home. After negotiations, the mercenaries were allowed to march north only to face continuous harassment by the mountain people and the Armenian army while scrimmaging for food and supplies. At the end 8600 Greeks made it home.[265]

After Cunaxa, the Achaemenids set out to reestablish their authority in Asia Minor. The Spartans sent an army to block their efforts, but the Persians were able to surround them. Desperate and trapped in hostile territory, the Spartans could only reduce their efforts to plundering the region in order to survive. Their constant fear was to run out of food and supplies. The Persian commanders planned to let the Spartans wander the countryside until they were forced to return to the coast.[266]

According to Sun Tzu, armies need drums to hear better and banners to locate and signal.[267]

The Achaemenids usually chanted during campaigns, and used banners to locate contingents and carry out orders and maneuvers. The magis or Zoroastrian priests accompanied the kings on campaigns. They interpreted solar eclipses and dreams. They poured libations, handled religious ceremonies, and sang spiritual hymns during the march. In the Persian army, each regiment commander had his own standard to easily receive or route orders and messages.

---

[263] Burn, p. 371.
[264] Sun Tzu, p. 123.
[265] Vasseghi, p. 33.
[266] Briant, pp.641-642.
[267] Sun Tzu, p. 119.

A regiment moved forward when its standard was raised. The royal Achaemenid standard showed a golden eagle or falcon upon a shield that was raised on a pole.[268]

According to Sun Tzu, local guides are the key to gaining advantage on enemy territory.[269] Having spies is the most efficient way to make appropriate and timely strategic decisions. Sun Tzu even considers it inhumane not to use spies, and encourages good leaders to reward spies accordingly.[270]

At the battle of Thermopylae in 480, the Persians overpowered the Greeks by rewarding a local man in showing them an alternate route. The Achaemenids used locals when in enemy territory. The famous "Eyes and Ears" of the king or spies were positioned across the empire to ensure governors followed local laws and the orders of central government. Anything out of the ordinary was immediately reported to the court. These individuals helped with intelligence gathering which directly affected law and order. Prior knowledge is mandatory to every matter. Knowledge gained from local guides and spies minimized undesirable conditions or unnecessary violence and disruption. Having spies within the inner circles kept the governors and local rulers in check as far as committing unlawful acts or organizing rebellions.[271]

Sun Tzu stresses the importance of loyal and devoted generals. Sun Tzu claims a nation's victory rests on the full cooperation from their military leadership.[272]

Contrary to Greek portrayal of Persian command structure, evidence shows under the Great King's supreme authority, the Persian commanders retained control and had the responsibility to take possession of a city in the name of the king.[273] The Persians made military preparations in advance. To obey the commanders unconditionally, the troops expected the leaders to make plans in advance so the campaign would follow an orderly fashion. The leaders

---

[268] Sekunda, N. 1992. *The Persian Army: 560-330 BC*, Oxford, UK: Osprey Publishing, p. 12.
[269] Sun Tzu, p. 117.
[270] Sun Tzu, p. 168.
[271] Briant, p. 364.
[272] Sun Tzu, p. 78.
[273] Briant, pp.788-789.

had to plan when to lead the army on its march, how to prepare for different terrains, how to manage logistics, how to set up camp, and what to do in case of advance or retreat when in action.[274] After the battle of Cunaxa in 401, when the Spartan army was marching through Asia Minor trying to push the Achaemenids out of the region, they soon realized no citadel commander was going to turn his back to the Great King rendering the Spartan efforts in taking control of the cities virtually impossible.[275]

During his retreat at the battle of Gaugamela in 331, Darius III ordered all satraps to preserve their royalty to him and fortify the major cities. Darius needed enough time to prepare a new army. Instead when Alexander arrived at Babylonia, the satrap did not organize a resistance. The satrap of Susa followed suit.[276] Later Alexander pushed back Ariobarzanes and his forces at the Persian Gates. The Macedonians were then on their way to Persepolis, the spiritual center of the Persian Empire.[277] The Persian official Tiridates in charge of the rich capital surrendered the city which was later burnt to the ground by Alexander and his army. In spring 330, despite his amazing progress, Alexander was still anxious about Darius's ability to gather another massive army which explains his forced march to Media only to find that Darius had retreated to the interior of the Empire.[278]

Darius III expected to draft troops from the eastern regions of the Empire. With news of Alexander's successful campaigns, the royal army started to collapse as contingents began to desert Darius. Capitulation of important cities without resistance and the burning of Persepolis caused a major damage to Darius' authority. These events placed Darius at the mercy of his eastern satraps. The Great King soon became the hostage of Bessus, the satrap of Bactria. Besus was in complete control of his cavalry contingency. He and other powerful conspirators

---

[274] Xenophon, I(6)57-8.
[275] Briant, pp. 641-642.
[276] Briant, pp. 840-842.
[277] Briant, p. 850.
[278] Briant, p. 842.

killed Darius in order to strike a deal with Alexander and maintain their status.[279] Lack of cooperation and loyalty by several Persian commanders led to the murder of Darius III, and played a major role in the fall of the Achaemenid Empire.

Conclusion

The Art of War has been a revered guide used by warriors and politicians since ancient times. The Achaemenid military grand strategy created a phenomenon -- a world empire lasting over 220 years. Based on the foundation of the Achaemenid Empire, Iranians remained a superpower from 6th century BCE to 7th century CE (excluding the Seleucid period (312-247 BCE)). Given their origins, the contemporary conflict resolution methodologies of Sun Tzu and the Achaemenids were presumably developed independently. Yet, their fundamental strategy and various options in dealing with conflict mirror each other.

Prior to the migration of Aryans to the Iranian plateau around 12th century BCE, their ancient homeland *Iranvej* is believed to have been in Kazakhstan. Centuries later, similar military tactics such as the Parthian Shot were noted between the Achaemenids and Central Asian Iranian nomads. Further, the Chinese use of cavalry was not observed prior to the Warring States Period (476-221 BCE). It is around the time of Sun Tzu that the Chinese were introduced to the use of cavalry and related military strategies as they faced an influx of Central Asian nomadic incursions.[280]

The Art of War is one of the greatest manuals for military victory and survival. The greatest achievements of the Achaemenids were their creation of the first world empire and its maintenance for more than two centuries. Cyrus the Great, who set the tone for the Achaemenid grand strategy, is one of the greatest role models for leadership. More information is needed regarding contact between the Chinese and people of Iranian stock from 6th to 3rd

---

[279] Briant, pp. 865-866.

century BCE. With further research perhaps there can be a better understanding of the connection, if any, between *The Art of War* and the Achaemenid military practices.

Recently, the British Museum has announced the discovery of two fossilized horse bones bearing cuneiform inscriptions that were found in China. The bones were donated to the Palace Museum in 1983 by a private collector, who thought they bore an ancient Chinese script. However, it has been determined that the mysterious cuneiform inscriptions on both bones were extracts from the Cyrus Cylinder. Despite some skepticism, experts are convinced of their authenticity. The finding is incredible as it will affect the common view that the Cyrus Cylinder was a unique, ceremonial object which was not distributed outside of Babylon. In studying and comparing the cuneiform strokes and shapes on the bones, they match the method used by Persian scribes rather than Babylonian. Therefore, it appears the copier used another version of the Cyrus Cylinder that may have been originally written in Persia. It is believed the "Persian" copy of the Cyrus Cylinder used as a model for the bones may have been distributed to the Far East during the reign of Cyrus.[281]

This finding is of great interest for various reasons. Not only does it add value to the argument that the Cyrus Cylinder was a policy not a ceremonial object, but it suggests the Achaemenid policies may have reached China as early as 539-530 BCE. The study of Achaemenid warfare should supplement *The Art of War*'s teachings since they actually implemented what is taught in the manual.

---

[280] Graff, D. A. 2002. *Medieval Chinese Warfare, 300-900*, London, UK: Routledge, p. 22.

[281] Bailey, M. 2010. "Extracts of Cyrus Cylinder found in China: British Museum curator has identified cunieform text inscribed on horse bones," Issue 215
(http://www.theartnewspaper.com/articles/Extracts+of+Cyrus+Cylinder+found+in+China+/21147
http://www.theartnewspaper.com/articles/Extracts-of-Cyrus-Cylinder-found-in-China).

Zen Buddhism and Mithraism by Dr. Masato Tōjō

Chairman of Mithraeum Japan

Tokyo, Japan

Abstract

Although Zen Buddhism (Abbreviated as Zen) is the most popular branch of Buddhism in the West, its relation to Iranian religion (Mithraism) is little known. This article provides both archaeological and textual evidences for its relation to Mithraism. Evidences are shown in two steps. In step one (chapter 1), two evidences about Mithraic influence upon Mahāyāna Buddhism are shown. One is Maga-Brahmins, the other is the religious situation of Central Asia at the time of formation age of Mahāyāna Buddhism. In step two (chapter 2 to7) Mithraic influence upon Zen is shown. Characteristic elements of Zen, i. e. the founder of Zen, Kegon-kyō, the Vijnāna-vādin, Mādhyamaka philosophies, the Prajñāpāramitā literatures and Ten Bull Pictures are examined in the context introduced by step one to show their Mithraic connection respectively. In chapter 2 an overview of Zen is provided. In chapter 3 the evidence of the Zen founder's Persian origin is shown. In chapter 4 direct link between Zen and Roman Mithraism is shown. In chapter 5 and 6 close link between Iranian Mithra and the Vijnāna-vādin, which is an important element incorporated into Zen, is shown. In chapter 7 a close parallel between Mysteries of Mithra and Ten Bull Pictures, which is an important Zen meditation tool, is shown.

1. Mithraic Influence on Mahāyāna Buddhism in General

1. 1 Lord Buddhas

Buddhism can be classified into three schools (Table 1. 1); Theravāda 上座部, Mahāyāna 大乗 and Vajirayāna 金剛乗. Theravāda is the oldest Buddhist school (250 BC). Mahāyāna arose in the area which encompasses northwest part of India, Pakistan, Afghanistan, east part of Iran (1st BC-1st AD) under the strong influence of Iranian culture. Esoteric Buddhism[282] arose until the 7th Century in the above area and spread to Tibet, Central Asia, China and Japan. Shingon-sect 真言宗and Tendai-sect 天台宗 are its two major sects. Vajirayānā 金剛乗 (Tibetan Buddhism) is its later form. They are also under the strong Iranian influence.

---

[282] In Chinese, Esoteric Buddhism is called Mi-jiao密教 (Jp. Mi-kkyō). In Chinese, Mi 密 means both closeness (friendliness) and secret, and is used also as a transcription of Mithra's name Mihr/Mir. Jiao 教 means teaching. Therefore Esoteric Buddhism means Teaching of Mithra in both Chinese and Japanese.

Table 1. 1 shows Lord Buddha (Lord God) of three schools mentioned above with their corresponding Iranian deities. The corresponding is inferred from speculations on the names, iconographical considerations, circumstantial evidences (such as Maga-Brahmins) and archaeological discovery in Bamiyan Buddhist site.

Amitābha 阿弥陀 (Jp: Amida) makes a triple with Avalokiteśvara 観音 (Jp: Kannon) and Mahāsthāmaprāpta 大勢至 (Jp: Daiseiši). According to Manichaean scriptures Avalokiteśvara is identical with Sraoša, Mahāsthāmaprāpta with Rašnu[283]. In Zurwanite *Bundahišn*, Mithra, Sraoša and Rašnu make a triple called "Three Judges"[284]. Therefore Amitābha's counterpart in Iranis Mithra. In Buddhist iconology, Amitābha's holy animal is peacock. Iranian Mithra has ten thousands of eyes (Mihr Yašt 7; 53; 73) which reminds us of many eyes of Peacock tail feathers. Amitābha means "Limitless Light" in Sanskrit. Iranian Mithra is Sun God the Source of Limitless Light.

Identification of Vairocana 毘廬遮那 (Jp: Birušana; identical with Mahāvairocana 大日 (Jp: Dainichi)) with Mithra is circumstantial. Etymologically Vairocana Buddha means "Buddha who is like the Sun" in Sanskrit. Mahāvairocana Buddha means "Great Buddha who is like the Sun" in Sanskrit, "Great Sun Buddha" in Chinese, Japanese and Korean[285]. Mithra was the sole God who is dominant Sun God in the forming age of Mahāyāna Buddhism (3-4 AD). Identification of the two is also inferred from icons of Bamiyan Buddhist site (see 4. 2) and Manichaean sources. According to Manichaean sources, Mahāvairocana, who is the later form of Vairocana, is identical with Zurwan-Mithra[286].

---

[283] Chinese Hymnscroll (H 391) (Klimkeit. *Gnosis on the Silk Road*, p. 5)

[284] Zaehenr, R. C. *Zurvan*, Biblo & Tannen, 1972, p. 317 (31). It should be remembered that in Roman Mithraism Mithra, Cautes and Cautopates make a triple too.

[285] Dainichi is the abbreviation of Dainichi-nyorai 大日如来. Dai 大 means "great", whose Sansktit origin is "mahā". Nichi 日 means "the Sun", whose Sanskrit origin is "Vairocana". Nyorai 如来 means "Buddha", whose Sanskrit origin is "Tathāgata". Therefore Dainichi- nyorai 大日如来 means "Great Sun Buddha". This is a typical example of Chinese translation-by-meaning of Sanskrit.

[286] In Early Esoteric Buddhism, its Root Buddha was called Vairocana. But later its Root God became to be called Mahāvairocana (Tanaka. *Iconology of Mandala*, pp. 65-69). According to its teaching, Mahāvairocana emanates Five Transcendental Buddhas 五智如来 (Jp: Gochi-nyorai; Vairocana 毘廬遮那 (Jp: Birušana), Ratnasambhava 宝生 (Jp: Hōšō), Amogašiddi 不空成就 (Jp: Hukūjōju), Amitābha 阿弥陀 (Jp: Amida) and Akṣōbya 阿閦 (Jp: Ašuku)). According to Manichaean sources, this Vairocana, who is not Universal Buddha mentioned in *Kegon sutra*, but one of Five Transcendental Buddhas, is identical with Sraoša (Lieu. *Manichaeism in Central Asia & China*, p. 54), and Sraoša (the Column of Glory) is the first emanation of Sun God Mithra (*Kephalaia* 7.35.11-13). From these, the emanator of Sraoša i. e. Mithra is inferred to be identical with Mahāvairocana logically. In Manichaeism, Zurwan and Mithra are identical and the same one body. Mithra is the perfect Image of Zurwan, and has the same power as Zurwan (*Psalm Book II* 138.59-65, *Kephalaia* 7.35.7-8; 10.43.17-20). Zurwan, who is Root God and has Five Light Limbs, occupies the same ontological position as Mahāvairocana. From these, Mahāvairocana is identical with Zurwan-Mithra. In Esoteric Buddhism, Sun God Mithra (the Third Messenger) and Creator Mithra (the Living Spirit) is one and the same. About Manichaean two Mithras, see Sundermann's "The Five Sons of the Manichaean God Mithra".

Identification of Amitāyus 無量寿 (Jp: Muryōju) with Zurwan (Zurwan Akarana) is based on etymological consideration and comparison of their theogonical positions and characteristics. Both names mean "Limitless Time". Amitāyus is Root Buddha (God) living in Pure Land of Light. According to Manichaean scriptures such as *Šābhuragān*, *Kephalaia* and Chinese *Hymnscroll*, Zurwan also is Root God living in Land of Light. In Mahāyāna Buddhism Amitāyus is identical with Amitābha. In Roman Mithraism, Mithras is both Sun God and God of Time[287].

Identification of Kālacakra with Zurwan-Mithra is based on etymological, ontological and historical consideration. Etymologically Kālacakra means "Wheel of Time", i. e. "Limitless Time". Zurwan Akarana means "Limitless Time". Ontologically Kālacakra is Tantra-lized Mahāvairocana (*The Guhyasamājatantra; The Kālacakratantra*). Historically Vajirayānā is the Tantric form of Esoteric Buddhism.

Table 1.1 Three Schools of Buddhism

School		Birth	Lord Buddha	Corresponding Iranian Deity
Theravāda 上座部		3 BC	Gautama	None
Mahāyāna 大乗	Pure Land 浄土	1-2 AD	Amitābha/Amitāyus	Mithra/Zurwan
	Mādhyamaka 中観	3 AD	None	None
	Kegon 華厳	3-4 AD	Vairocana	Mithra
	Vijnāna-vādin 唯識	3-4 AD	Maitreya	Mithra
	Zen 禅	7 AD	Vairocana	Mithra
	Esoteric Buddhism -Shingon 真言 -Tendai 天台	7-8 AD	Mahāvairocana	Zurwan-Mithra
Vajirayāna 金剛乗		10 AD	Kālacakra	Zurwan-Mithra

I suppose for the eyes of those who are accustomed to the western methodology, evidences shown above are too little and weak. So I think it's better to give an apology for this:

---

[287] Vermaseren. *Mithras the Secret God*, 12.

(1) Mahāyāna Buddhism uses intentionally general names such as Vairocana (Sun God), Amitābha (Limitless Light), Amitāyus (Limitless Time), etc on appellation of deity names in order to erase all the ethnic elements.

(2) The Indo-Iranian tradition preserves their religious literatures by oral tradition. Therefore after Islamization, pre-Islamic Iranian tradition is almost lost.

In spite of such a situation, the evidences shown above shouldn't be disregarded as mare speculations. For Iranian influence upon Mahāyāna Buddhism is supported widely among Japanese scholars, and is now gaining more circumstantial evidences by the archaeological excavations in Bamiyan valley and its surrounding area by Japanese archaeologists.

1. 2 Maga-Brahmins

There is a legend of Mithra's magi in the area (Afghanistan, Pakistan and north-west India) where Mahāyāna Buddhism was formed. It is a legend about the Maga-Brahmins, who are also called atarvan Maga, Bhojaka or Sakaldwipiya Brahmins. They claim they are descendants of Jarashabda (Zoroaster?), who is a son of Sun God Mihir (Mithra), and that they are His magi (Maga-Brahmins) came from Saca[288] (Shakadwipa), where is the birth place of Gautama (Shyakamuni). Their major centers are in Rajasthan in Western India and near Gaya in Bihar. According to *Bhavishya Purana* and other texts, they were invited to settle in Punjab to conduct the worship of Lord Sun Mihir (Surya). *Bhavishya Purana* explicitly associates them to the rituals of the Zurvanism. The members of the community still worship in Sun temples in India. They are also hereditary priests in several Jain temples in Gujarat and Rajasthan. Bhojakas are mentioned in the copperplates of the Kadamba dynasty (4-6th) as managers of Jain institutions. Images of Lord Sun Mihir in India are shown wearing a central Asian dress, complete with boots. The name "Mihir" in India is regarded to represent the Maga influence. Here is the summary of *Bhavishya Purana* 133:

When Krishna's son Samba suffered from leprosy, he recovered from it after he worshiped Surya (Hindu Sun god). To express gratitude, he built a temple for Surya on the banks of the river Chandrabhaga, but he couldn't find Brahmins who are able to perform the role of priests in his temple. So he sought help of Gauramukha, the adviser of the yadu chief, Ugrasena. Gauramukha suggested him to go to Saca (Shakdvipa) in order to invite their priests to

---

[288] Also called Sacastan. *Shakyamuni* the title of Gautama means "sage of the Sacas".

worship Surya. Further, he asked another question, "tell me, oh Brahmin, what are the antecedents of these worshipers of the Sun?" Gauramukha replied to say, "the first of the Brahmins amidst the Sacas (Shakhas) was called 'Sujihva.' He had a daughter whose name was Nikshubha. She was so enamored of Surya that she became pregnant by him and gave birth to Jarashabda (Zoroaster?) who was the founding father of all the *Maga-Acharya*. They are distinguished by the sacred girdle called the *Avyanga* that they wear around their waist." After receiving the answer, Samba called on Krishna to send him Garuda. He rode on Gauda and flew to Saca. He collected the *Maga-Acharya* there, brought them back to India and installed them as priests of his Surya temple. The *Maga-Acharya* who came to India was called Maga-Brahmins. Their descendants came to be known as Bhojakas, for they married Bhoja vamsa women.

The following points should be remembered:

(1) Mithra

Images of Sun God Mihir in India are shown wearing a central Asian dress, complete with boots. The same image of Mithra is depicted in the large mural paintings in Bamiyan's Mahāyāna Buddhist site (300-400 AD). Interestingly Bamiyan's Mithra has strong Hellenistic tint. For example Mithra is accompanied by the twin gods Cautes and Cautopates as Roman Mithras[289].

(2) Maga-Brahmanas

By Japanese researchers, they are considered to be Indo-Scythians (the Sacas), and Gautama Buddha was the prince of them. They are religiously very active during 45 to 450 AD. It corresponds to the forming age of Mahāyāna Buddhism[290].

1. 3 Central Asia

At the time when Zen were transmitted along the trans-Asian trade route known as the Silk Road, various religions such as Mithraism, the cult of Mithra and Anahita, Zoroastrianism (Mazda worship), the Greek polytheism, early Mahāyāna Buddhism, Hinduism and the Nestorian Christianity flourished along this route.

---

[289] Maeda. *The Golden City Bamiyan Revived by Hi-vision Digital*; Odani. "The Colossal Buddha and Maitreya Cult in Bamiyan".
[290] Kurimoto. *Asuka: the Capital City of Sirius*, pp. 309-326. Also Aoki. *A History of Zoroastrianism*, p. 100.

The major transmitters of Buddhism to China were the Iranian peoples of Parthia, Bactria, and Transoxiana, whose convenient position between east and west enabled them to serve as middlemen along the Silk Road. The latter group in particular, known as the Sogdians, established communities along the trade routes from Iran and India all the way into China.

Actually many important features of Mahāyāna Buddhism show Iranian influences, such as Maitreya 弥勒 (Jp: Miroku; Buddhist Saošyant), swastika 卍 (Jp: Manji)[291], Pure Land 浄土 (Jp: Jōdo; Manichaean Paradise of Light) and the Buddha-nature 仏性 (Jp: Busšō; Manichaean particle of Light). Central deities also had Iranian origins (Table 1. 2).

The culture of Iranian people in Central Asia was Simorghian, which is the original culture of them which predates Zoroastrianism[292]. Mihr (Mithra), Anahita, Bhaga, Farrox, Mah, Haoma, Ohrmizd (Ahura Mazda), Yima and Zardušt (Zoroaster) were the gods in its pantheon. Mihr and Anahita worship were prominent. Ohrmizd was not the supreme god. Ohrmizd worship was a mare branch of it[293].

Table 1.2 Buddhas and their Iranian Origins

Buddha			Iranian Origin
Sanskrit	Chinese/Japanese	Meaning of Name	
Maitreya	弥勒 Miroku	Friend, Loving One	Mithra
Vairocana	毘盧遮那 Birušana	Sun God	Mithra (Mithras)
Mahāvairocana	大日 Dainichi	Great Sun God	Mithra (Mithras)
Amitāyus	無量寿 Muryōju	Limitless Time	Zurwan
Amitābha	阿弥陀 Amida	Limitless Light	Mithra (Mithras)
Avalokiteśvara	観音 Kannon	Lord who gazes down (at the world)	Sraoša
Mahāsthāmaprāpta	大勢至 Daiseiši	Great Power	Rašnu

Considering in the chronological order of the births of Mahāyāna sects, it is evident that the incorporation of Iranian Mithra into Buddhism was done in two steps:

---

[291] Swastika is a symbol of Dharma, the law of cause and effect, the law of karma, and fortune in Buddhism (Nakamura et al. ed. *Iwanami's Dictionary of Buddhism*). It is a symbol of Mithra and the sun in Iran, and is called "garduneh-e Mihr".

[292] Jamshid. *farhang-e iran*; http://www.shamogoloparvaneh.com/farhang.html

Step 1

Mithra was incorporated as the sole successor of Gautama the World Teacher. Alexander the Great (356–323 BC) brought Greek culture to Central Asia. This gave certain influence upon early Buddhism. Buddhists developed Gandhāra style art, which was a merger of Greek, Syrian, Persian, and Indian arts. This development began during the Parthian Period (50 BC – AD 75). Gandhāra style flourished and achieved its peak during the Kushan period (60 BC-375 AD). It might have affected the rise of Maitreya cult too. Maitreya cult developed during the period from 2nd BC to 2nd AD under the reign of Bactria (265-125 BC) and Kushan (60 BC-375 AD). Sutras called "Maitreya trilogy" 弥勒三部経 (Jp: Miroku-sanbukyō) were also formed during this period. The state religion of Bactria was Mithraism. Kushan adopted this policy too.

Step 2

Persian culture penetrated into the area west to Iran. During its westward penetration, it absorbed various elements from Greco-Roman culture and formed Roman Mithraism. By a series of decrees called the "Theodosian decrees", Christianity became the state religion of Roman Empire, while proscription was sentenced to all the other religions (392 AD). Until then Roman Mithraism brought back Hellenistic culture to its homeland (Iran and Central Asia). Merging with Manichaeism in Simorghian culture, it strengthened Sun God aspect of Mithra and His worship. It penetrated into Buddhism and formed new religion which we call Mahāyāna Buddhism. Mithra became Lord God of newly formed Buddhism (i. e. Mahāyāna Buddhism), and became to be called Vairocana (Sun God). The identification of Maitreya with Vairocana was assured in the doctrine[294].

2. Overview of Zen

2. 1 Etymological Origin

Zen 禅 is a school of Mahāyāna Buddhism. Both Japanese and Chinese use the same Chinese character "禅", however its pronunciation differs. Chinese pronounces it "Chán", Japanese "Zen". Japanese pronunciation preserves old Chinese pronunciation, and retains its etymological original Sanskrit pronunciation *dhyāna*, which means "meditation".

---

[293] Aoki. *A History of Zoroastrianism*, pp. 194-204; Kyō. *History of Zoroastrian Arts in China*.
[294] See 4.1.

2. 2 Charactersitics

Zen focuses on attaining enlightenment (bodhi) through meditation. It teaches that all human beings have the Buddha-nature 仏性, and the potential to attain enlightenment, within them, but the Buddha-nature is clouded by ignorance. To overcome this ignorance, Zen claims meditation is the best way. It is less effective to read scriptures, to perform religious rites, to do devotional practices, and good works. Training in the Zen path is usually undertaken by a disciple under the guidance of a master just like sufi training.

2. 3 Transmission

China

Zen is traditionally credited to be established at the Šaolin temple 少林寺 in China by a Persian wandering monk Bodhidharma 菩提達磨 (Jp: Daruma). He came to China to teach a "special teaching unwritten in the scriptures". The reason why it was not written was that the teaching is so subtle that it is impossible to transmit it by the words.

Zen is thought to have developed as an amalgam of various currents in Mahāyāna Buddhist thoughts—among them the Vijnāna-vādin 唯識 (Jp: Yuišiki), Mādhyamaka 中観 (Jp: Chūgan) philosophies and the Prajñāpāramitā 波羅蜜多 (Jp: Haramitta) literature—and of several traditions in China, particularly Taoism and preceding Mahāyāna Buddhism sect Kegon-šū 華厳宗 (Ch: Huáyán-zōng). The first document which mentioned Zen as a distinct school of Buddhism was written in 7th Century. From China Zen subsequently spread south to Vietnam, and east to Korea and Japan.

Japan

Zen arrived in Japan as early as the 7th century, but didn't develop significantly there until the 12th century. Zen has since been an important force in Japan. It has had considerable influence on Japanese culture such as gardening, calligraphy and the tea ceremony. In medieval age, Zen temples became training center of political and military elites. Therefore many warlords and warriors trained themselves in Zen temples. Even monk-soldiers appeared and became a strong force in medieval Japan. Zen is still one of the most popular Buddhist branch in Japan today.

Western World

Zen is probably the most well-known school of Buddhism in America. Its concepts have been influential on western world since the latter half of the 20th Century. Numerous Zen groups have developed in North America and Europe within the last century.

2. 4 Scriptures

(1) Scriptures of Kegon-šū 華厳宗

-Kegon-kyō 華厳経 (Skt: Buddhāvatamsaka-nāma-mahāvaipulya-sūtra) 3rd AD

(2) Scriptures of the Vijnāna-vādin 唯識

- Gejinmik-kyō 解深密経 (Skt: Samdhi-nirmacana-sutra) 3rd AD

- Yuishiki-sanjū-ju 唯識三十頌 (Skt: Triśikā Vijnaptimātratāsiddhih) 4-5th AD

- Yuišiki-nijū-ron 唯識二十論 (Skt: Vimśatikā Vijnaptimātratāsiddhih) 4-5th AD

(3) Mādhyamaka 中観 philosophies and the Prajñāpāramitā 波羅蜜多 literatures

-*Chūron* 中論 (Skt: Mādhyamaka-kārikā) 2nd-3rd AD

-The Heart Sutra 般若心経 (Skt: Prajnāpāramitāhrdaya)

(4) Meditation 瞑想

-The Treatise on the Two Entrances and Four Practices 二入四行 (Jp: Ninyū-shigyō-ron; Ch: Erh-ju ssu-hsing)

-Ten Bull Pictures 十牛図 (Jp: Jūgyūzu)

(5) Others

-The Record of the Buddhist Monasteries of Luoyang 洛陽伽藍記 (Jp: Rakuyō-garan-ki ; Ch: Luòyáng Qiélánjì)

3. Bodhidharma the Founder of Zen

3.1 Profile

The Founder of Zen is Bodhidharma 菩提達磨 (470-543). He is said to be the twenty-eighth patriarch after Gautama Buddha in the Indian lineage, and the first Chinese patriarch (i. e. the founder) of Zen 禅 Buddhism.

There are two legends about his biography. One says he is a Persian, the other says Indian. Most Japanese scholars and Buddhist monks think he is a Persian. In Japan, even in popular books and internet articles he is introduced as a Persian.

His nickname is an evidence for his Persian origin. He is said to be a blue-eyed Persian 碧眼胡僧 (Hekigan-kosō) in Zen tradition. "Blue-eyed Persian" means Hellenized Persian, and/or a Persian who has plenty of knowledge about western culture. Mithra's magi are such Persians.

Note

Bodhidharma's Indic origin legend is written in a short preface to the *Two Entrances and Four Acts* by Tánlín 曇林 (506–574). According to it, he was from the southern region of India, born as the third son of a great Indian king of the Pallava dynasty. He left his kingdom after becoming a Buddhist monk and travelled through Southeast Asia into Southern China.

Those who want to have a definite lineage of Zen tend to stick to Indic origin theory. But this theory is highly dubious. For there is no room for doubt that Mahāyāna Buddhism including Zen was developed in Central Asia and there is no evidence to show its close link to South India.

3. 2 The Record of the Buddhist Monasteries of Luoyang 洛陽伽藍記 (Ch: Luòyáng Qiélánjì; Jp: Rakuyō-garan-ki)

3. 2. 1 Bibliography

This was compiled in 547 by Yáng Xuànzhī 楊衒之 (Jp: Yō-gen-ši). Who lived sometime between the time of North-Wei 北魏 (386-534) and East-Wei 東魏 (534-550). Bodhidharma seems to have stayed in Luoyang between 516 and 526[295], when the temple referred to—Yǒng-níng-sì 永寧寺—was at the height of its glory.

Japanese scholars and monks think this book is more reliable than *The Treatise on the Two Entrances and Four Practices* 二入四行 (see 3. 3).

3. 2. 2 English Translation

At that time there was a monk of the Western Region named Bodhidharma, a Persian Central Asian. He traveled from the wild borderlands to China. Seeing the golden disks [on the pole on top of Yung-ning's stupa] reflecting in the sun, the rays of light illuminating the surface of the clouds, the jewel-bells on the stupa blowing in the wind, the echoes reverberating beyond the heavens, he sang its praises. He exclaimed: "Truly this is the work of spirits." He said: "I am 150 years old, and I have passed through numerous countries. There is virtually no country I haven't visited. Even the distant Buddha realms lack this." He chanted homage and placed his palms together in salutation for days on end.[296]

3. 3 The Treatise on the Two Entrances and Four Practices 二入四行 (Ch: Erh-ju ssu-hsing; Jp: Ninyū-shigyō-ron)

3. 3. 1 Bibliograpgy

This was written by Tánlín 曇林 (506–574). Tánlín's brief biography of the "Dharma Master" is found in his preface to *The Two Entrances and Four Acts* 二入四行, a text traditionally attributed to Bodhidharma. Tánlín has traditionally been considered a disciple of Bodhidharma, but it is more likely that he was a student of Huìkě, who in turn was a student of Bodhidharma.[297]

Though this text was attributed to Bodhidharma, a great deal of material was added to it, probably around the 8th century, by the monks and/or other anonymous groups including Taoist. Therefore Japanese scholars think this text is less reliable than *The Record of the Buddhist Monasteries of Luoyang*[298].

---

[295] Broughton, Jeffrey L. *The Bodhidharma Anthology: The Earliest Records of Zen*, University of California Press, 1999, p. 138.
[296] Ibid., pp. 54-55.
[297] Ibid., p. 53.
[298] Atsushi, Ibuki. "Is the Treatise on the Two Entrances and Four Practices Truly the Record of Bodhidharma's Teaching?", Journal of Indian and Buddhist studies 55(1) pp. 127-134, 2006. Dec. 20.

3. 3. 2 English Translation

The Dharma Master was a South Indian of the Western Region. He was the third son of a great Indian king of the Pallava dynasty. His ambition lay in the Mahayana path, and so he put aside his white layman's robe for the black robe of a monk [...] Lamenting the decline of the true teaching in the outlands, he subsequently crossed distant mountains and seas, traveling about propagating the teaching in Han and Wei.[299]

3. 4 Unwritten Teaching

Zen is a teaching of Gautama which has been transmitted without scriptures. This is called the doctrine of Huryūmonji 不立文字[300]. Huryūmonji means "teaching established without written scriptures". Later this doctrine was supplemented by a legendary story about the Flower Sermon (14th AD). It said that Gautama gathered his disciples one day for a dharma talk. When they gathered together, he kept silence, uttering no word. Some of the disciples speculated that he was tired or ill. After a certain time has passed, he silently held up to twirled a flower and twinkled his eyes. Some disciples tried to interpret what this meant, though none of them were correct. One of Gautama's disciples, Mahākāśyapa, silently gazed at the flower and broke into a broad smile. Gautama then acknowledged Mahākāśyapa's insight by saying: I possess the true Dharma eye, the marvelous mind of Nirvana, the true form of the formless and the subtle dharma mystery that is impossible to write down for no words can express it. This unritten mystery I entrust to Mahākāśyapa[301].

From Persian point of view, it is more likely that the true intention of the doctrine of Huryūmonji is to hide its Persian origin.

3. 5 Wandering Zen monks

In Zen tradition, monks are wandering practitioner-preachers. They wander from place to place without staying long in one place. This behavior reminds us of Persian sufis (wandering dervishes). This parallel should not be disregarded. It should be considered with other points from holistic Simorghian view.

---

[299] Broughton, Jeffrey L. *The Bodhidharma Anthology: The Earliest Records of Zen*, University of California Press, 1999, p. 8.
[300] Nakamura, Gen et al. ed. *Iwanami's Dictionary of Buddhism*

3. 6 Zen and Roman Mithraism

The Šaolin temple 少林寺 (Jp: Šōrin-ji) is famous for its martial arts. There were many monk-warriors in the Šaolin temple. There were also many monk-soldiers (僧兵 sōhei) in Japanese Zen temple Eihei-ji 永平寺. Believers of Roman Mithraism were mainly military people. This parallel is not a coincidence, but a tendency of Mithraism.

4. Kegon-kyō

4. 1 Doctrine of Universal Buddha and His Avatars

Kegon-kyō 華厳経 (Skt: Buddhāvatamsaka-nāma-mahāvaipulya-sūtra, Shortened name: The Avataṃsaka Sūtra) is formed in late 3rd to 4th Century in Central Asia by assembling various teachings of Mahāyāna Buddhism widely spread in Central Asia. It became an important scripture of Zen[302]. According to Kegon-kyō, Buddha Vairocana (Sun God) is Universal Buddha. Gautama is his first avatar. Maitreya is the next and the last avatar. Although there is no direct identification of Vairocana with Mithra, in the religious context of Central Asia at that time, there was no God but Mithra who deserved to be called Vairocana (Sun God).

Maitreya as the last avatar of Mithra (Vairocana) is one of the essential doctrine of Esoteric Buddhism, and is called the doctrine of identification of Maitreya with Vairocana (Dainichi-Miroku-dōtai 大日弥勒同体). The first monk who brought this doctrine from Central Asia to China is Zenmukon 善無根. Zenmukon wrote a scripture *Manthra Zikr Practice of the Loving One (Miroku)* 慈氏菩薩略修愈言我念誦法 in two volumes. He wrote it in this scripture. The doctrine was succeeded by Kongōchi 金剛智, Keika 恵果 and Kūkai 空海 (774-835). Kūkai is a Japanese monk. He brought it back to Japan.

4. 2 Bamiyan Buddhist Site

The tradition mentioned in 4.1 is also supported by the archaeological findings in the large Buddhist site in Bamiyan valley, which was the center of Mhāyāna Buddhism in the same age when Kegon-kyō and Zen were formed.

In Bamiyan Buddhist site, there are two great stone images of Buddhas in Bamiyan valley. The east Buddha is Gautama (Shyakyamuni) 38m in height, the west Buddha is Maitreya 55m in height. These are created during 4th to 6th^{h} century.

---

[301] Dumoulin, Heinrich. *Zen: A History*. vol. 1 India and China, pp. 8–9, 68, 166–167, 169–172.
[302] Nakamura. *Iwanami's Dictionary of Buddhism*, p. 222.

Sun God Miiro (Mithra) is drawn above the head of the east Buddha (Gautama). Two servant-gods in front of Miiro bear torches. They are Cautes and Cautopates of Roman Mithraism. Greek Athena is drawn to protect Miiro. The painting of Miiro above the Gautama indicates that Gautama is a friend of or an avatar of Miiro, just like Roman emperors who are friends of Mithras. This is the doctrine of the Buddhists of Bamiyan[303].

The scheme of the mural painting above the head of the west Buddha (Maitreya) represents the heavenly world. The combination of the statue (the west Buddha) and the painting represents their doctrine that Maitreya will come as a messiah Buddha from the Sun sphere in the far future[304].

Between the two great images lies a great stone image of dying Gautama. The alignment of these three images –from east to west, East: Gautama, Middle: dying Gautama, West: Maitreya- seems to represent succession of World Teacher-ship from Gautama to Maitreya, i. e. first avatar to second avatar of Vairocana (Mithra).

5. The Vijnāna-vādin

5. 1 Origin

The Vijnāna-vādin 唯識派 (Jp: Yuishikiha), also called Yogācāra 瑜伽行派 (Jp: Yugagyōha) was founded by Maitreya 弥勒 (Jp: Miroku), succeeded and expanded by Asanga 無着 (Jp: Mujaku). Maitreya is believed to have lived in 4th-5th centuries. Asanga lived in 4th century and came from a Brahmin family living in present-day Peshawar (Pakistan). The historicity of Maitreya is a matter of controversy. According to tradition Asanga received the inspiration for his teaching direct from Maitreya Buddha. They thought all the material creatures are illusion, there only exists manas (mind), ultimately the great manas. They practiced yoga to attain this recognition. Vijnāna-vādin is thought to have prepared philosophical and practical basis for the Esoteric Buddhism[305].

---

[303] Maeda. *The Golden City Bamiyan revived by Hi-vision Degital*;
http://bunka.nii.ac.jp/SearchDetail.do?heritageId=48345; http://silkroadbamiyan.com/bamiyan_jp.htm
[304] Miyaji. *Iconology of Buddhist Arts*.
[305] Fischer-Schreiber. *The Shambhala Dictionary of Buddhism and Zen*, p137, 12; Nakamura. *Iwanami Dictionary of Buddhism*, p. 810.

5. 2 Teachings

(1) Eight Types of Consciousness –Hasšiki 八識

According to the Vijnāna-vādin (Yogācāra) philosophy, the consciousness is divided into eight types (Table 5. 1). They are systematized into a layer structure shown in table 5. 2. The definition of each term is shown in chapter 7.

Table 5. 1 Eight types of Consciousness

Japanese	English	Persian Sufi Term
Arayašiki 阿頼耶識	Logos (Skt: Ālaya-vijñāna)	Hakk and 'Aql
Manašiki 末那識	Monad (Skt: Manas-vijnāna)	Soul at peace (Nafs-e mutma'inna)
Išiki 意識	Mind	Human soul (Nafs-e insānī) Rational soul (Nafs-e nātiqa)
Šinšiki 身識	Skin-sense	Animal soul (Nafs-e heiwānī)
Zetsušiki 舌識	Tongue-sense	
Bišiki 鼻識	Nose-sense	
Nišiki 耳識	Ear-sense	
Genšiki 眼識	Eye-sense	

Table 5. 2 Eight layers of Consciousness

The Vijnāna-vādin philosophy	Persian Sufism	Theosophy
Arayashiki 阿頼耶識 Âlaya-vijñāna	Hakk	Logos
	'Aql	Monad
Manashiki 末那識 Manas-vijnāna	Soul at peace (Nafs-e mutma'inna)	Ātmic body
Sikiun 識蘊 Vijnāna	Soul of the Friend of God (Nafs-e qudsi)	Buddhic body
Sōun 想蘊 Samjā	Human soul (Nafs-e insānī) Rational soul (Nafs-e nātiqa)	Mental body
Gyōun 行蘊 Samskāra		
Jyu'un 受蘊 Vedanā	Animal soul (Nafs-e heiwānī)	Astral body
Seiki 生気 Purāna	Vegetable soul (Nafs-e nabātī)	Etheric body
Šikiun 色蘊 Vijnapti	Nature (Tabī'at)	Physical body

(2) The Three Natures –Sanšō-setsu 三性説

The Yogācāra philosophy said there are three modes (stages) in our consciousness.

Parikalpita (Fully Conceptualized Consciousness):

This is the lowest stage of consciousness. It is erroneous in its nature. This mode of consciousness perceives things on its conceptualized view tinted by attachment and prejudice.

Paratantra (Other Dependent Consciousness):

This is the middle mode of consciousness. Its nature is partially liberated. Although its view is still deeply influenced by its conceptualization, it understands the conceptualized view is not absolute but is a consequence of environment (causes and conditions).

Pariniṣpanna (Fully Accomplished Consciousness):

This is fully liberated consciousness, the highest mode of consciousness. It can see things as it are free from any kind of conceptualization.

(3) Âlaya Only Exists Yuišiki 唯識

The Yogācāra philosophy said there exist only Ālaya (Hakk), all others are mare illusion blossoming out from it (Ālaya). The purpose of ascetic practices is to attain the highest mode of consciousness to experience it.

In Ancient Persian culture (Simorghian culture), everything comes from Universal Spirit[306]. This Universal Spirit is symbolized by Simorgh. This tradition is well preserved in Attār's best known work "the Conference of the Birds". There is a striking parallel between the Yogācāra philosophy and the Simorghian tradition. Combining this parallel with the fact two facts that (a) Maitreya-Mithra is the founder-teacher of the Vijnāna-vādin (Yogācāra) philosophy, (b) it developed in Central Asia where the Simorghian culture is dominant, the Yogācāra philosophy seems to be a philosohical expression of the Simorghian culture.

---

[306] Jamshidi. *farhang-e iran.*

5. 2 Link to Mithra

According to Manichaeism, Mihryazd (Mithra) is the creator of the cosmos, creatures and the reincarnation process. All of them he created by his maya. According to chapter 4, Maitreya is the second and the last avatar of Mithra. According to Manichaeism, Maitreya is the last avatar of Mithra. These indicate the teachings of Vijñāna-vādin are Mithra's teachings, i. e. Persian teaching.

6. Mādhyamaka philosophies and the Prajñāpāramitā literatures

6. 1 History

The Mādhyamaka school was founded by Nāgārjuna 龍樹 (c. 150-250), who was an Indian philosopher. His writings are the basis for the formation of this school. He is credited with developing the philosophy of the Prajñāpāramitā sutras.

6. 2 Teachings

(1) The Law of Cause and Effect

All phenomena are empty of "self nature" or "essence" (Skt: **Svabhāva**), meaning that they have no intrinsic, independent reality apart from the causes and conditions from which they arise. Everything in the Cosmos is linked by the chain of cause and effect (因果, Skt: Hetu-phala). The notion that everything in the Cosmos is a consequence of the causes and conditions is called Engi 縁起 (Skt: Pratīya-samutpāda).

(2) Middle Way

It is the best and correct way to accept (1) and reject the two extreme philosophies (Eternalism: the view that something is eternal and unchanging. Nihilism: the view that nothing is eternal, everything changes.). This is called Chūgan 中観 (the middle way) between the two extremes.

(3) The Best Method for the Perfection of Wisdom

Mādhyamaka is a source of methods for approaching prajñāpāramitā 般若波羅蜜多 (perfection of wisdom), the sixth of the Six Perfections of the bodhisattva path.

6. 3 Link to Mithra

The teachings of Mādhyamaka philosophies and the Prajñāpāramitā literatures are philosophical supplements to the teachings of the Vijnāna-vādin. The Law of cause and effect gives theoretical base for karma 業 (Jp: Gō) and Reincarnation 輪廻転生 (Jp: Rin'ne-tenšō). According to this law, the cause of the cause i. e. the first Cause is Vairocana (=Mithra the Sun). In this sense these also have a connection with Mithra's teachings.

The law of cause and effect in Mādhyamaka philosophy is a more scientific and detailed expression of what Roman Mithraism had expressed symbolically as Mithra's four winds.

According to Vermaseren, the mysterious statue of the lion-headed God is the Hellenistic theosophic image of syncretic God "Zurwan-Mithra", who is the highest God of Roman Mithraism. He is both Sun God and God of Time. He rules over four winds of four directions and four seasons. This is symbolized by his four wings. Sometimes four seasonal gods are depicted in the four corners in his icons[307].

The lion-headed God blows out four winds and a logos-fire from his mouth to move the cosmos. These winds and the logos-fire are Roman expression of fōhat. The function of four winds is to unite four elements (fire, wind, water, earth) in spite of their essential differences in order to make a physical body of a creature. The function of the logos-fire is to put a spark (spirit) into the physical body and give it a life. When its pre-determined time will pass, the bond will disappear. The spirit left the body, and return to the Heaven (Sun). The body will disintegrate into four elements and scatter among air, water and earth. (Plato. *Timaeus* 41-42; *Hermetica* XVI)

7. Ten Bull Pictures

7. 1 The Meaning of the Name

Jū 十 means ten, gyū 牛 means the bull, zu 図 means painting, therefore Jūgyūzu 十牛図 means Ten Bull Paintings. Jūgyūzu is a set of ten pictures which represents the path to enlightenment in Zen 禅宗.

---

[307] Vermaseren. *Mithras the Secret God*, 12.

7. 2 Origin

The earliest Jūgyūzu was made in Sui 宋 dynasty (960-1279). There are many Jūgyūzus, however, Kakuan (Ch: Kou-an) 廓庵's one is the most famous. Kakuan (fl. 1150) was born in He-chuan 合川 of Kansu 甘粛省. Kansu was a stronghold of Manichaeism. He lived in Hunan 湖南省.

There are earlier versions consisting of five or eight pictures in which the bull is black at the beginning, becomes progressively whiter and finally disappears altogether. This last stage is shown as an empty circle. But Kakuan, feeling this to be incomplete, added two more pictures beyond the circle to make it clear that the Zen man of the highest spiritual development lives in the mundane world of form and diversity and mingles with the utmost freedom among ordinary men, whom he inspires with his compassion and radiance like Miroku[308].

Considering in these facts, there seems to be no denying the influence of Persian culture (Mithraism) in Ten Bull Pictures.

7.3 Terminology

Before giving explanation about each picture of Ten Bull Pictures, it would be necessary to give clear definition of technical terms which will be used in the explanations. Table 7. 1 shows correspondence among technical terms of Theosophy, Buddhism and Sufism. In the explanation, technical terms of Theosophy are used for the convenience of the western readers.

Table 7. 1 Mystic Bodies

Theosophy	Buddhism	Persian Sufism
Logos	Arayashiki 阿頼耶識 Ālaya-vijñāna	Hakk
Monad	Arayashiki 阿頼耶識 Ālaya-vijñāna	ʻAql
Ātmic body	Manashiki 末那識 Manas-vijnāna	Soul at peace (Nafs-e mutma'inna)
Buddhic body	Sikiun 識蘊 Vijnāna	Soul of the Friend of God (Nafs-e qudsī)
Mental body	Sōun 想蘊 Samjā Gyōun 行蘊 Samskāra	Human soul (Nafs-e insānī) Rational soul (Nafs-e nātiqa)
Astral body	Jyu'un 受蘊 Vedanā	Animal soul (Nafs-e heiwānī)
Etheric body & Physical body	Seiki 生気 Purāna & Shikiun 色蘊 Vijnapti	Vegetable soul (Nafs-e nabātī) Nature (Tabī'at)

---

[308] Nakamura et al. ed. *Iwanami's Dictionary of Buddhism*, p391; Fischer-Schreiber, Ingrid et al. *The Shambhala Dictionary of Buddhism and Zen*, pp. 106-107.

Logos

It is Universal Spirit (Spirit of God). It is the supreme Root of all beings. There is no individuality in it, no "I" nor "You".

Monad

It is the first emanation (differentiation) of Logos. It dwells in Ākāśa. For Ākāśa is the lower part of Logos, when monad dissolves into Ākāśa, the seeker becomes one with Universal Spirit. Famous Persian mystic Mansur al-Hallaj (ca. 858-922) said "Ana al-Haqq" (I am Universal Spirit) to express this mystic union with Universal Spirit (Rūmī. Fī-hi Ma Fī-hi, 52).

Ātmic body

It is the highest part of a human being and the root of individuality. It generates I-ness (ego) in a human being. The annihilation of I-ness is called fanā' in Sufism. It occurs in the 8th stage of Ten Bull Pictures.

Buddhic body

It is the second highest part of a human being. It is the source of love, compassion and intuition. It is sometimes symbolized by the moon.

Mental body

It is the dwelling place of human consciousness. Human consciousness descends to the astral body when he becomes intoxicated. It ascends to the upper bodies when he purifies himself and practices meditation.

Astral body

It is also called animal soul. It is the source of passion and emotional turmoil, which pollute neighboring two mystic bodies (mental body and ether body). When the seeker succeeds in pacifying his astral body, two things occur. (1) Mental body and ether body are released from astral pollution (his passion and emotional turmoil). (2) His consciousness is released from astral pollution and gains power to ascend to the higher bodies (planes).

Etheric body and physical body

Etheric body forms and sustains the physical body by providing it with the vital energy. When the vital energy is exhausted, man can't maintain his physical body to die.

Other technical terms

Fanā, bakā, namu (nama), zikr, Tosotsuten, mir, etc are explained in the commentaries to the pictures.

7.4 The Story and the Commentaries

The story is written by the author basing on Ueda & Yanagida's *Ten Bull Pictures*. The commentaries are added by the author.

(1) Seeking for the Bull 尋牛

> Title: Jin 尋 means to seek, gyū 牛 means bull, therefore jingyū 尋牛 means to seek for the bull.
>
> Picture: The first picture shows a shepherd boy seeking for his lost bull.
>
> Commentary: The boy is the symbol of a soul (consciousness) who begins to tread his self-seeking path. The lost bull is the symbol of his astral body.

(2) Finding the Footprints 見跡

> Title: Ken 見 means to find, seki 跡 means footprint, therefore kenseki 見跡 means to find footprints (of the bull).
>
> Picture: The shepherd boy is at a loss in the wilderness. A thick mist covered everything. He prays Miroku 弥勒 for protection and guide, repeating "Namu Miroku-butsu 南無弥勒仏 [309]".
>
> Commentary: Footprints are the symbol of scriptures and commentaries. The thick mist is the symbol of the barzakh (veil) which covers the bull. The seeker reads many books. The

---

[309] Namu 南無 is transcription of Persian word "nama", which means "homage to". It is widely used among Mahayana Buddhism. Miroku 弥勒 means Mithras, butsu 仏 means Buddha. Therefore it means "Homage to Buddha Mithra".

more he read, the more his knowledge becomes rich. But he can't apply his abundant knowledge to his specific situation. He is so depressed that he prays Miroku (Mithras) for protection and guidance. By saying "Namu Miroku-butsu 南無弥勒仏" repeatedly, his consciousness recovers its stability. The origin of repeating the phrase is Iranian zikr.

(3) Seeing the Bull 見牛

　Title: Ken 見 means to see, gyū 牛 means the bull, therefore kengyū 見牛 means to see the bull.

　Picture: The shepherd boy sees the tail and the hind legs of the bull. He is running after the bull, but still can't see the whole bull.

　Commentary: This situation is the symbol of the seeker who got a clue to what he should do. During pursuit of the bull, he gradually recognizes he must catch the bull and tame it, but he forebodings it would be a tough work.

(4) Finding the Bull 得牛

　Title: Toku 得 means to catch, gyū 牛 means the bull, therefore tokugyū 得牛 means to catch the bull.

　Picture: The shepherd boy is catching the bull. The bull doesn't follow his order. The bull resist violently against the boy. The struggle continues.

　Commentary: This situation is the symbol of the seeker who is trying to pacify and tame his astral body. By pacifying his astral body, his passions and emotional turmoil will cease.

(5) Taming the Bull 牧牛

　Title: Boku 牧 means to tame, gyū 牛 means the bull, therefore bokugyū 牧牛 means to tame the bull.

　Picture: The shepherd boy successfully tamed the bull. The bull obediently follows the boy.

　Commentary: This situation is the symbol of the seeker who succeeded in pacifying his astral body. His astral body is in perfect accordance with his mental body now.

(6) Returning Home Riding the Bull 騎牛帰家

Title: Ki 騎 means to ride, gyū 牛 means the bull, ki 帰 means to return, ka 家 means home, therefore kigyūkika 騎牛帰家 means to return to home riding on the bull.

Picture: The shepherd boy returns to his home, riding on the back of the bull. He is playing the flute victoriously.

Commentary: This situation is the symbol of the seeker who succeeded in purification of his astral body. Riding on the bull is a symbolic expression of perfect accordance with his astral body. By the pacification of his astral body, his ether body is also purified. Returning home playing the flute is a symbolic expression of the end of the first half of meditation. The objective of the first half of meditation is to develop and purify his buddhic, mental, astral and ether body.

(7) Forgetting the Bull 忘牛存人

Title: Bō 忘 means to forget, gyū 牛 means the bull, zon 存 means to exist, nin 人 means person, therefore bōgyūzon'nin 忘牛存人 means that a person exists forgetting the bull.

Picture: The shepherd boy returns to his daily life (the mundane world) and forgets the bull. The moon, taking bull's place, begins to attract his consciousness. He raises his gaze upward toward the moon for the first time since he started his self-seeking.

Commentary: By pacifying his astral body, his consciousness was released from emotional turmoil. It affords his consciousness to ascend to his higher subtle bodies. Forgetting the bull and seeing the moon is a symbolic expression of this situation.

(8) Forgetting the Person and the Bull 人牛俱忘

Title: Nin 人 means a person, gyū 牛 means the bull, gu 俱 means both, bō 忘 means to forget, therefore ningyūgubō 人牛俱忘 means to forget both the person and the bull.

Picture: One day, the shepherd boy forgets both himself and the bull.

Commentary: This situation is called "fanā[310]" in Persian sufism. Fanā means annihilation of the individual ego. The seeker's consciousness ascends to Tosotsuten 都率天[311]. Before

---

[310] Its Japanese translation is muka 無化 and/or jigašōmetsu 自我消滅. Mu 無 means null, ka 化 means -lify/-lize, therefore muka 無化 means nullify (annihilation). Ji-ga 自 means individual, ga 我 means ego, šō-metsu 消滅 means extinction, therefore jigašōmetsu 自我消滅 means extinction of individual ego.

entering Tosotsuten, the consciousness of the seeker loses its grip of I-ness. As soon as he loses I-ness, his consciousness dissolves into Universal Spirit (Hakk).

(9) Returning to the Root 返本還源

Title: Hen 返 means to return, bon 本 means the Root (Hakk), gen 還 means to return, gen 源 means the Source (Fountain, Hakk), therefore henbongengen 返本還源 means to return to the Root.

Picture: The consciousness of shepherd boy wonders joyously in Universal Spirit. The richness of Universal Spirit is expressed as a beautiful landscape in the picture. For there is no individuality, there is no one in the picture.

Commentary: This situation is called "bakā[312]" in Persian sufism. Bakā means wandering within Ākasha. The seeker enjoys eternal life within Ākāśa. Monad wanders in Ākāśa. For there is no individuality, monad and Ākāśa are one. Monad enjoys mystic unity.

(10) Entering the Mundane World to Give Hand 入鄽垂手

Title: Nit 入 means to enter, ten 鄽 means shop (symbol of the mundane world), sui 垂 means to give, shu 手 means hand, therefore nittensuishu 入鄽垂手 means to enter the mundane world to give hand (to the people).

Picture: After returning from bakā, the shepherd boy finds that he becomes Bu-dai, an avatar of Miroku (Mithra). He goes out to the town and begins to save people. Commentary: The seeker becomes Miroku-tenze 弥勒転世. Miroku 弥勒 means Mithra, ten 転 means to reincarnate, ze 世 means the mundane world, therefore Miroku-tenze 弥勒転世 means Miroku reincarnated in the mundane world. He is a Persian mir (imam).

Commentary: Bu-dai 布袋 (Jp: Hotei) is a Zen monk, said to have lived in the late Tang (Jp: Tō) 唐 dynasty (705-907). His name comes from his wandering through the towns with a hempen beggar's sack on his back. According to the Chinese legend Bu-dai is an avatar of

---

[311] Tosotsu 都率 is transcription of Sanskrit "Tusita", which means the Sun sphere. Ten 天 means heaven (sphere). Therefore Tosotsuten means the Sun sphere. His consciousness ascends to the Ātmic plane and finally loses its grip of I-ness and melt into Ākāśa. This is the fanā.

[312] Its Japanese translation is shōyō 逍遥. Both shō 逍 and yō 遥 means to wander, therefore shōyō 逍遥 means wandering.

Milo 弥勒 (Miroku=Mithra). He showed his true image when he died. His wandering preaching reminds us of wandering dervish of Sufism.

7. 5 Relation to the Simorghian Culture

Ten Bull Pictures is a Miroku Buddhism version of the Simorghian tradition. It is attested by comparison with the following works which retains the Simorghian tradition:

Avicenna[313]'s mystic story "the Recital of Bird"

Nezāmi-e Ganjavi[314]'s poem "Haft Paykar".

Attār[315]'s best known work "the Conference of the Birds"

Suhrawardi[316]'s mystic story "the Treatise of the Birds"

Rūmī[317]'s *Mathnawi*

Attār

In Attār's poem '*the Conference of the Bird*', thirty birds journey through seven valleys to meet Simorgh. Thirty birds are the symbolic expression of seekers. The seven valleys are the symbolic expression of seven spheres. Simorgh is the symbol of Hakk (Universal Spirit). The following is a synopsis of their (thirty birds') journey:

> When thirty birds arrived at the Threshhold of the Eternal One (Universal Spirit), a winged harbinger of flame appeared suddenly and asked them, "Who are you? Whence and why do you come here?" Their spokesman answered, "Let us see the Fount from which we flow, and, melt (annihilate) ourselves therein!" Before the word was uttered, the portal open flung. They were within. Before the Throne, when they awfully raised their eyes to see the Eternal One on the Throne, they saw Sun-like Simorgh (themselves)

---

[313] Latinized name of Ibn Sina, c. 980-1037. Persian polymath, physician and philosopher.
[314] 1141-1209. Persian polymath and poet.
[315] 1145/46- c. 1221. Persian Sufi and mystic poet.
[316] 1155-1191. Persian theosophist, philosopher.
[317] 1207-1273. Persian mystic and philosopher.

in the center of the glorious blaze. It was them, they are it. Another, yet the Same. Dividual, yet One. Yes, this is their goal. They finally attained the perfect mystic union with the Eternal One.

The mystic union with the Simorgh is the same kind of mystic union as Ten Bull Pictures.

One of characteristic features of the Simorghian tradition is its symbolism of birds. It is retained in Roman Mithraism. Roman Mithraism put bird name to its lowest and highest initiation ranks. The name of the lowest rank is Corax (Raven), and the name of the highest rank is Aquila (Eagle). The initiate begins his journey as a raven and ends it as an eagle. This scheme is quite parallel with Attār's poem. Although birds don't appear in Ten Bull Pictures, the step by step ascension of initiation ranks in Roman Mithraism has great similarity to the meditation steps in Ten Bull Pictures.

Rūmī

In the Rūmī's *Mathnawi* III 3901-06 the ascension of a soul is explained as follows:

I died as a mineral and became a plant,

I died as a plant and rose to an animal,

I died as animal and I became Adam (Man).

Why should I fear? When was I less by dying?

Yet once more I shall die as Man, to soar among the angels;

But even from the state of angel

I must pass on: all except God doth perish.

When I have sacrificed my angel-soul,

I shall become what no mind ever conceived.

I shall become Non-existence.

Non-existence saith to me in organ tones,

Verily unto Him we shall return.

In the verse the soul ascends by transmigration from a mineral to God (Universal Spirit), via vegetable, animal, human-being and angel. This step by step ascension corresponds seven layers of Table 7. 1.

7.6 Relation to Mysteries of Roman Mithraism

Although the system of Roman Mithraic initiations is not a system of meditation, there seems to be a sort of correspondence between it and Ten Bull Pictures. Table 7. 2 shows the result of a consideration on the correspondence. It seems to me the correspondence can't be accidental, for both systems developed from the same Iranian tradition. The following is a speculation on the correspondence.

Table 7. 2 Seven Initiation Ranks of Roman Mithraism

Initiation Ranks	Gigaku Namings	Guardian Planets	Corresponding Ten Bull Pictures	Mysteries
Aquila (Pater)	Gokō 呉公	Saturn	(10)	Major mystery
Heliodromus	Chidō 治道	Sun	(8), (9)	
Perses	Suiko'ō 酔胡王	Moon	(7)	
Leo	Shishi 獅子	Jupiter	(6)	Minor mystery
Miles	Kongō 金剛	Mars	(4), (5)	
Nymph	Gojo 呉女	Venus	(3)	
Corax	Karura 迦楼羅	Mercury	(1), (2)	

Gigaku 伎楽 is a ritual masque of Roman Mithraism transmitted to Japan. According to *Shokunihongi* 続日本紀[318] (A Sequel to the History of Japan), Mimashi 味摩之 of Bekje 百済 brought gigaku from south China district Go 呉 in 612 AD. He organized a group of boys (gigakudan 伎楽団) and performed ritual dance in major Buddhist temples. It was incorporated into National Ritual Institution Utainomainotsukasa 雅楽寮 in 701 AD.

Corax is called Karura 迦楼羅, which means crow. Nymph is called Gojo 呉女, which means Persian woman (girl). Go 呉 is equivalent to ko 胡, and means Persian. Jo 女 means woman

---

[318] Edited by Sugano Mamichi 菅野真道 and Fujiwarano Tsugutada 藤原継縄 in 797 AD. 40 vols.

and/or maid. It is a name reflecting the meaning of Nymph (bride of Mithras). In Gigaku Pater 呉公 and Nymph 呉女 make a pair: Persian Lord (Mir) and Persian maid, Mithras and his male bride. Miles is called Kongō 金剛. Kongō means Deva king, who is the conqueror of death and the keeper of the gate to the Heaven. Leo is called Šiši 獅子, which means lion. Šiši is also called Šōša 笑者, Šōša 勝者 and Kōša 輝者. Šō 笑 means laughing, ša 者 means one (man), šō 勝 means victory and kō 輝 means shining, therefore Šōša 笑者 means the laughing one, Šōša 勝者 means the victor, Kōša 輝者 means the shining one. Perses is called Suiko'ō 酔胡王, which means intoxicated Persian king. Sui 酔 means intoxicated, ko 胡 means Persian and ō 王 means king. Suiko 酔胡 (Intoxicated Persian) reminds us of famous Persian mystic-poet Hāfez. Heliodromus called Chidō 治道, which is a name reflecting the meaning of Heliodromus. Pater is called Gokō 呉公, which means magi. Go 呉 is equivalent to ko 胡, and means Persian. Kō 公 means lord. Therefore Gokō 呉公 means lord of Persian, namely mir.[319]

8. Concluding Remark

Mahāyāna Buddhism is formed under the influence of Mithraism. Zen is not the teaching of Gautama (Shyakamuni) but Iranian Sun God Mithra (Vairocana). This Sun God Mithra is not Mazdaean but Simorghian with strong Hellenistic tint (Roman Mithras).

From the Simorghian point of view, it is possible to say that Simorghian magi absorbed Buddhism to develop their new religion (i. e. Mahāyāna Buddhism) in Central Asia. Its central deity is Iranian Mithra with Hellenistic tint. The reason behind the fact that there is no dualistic tendency in Mahāyāna Buddhism (including Zen) is that Persian culture which gave influence upon Buddhism was not Mazdaean but Simorghian.

Some researchers tend to think that the Simorghian culture was extinguished by Zoroastrianism and Islam, therefore today people can only see its fragmental reflections in various esoteric traditions such as Yezidism and Persian Sufi literatures. But it isn't true. We can see its evolved (sophisticated) form in Zen.

Some researchers on Mithraism tend to put Mithraism in the mirror image of Christianity and/or Zoroastrianism. But this is also misleading. Persian Sufism, Zen and Roman Mithraism,

---

[319] Ogawa, Hideo. *A Study in Mithraism*, Lithon, pp. 65-68; 小川英雄『ミトラス教研究』リトン社, 1993.

these three are to be seen as three branches of one same tree, with its root the Simorghian culture.

Lastly, some members of Mithraeum Japan wrote me that there is something common among warriors of Zen, Roman Mithraism and jedi knights of SF movie the Star Wars. This fact may cast a light on the ideal model of a man in Mithraism. A Buddha awakes from his meditation to take his sword for the benefit of mankind. It is possible to say that such kind of image of ideal Mithraist is formed in the minds of some Japanese Mithraists.

Abbreviations

Ch ……. Chinese, Jp ………Japanese, Skt …….Sanskrit

Bibliography

Aoki. Ken. *A History of Zoroastrianism*, Tōsui Shobō, 2008; 青木健『ゾロアスター教史』刀水書房, 2008.

Atsushi, Ibuki. "Is the Treatise on the Two Entrances and Four Practices Truly the Record of Bodhidharma's Teaching?", *Journal of Indian and Buddhist studies* 55(1) pp. 127-134, 2006.

Attar, Farid ud-Din. Edward FitzGerald trans. *Bird Parliament*, Macmillan and Co., 1889.

'Attār, Farīd ud-Dīn. Afkham Darbandi and Dick Davis trans. & intro. *The Conferrence of the Birds*, Penguin Books, 1984.

Bivar, A. D. H. *The Personalities of Mithra in Archaeology and Literature*, Bibliotheca Persica Press, 1994.

Broughton, Jeffrey L. *The Bodhidharma Anthology: The Earliest Records of Zen*, University of California Press, 1999.

Dumoulin, Heinrich. *Zen: A History. Vol. 1, India and China.* Trans. by James W. Heisig and Paul Knitter, with Intro. by John McRae. N.p.: World Wisdom, 2005.

Fischer-Schreiber, Ingrid et al. *The Shambhala Dictionary of Buddhism and Zen, Shambhala*, 1991.

Gardner, Ian. *The Kephalaia of the Teacher*, E. J. Brill, 1995

Iqbal, Afzal. *The Life & Work of Jalaluddin Rumi*, the Octagon Press, 1983 (1956).

Jamshidi, Jamshid, Dr. *farhang-e iran*, 2005.

_____ http://www.shamogoloparvaneh.com/farhang.html

Klimkeit, Hans-Joachim. *Gnosis on the Silk Road*, HarperSanFrancisco, 1993.

Kurimoto, Shin'ichirō. *Asuka: the Capital City of Sirius*, 2005; 栗本慎一郎『シリウスの都飛鳥』たちばな出版, 2005.

_____ *Economy and Anthropology of Eurasia*, Tokyo University of Agriculture Press, 2007;栗本慎一郎『シルクロードの経済人類学』東京農業大学出版会, 2007.

Lieu, Samuel N. C. *Manichaeism in Central Asia & China*, Brill, 1998

Kyō, Hakukin. *History of Zoroastrian Arts in China*, Sanlien Shudian, 2004; 姜伯勤『中国祆教芸術史研究』三聯書店, 2004.

Maeda, Kōsaku. *The Golden City Bamiyan Revived by Hi-vision Digital*, NHK, 2006; 前田耕作監修『ハイビジョンデジタルでよみがえる黄金の都バーミヤン』NHK, 2006.

_____ http://bunka.nii.ac.jp/SearchDetail.do?heritageId=48345

_____ http://silkroadbamiyan.com/bamiyan_jp.htm

Nakamura, Gen et al. ed. *Iwanami's Dictionary of Buddhism*, Iwanami-shoten, 1989; 中村元他編『岩波仏教辞典』岩波書店, 1989.

Odani, Nakao. "The Colossal Buddha and Maitreya Cult in Bamiyan", *Journal of the Faculty of Humanities, Toyama University,* University of Toyama, Faculty of Humanities, 2002; 小谷仲男「バーミアーン石窟と弥勒信仰」富山大学人文学部紀要, 2002.

Ogawa, Hideo. *A Study in Mithraism*, Lithon, 1993; 小川英雄『ミトラス教研究』リトン社, 1993.

Rūmī, Jalāl ad-Dīn Muḥammad Balkhī. Izutsu Toshihiko trans. *Fī-hi Ma Fī-hi*, Chūōkōronsha, 1993; ルーミー. 井筒俊彦訳『ルーミー語録』中央公論社, 1993.

Sundermann, Werner. "The Five Sons of the Manichaean God Mithra", in Ugo Bianchi ed. *Mysteria Mithrae*, E. J. Brill, 1979.

Tanaka, Kimiaki. *Iconology of Mandala*, Hirakawa-shuppansha, 1987; 田中公明『曼陀羅イコノロジー』平河出版社, 1987

Ueda, Shizuteru and Yanagida Seizan. *Ten Bull Pictures*, Chikuma-shobō, 1982; 上田閑照・柳田聖山『十牛図』筑摩書房, 1982.

A New Archaeological Research of the Sassanian Fire Temple of Rivand in Sabzevar, by Hassan Hashemi Zarjabad,[320] Farhang khademi Nadooshan,[321] Seyed Mehdi Mousavi,[322] Javad Neyestani,[323] Syed Sadrudin Mosavi Jashni,[324] Barbara Kaim[325]

Abstract.

The fire temples and square domes (*Chahartaghys*) of the Sassanian dynasty are certainly of great importance in Archeological studies, particularly in the field of religious research. Fire is one of the sacred elements in Zoroastrian teachings. During the five centuries of the Sassanian Dynasty's rule, a large number of fire temples and square domes were constructed across the kingdom to protect the flames of the sacred fire. The square dome of Rivand in Sabzevar is one of the most important religious monuments remaining from the Sassanian era, which has been referred to by some Pahlavi Texts and documents as the Azar Barzin Mehr Fire Temple - one of the three prominent fire Temples of Sassanian Dynasty. Given the importance of the issue and the position of the fire temple of Azar Barzin Mehr in the Iranian history, and culture, during the Sassanian Dynasty and due to the fact that this monument has not been thus far scientifically studied by archeologists, its study is of great use to the scholars and researchers.

For the first time an Iranian-Polish Archeology Team began to study and explore the square domes in Rivand in two seasons, but the studies were not complete. Attempts have been made in the present study to shed light on different aspects of archeological significance of the fire temple which can serve as a contribution to the study of religious monuments of the Sassanian Dynasty.

Keywords: Sassanian, square dome, architecture, religion, Sabzavar, fire temple

1) Introduction

Sassanian religious architecture has been talked about mostly based on square domes and fire temples. The religious fire temples were such an important landmark in the Sassanian era that

---

[320] PhD Student, Dept of Archaeology, Tarbiat Modares University.

[321] Associate Professor, Dept of Archaeology, Tarbiat Modares University, Tehran, Iran.

[322] Assistance Professor, Archaeology department, Tarbiat Modares University.

[323] Assistance Professor, Archaeology department, Tarbiat Modares University.

[324] Assistant Prof, Department of Political Thought, Imam Khomeini and Islamic Revolution Research Institute and Department of Indian Studies, Faculty of World Studies, University of Tehran.

[325] Dept of Near Eastern Studies, Warsaw University, Poland.

each Sassanid king during his coronation endowed a fire temple, as a symbol of his kingship. During the Sassanian era, Zoroastrianism was the state religion, thus the fire temple was a place of worship. During the five centuries of the Sassanian dynasty countless fire temples and square domes were built around the country. *Ebne Hughal*, a geographer of fourth century states: "there is no city and no place that has no fireplace (*Ebne Hughel, 1366, p.35*). The fire temples, particularly the three well known fire temples, to the Sassanian represented worship, human accomplishments and attainment. The Pahlavi texts indicate that the fire temples were highly sanctified. The *Azar Farnbagh, Azar Goshnasb, Azar Barzin Mehr* and other Azar and Atashes (fire temples) were highly honored by the people. According to Avestan texts, the three mentioned fire temples preserved the flame of the fire of *Bahram* and kept it alive. Hence, they were considered highly sacred by the people who accorded due respect to the flames of the *Bahram* fire kept in these temples. These fire temples enjoyed a high status among different classes of society in the Sassanian community. Christensen maintains that the fire temple of *Azar Franbach*, devoted to clerics and priests, was located in Karian region in Fars province (*Christensen, p.119*). The fire temple of *Azar Goshnasb,* called a royal fire temple, was specifically allocated to the kings, commanders, royal figures and wealthy classes of Sassanian age. This fire temple, located in Shizz in Azarbayjan (*Mashkoor, 1347, p.135*), was of great importance. Commenting on the Azar Goshasb fire temple, *Ibn kherdad beh* writes: the Sassanid kings after coronation went such a long way on foot from Tisfon to the fire temple of Azar Goshnasb for pilgrimage *(Moein, 1355, p. 317)*. The fire temple of Azar Barzin Mehr, located in the Rivand high land of Sabzevar, was particularly designated to the peasants and farming class (*Bahar 1375, p.13-14*). General studies on Sassanid religious monuments show that the religious structures of this era were characterized by their own architecture and have their own specific customs, so that most of the famous religious structures of this era have a square dome plan. *Schippmann* following studies on square domes divides Sassanid square domes into two major groups: the first group are the kinds of square domes which are related to great structures (e.g. *Takht Suleiman*); the second group are the individual square domes to which fire temples or other secondary chambers are added (e.g. Niasar fire temple) (*Schippmann 1972, pp. 353-364*). Other researchers have introduced different patterns in identifying the square domes. For example, Gropp suggested three models concerning the usage of old fire temples. The first model is a rectangular construction in which there is a square and domed chamber named Adriyan which is surrounded by a hallway. In one side of Adriyan (the master domed chamber), there is another room which is named Yazeshgah. This room either directly, or through a hallway, is connected to the main chamber. The second type is a fire temple which has a domed square chamber surrounded by a hallway. This type of fire temple has no Yazeshgah. The third type is a fire temple which is consisted of one or more

Yazeshgah without Adriyan space (the master domed chamber) (*Gropp, 1969, pp 166-173*). Pope also divides the Sassanid fire temples functionally into two groups: the first groups where the fire temples were for public prayer and usage and the second group are the fire temples which were made for keeping the holy fire and were only available for Zoroastrians and priests (*Pope, 1388, p.55*). Mary Boyce believed that the fire temples depending on the importance of the kind of fire in them were classified into three groups of Anooran fire, Dadgah fire and Bahram fire (*Boyce.M., 1375, p. 98*). So in order to identify the structural analysis of square dome of Rivand, its antiquity and precise function, as well as to find out whether the square dome of Rivand was single or complex, and, most importantly to explore whether the square dome of Rivand was the very well-known fire temple of Azar Barzin Mehr of Sassanid the archeological team of Iran-Poland was formed to study and explore this important but unknown archeological monument (Pic. 1&2).

Pic1: South view of the heights of Rivand square dome, Sabzevar.

Pic2: square dome's southern interior part

2) Geographical study of the location of Rivand square dome in Sabzevar

Sabzevar, which is located in western part of the *Khorasan Razavi* province is surrounded by the cities of JaJarm and Esfarayen in the north, by *Nayshabour* in the east, by the cities of Kashmar and Bardeskan in the south and by the city of Shahrood in the north which is in Semnan province. The weather in Sabzvar is moderate and dry. Some 40 km northwest of Sabzevar and 5 km north of Fashtangah village within the highlands of Rivand, a tremendous pile of rock emerges from the riverbed in Rivand which is 100m in height. High on the very summit of the remnants of Sassanid monuments, there is the remains of a building which is known as the Devil's House to the people of the region and as the fire temple of Azar Barzin Mehr to the archeological community.

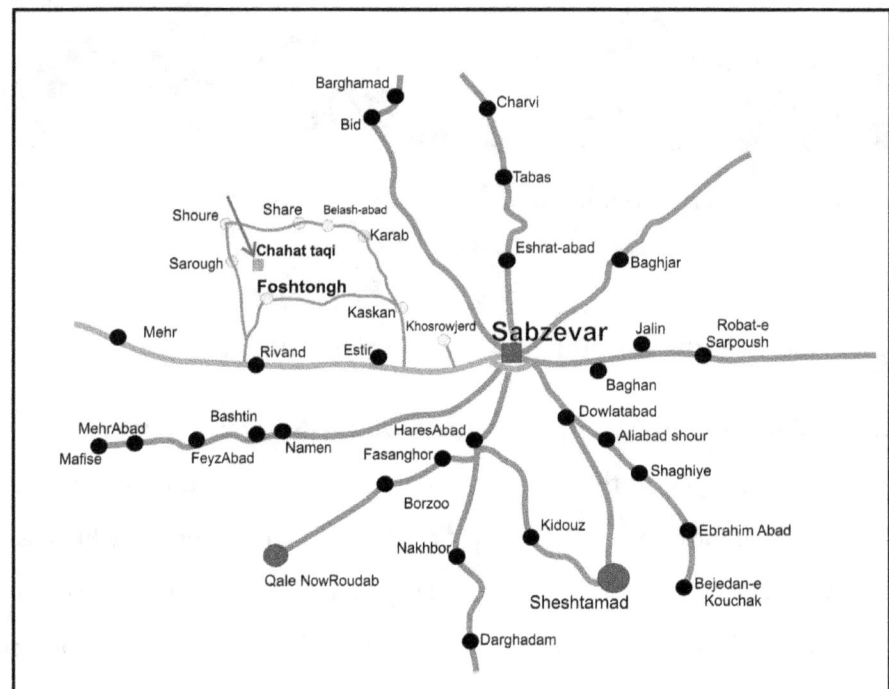

Figure1 & 2: Location of Sabzevar and Rivand

3) Background:

Until the archeological studies and excavations of Iran-Poland expedition in Rivand square dome, no scientific excavation had been done in this building and most of the researches were restricted to some moderate visits and searches. In 1967, Fayegh Tohidi in his archeological study of the Sabzevar region referred to the Rivand four domes. According to his reports, Four domes, called the Devil (Demon)'s House is located in Rivand heights which is the same as the

Sassanian Azar Barzin Mehr fire temple (*Tohidi 1356*). Hassan Ghareh Khani, an Iranian archaeologist, in his book entitled *Ancient Ruins and Holy Mausoleum Around Sabzevar and Esfarayen* produces an extensive report on the plan of the building (*Ghareh khani 1363*). Also Ali Aldeghy, Ghasem Jaghty and Rahmane Geraili in 2001 produced another plan of the square dome (*Mashhad Cultural Heritage: not reported*).

A Japanese expedition under the supervision of Tagaya Sohi Gigy visited and studied shrines adjacent to Silk (Abrisham) Road and also visited the Rivand square dome in 2006 (Sabzevar Cultural Heritage not published). Finally, the Iran-Poland archeological expedition under the supervision of Barbara Kaim from Warsaw University and Hassan Hashemi started to excavate this site in two seasons (2008-2009).

Pic3: Aerial photos and access route to Rivand square dome

4) Square dome of Rivand or Azar Barzin Mehr fire temple.

The fire temple of Azar Barzin Mehr, which was called Ature-Burzin Mihr (that is, the fire temple of Mehr Balandeh), is one of the three important fire temples of Sassanian era. According to the Pahlavi texts, the fire temple of Niyayesh was in Rivand in Khorasan and was specified for the farmers. As mentioned earlier, some researchers introduced the square dome located in the highlands of Rivand in Sabzevar as the fire temple of Azar Barzin Mehr. This narration is based on the Pahlavi texts of Band Heshen, which speak about the fire temple. However, on the basis of some quotations from the Avesta, the fire temple of Azar Barzin Mehr was located in Rivand in Khorasan. As it is said in Fargard 12 and paragraph 8 of Band Heshen, the mount of Rivand is located in Khorasan and Azar Barzin Mehr is seated on it and Rivand, a magnificent building regarding its height in this part and the mount of Binalood, holds a sacred fire temple in itself (*Bahar, 1375, pp.13-14*). The oldest references, such as the history of Beyhaghi state: Zoroaster, who was the owner of monarchy (magus), asked for the plantation of two Cedar trees, one in the village of Keshmar (Kashan) and another in the village of Faryoomad and those trees were planted by the Zoroaster (*Beyhaghi 1317, pp.281-282*). It was written in Pahlavi text, that the Azar Barzin Mehr fire temple was the place for the prayers of farmers in the mountains of Rivand. Today, with regard to the myth of plantation of the trees by Zoroaster in Khorasan, the attribution of this fire temple to farmers of the time is much more plausible and acceptable.

Azar Barzin Mehr was one of the three heavenly fires sent to the earth to help mankind. It was introduced in Ferdosi's Shahnameh along with other fire temples:

"*Cho Azar Gashto khaordad o Mehr*
Forozan Cho Bahram o Nahid o Mehr."

Christensen writes: 'Azar Barzin or the fire of farmers was located in the eastern part of the Sassanid Empire in the River Mountains and in north western Neyshabour.'

Lazar Faei called the Rivand village the village of magus. In Jakson's opinion, the place of Fire temple had been in Mehr village which was on the way to Khorasan near Sabzevar (P. Christiansen, p 118, 1385). Also, the Archeological studies of Khorasan Cultural Heritage experts on Sabzevar and its surrounding regions introduce the existing square dome as the Azar Barzin fire temple. The accomplished diggings and archeological studies on the square dome of Rivand can help the acceptance or rejection or this notion.

Pic. 4: west view of the heights of square dome, Rivand, Sabzevar.

The site has been dated in accordance with a coin of Sassanian king. The coin, which belongs to Khosrow II (590 AD) Sassanian king is silver and was found in the threshold of the southern side of the square dome which undoubtedly is a valid document for relative dating of the square dome.

Pic 5: Sassanian coin related to Khosrow II, 590 AD, 29 in diameter, silver, rediscovery place found in the threshold of the southern side of the square dome.

In addition to the coins, Sassanian architecture was greatly decorative. This can be seen in the multiplicity of the stuccos (Azarnoush 2002: 275) in the process of the excavation of the trench in which some plaster was found, and it is comparable with other of decorative elements of the Sassanian period. This kind of design in Iran has a long history because in the excavations of Tepe Damghaty of Sabzevar, which was done by an Iranian-French expedition, a rock with meander design was found which showed the continuous use of these kinds of designs in stuccos in many Sassanian holy buildings and palaces(postscript 3). The two chalk pieces obtained from chartaghy which shows the designs meander and flower can be compared with the beautiful Sassanian buildings (Bandian of Dargaz) (postscript 4) in north of Khorasan and Tisfoon palace (Pic 6 &7).

Pic 6: plaster piece/fragment with herbaceous and meander designs

Pic 7: The stuccos of Sassanian building (Bandian Dargaz) in north of khorasan

Potsherds finding in different trenches are divided into two groups of enameled and non-enameled. These potsherds have incised geometrical and stamped patterns. There is a potsherd in the findings which might be a part of a vessel's lid and it has an interesting design like the letter M on it. Enameled crocks are green, yellow and turquoise. The indecision point is that only a few of the pottery obtained were of the Sassanian period and most of them belong to Islamic period. (Pic. 8a-8b)

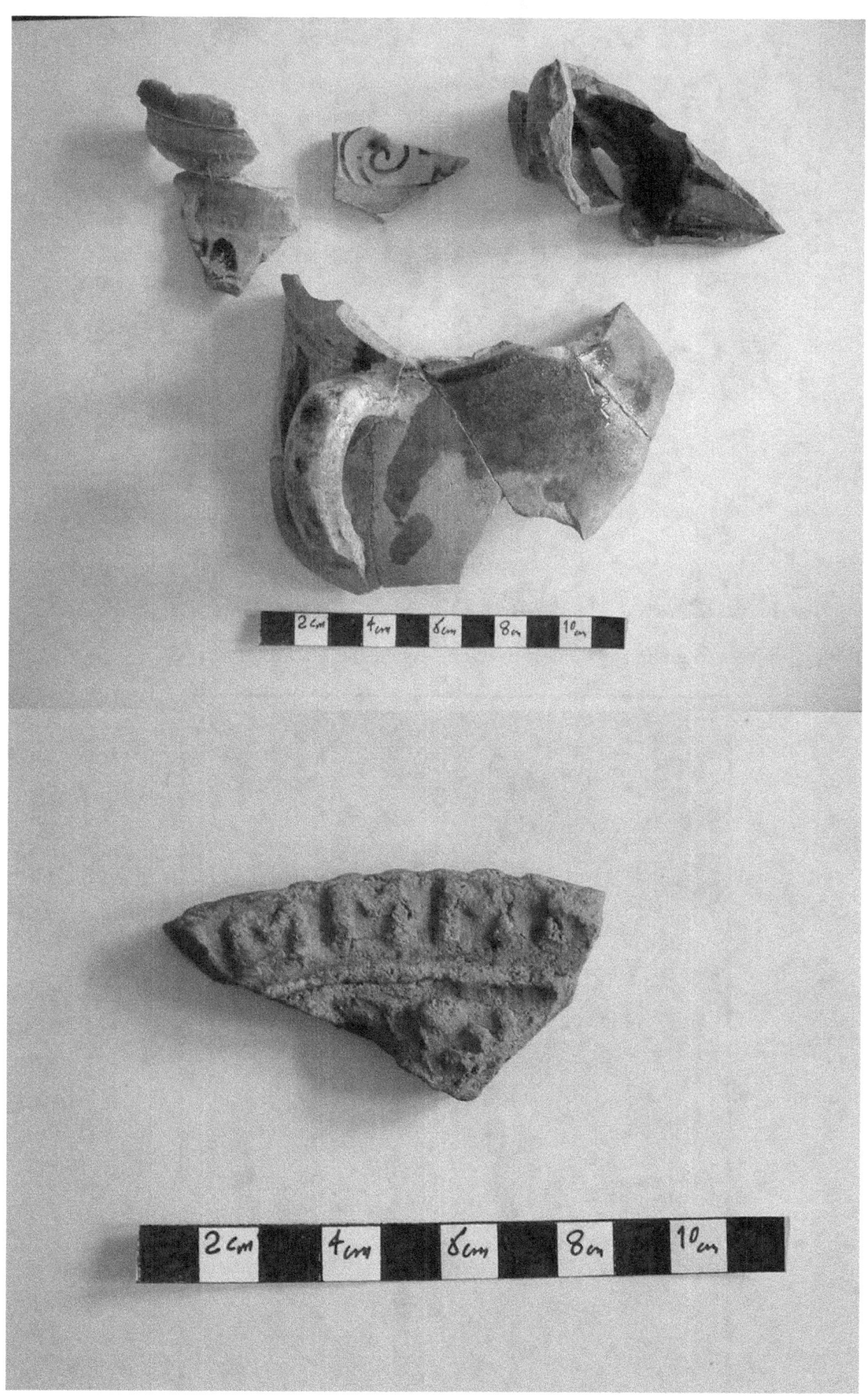

Pic8a: Plaster pieces found in square dome with M design and enameled

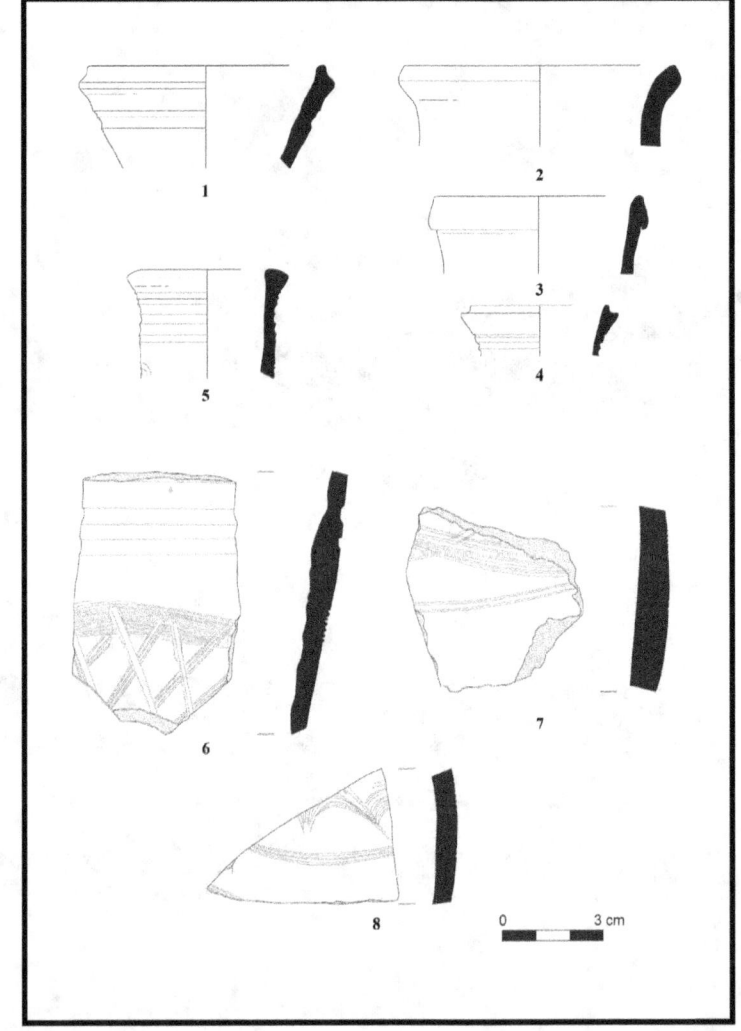

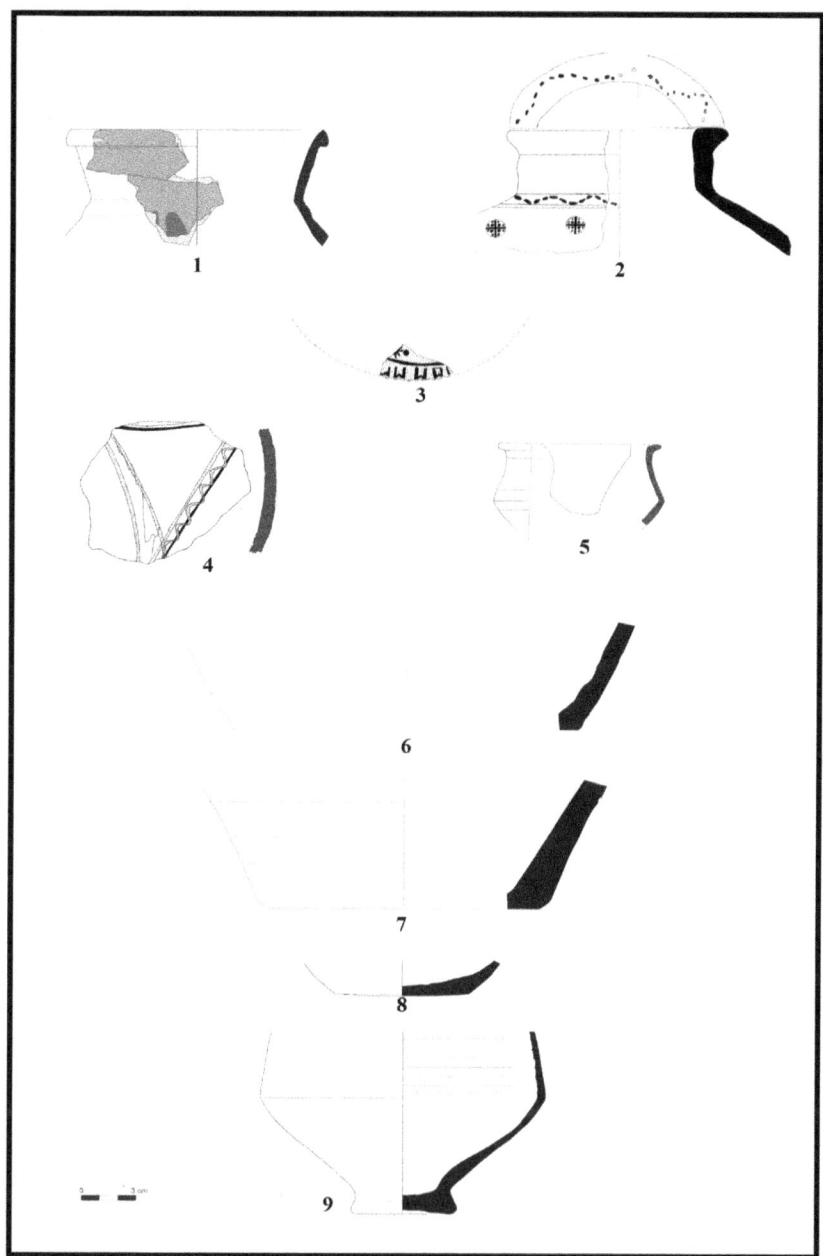

Figure 8b: Drawings of plaster pieces found in square dome

5. Discussion

As mentioned previously, ruined square dome of Rivand which is called the devil's house by native people is located in an area of the Rivand Mountains, in the north of Fashtang village, in a skewed path on top of a cliff with 100m height. In the first place, the expedition started to provide a topography map of the square domes (figure3). Then the expedition started to probe into different parts of the square domes in order to understand the typology and architectural spaces of the square domes, which led to the finding of other cultures.

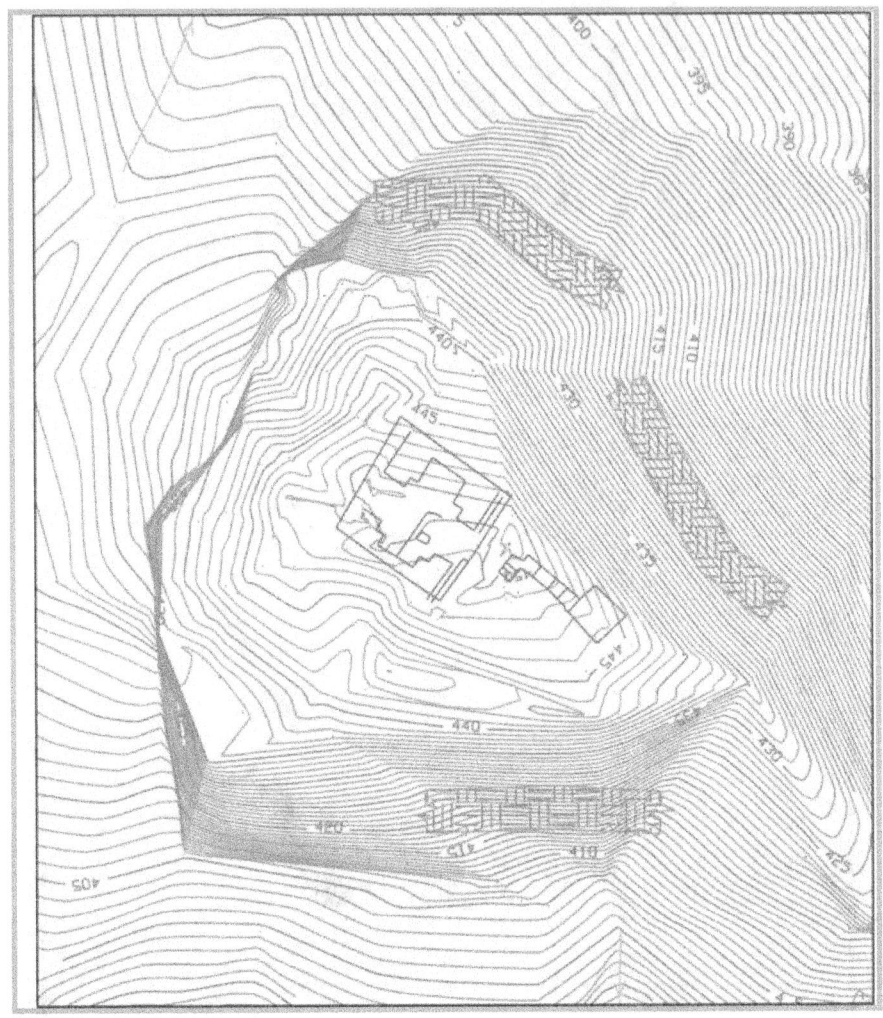

Figure 3: Topography of Rivand square dome

Despite the fixed factors and patterns in Sassanian constructions, especially square domes and fire temples, each of them has peculiar features; hence no two temples are completely similar in their plans. However, most of the square domes and fire temples have special architectural properties such as thick pillars, four wide mouth in pillars, a dome-like roof, a cross square plan and a hall on one side or around the square domes *(Kazemi 1386, p. 292)*.

The plan of the Rivand square dome is simple and rectangular with the dimensions of 13.29X12.46 m, the corner of the walls point toward the four main sides. The entrance of the building is at the north side. The main room of square dome is 6/6 m^2 . The dint of the northwest wall has 2.63m depth and 4.32 m width; the dint of southeast wall of the square dome is just 1.13 m deep and 4.32m wide. The dint of southwest wall has 4.32m width and 2.56m depth. In northeast of the square dome, there is a very narrow corridor with 80 cm dimensions. Its function probably is to access the main room and also the south area of square dome.

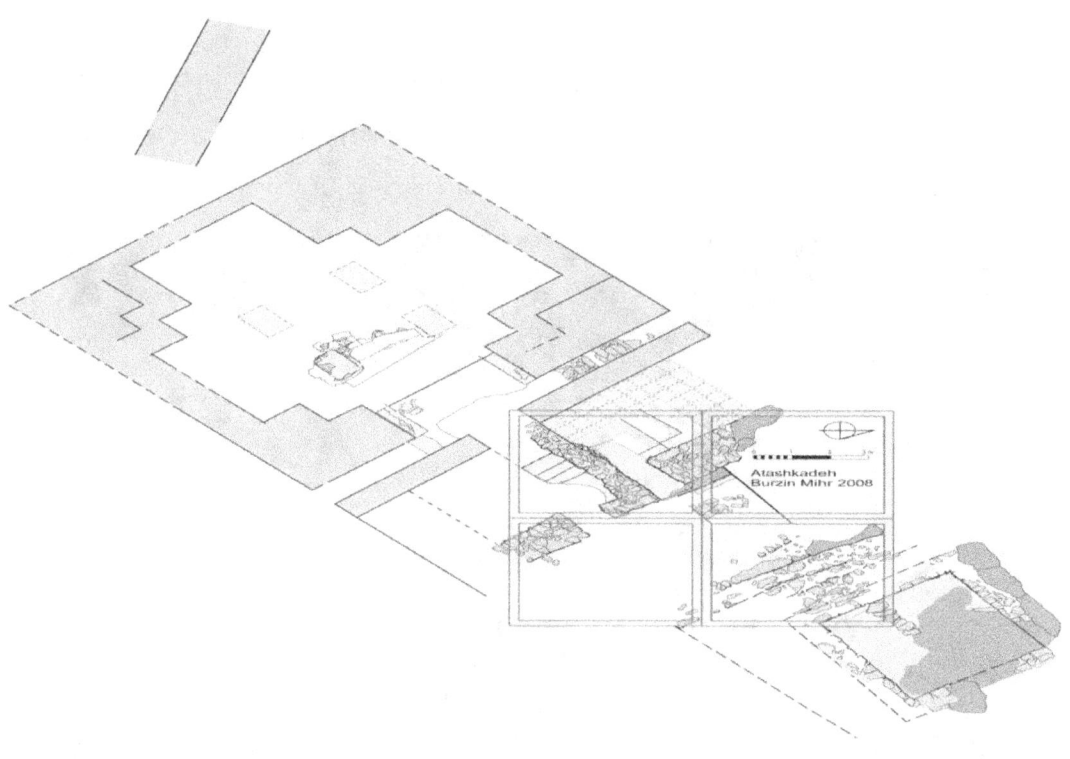

Figure 4: square dome plan and exploration of the space

Pic 9: Corridor in chartaghy

During the two seasons of excavation, the expedition team succeeded in discovering interesting architectural spaces like Odon and Brasmdan platforms, corridors or entrance hall, water reservoir or Patav, waiting room, rest room and entrance stairs of *Chahartaghy*.

Pic10: one of the platforms within explore *Chahartaghy*

Pic 11: the discovered room, a waiting room and the renovation activities after the excavation.

Revelation of the discovered spaces and the studies show that the square dome consists of three different spaces.

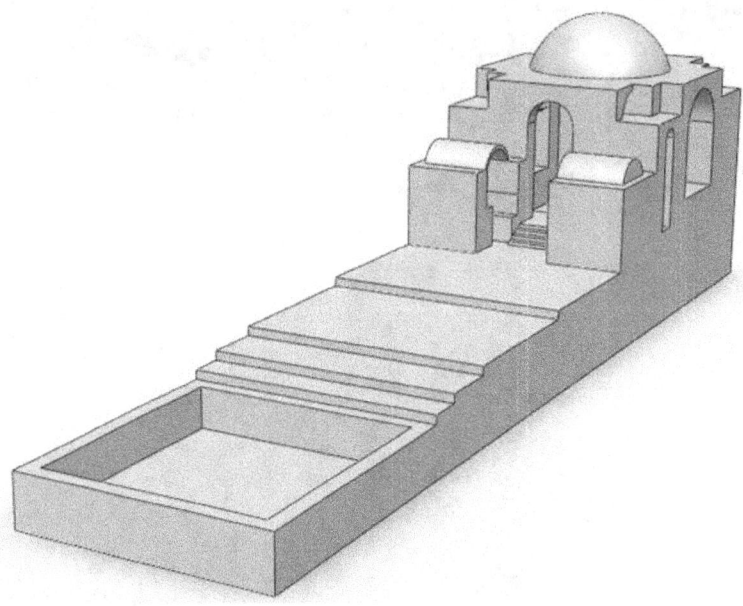

Figure 5: Space of exploration

This section plays the main interactive role of the construction from entrance portico and it is possible to have two entrances, which is inferred from the social classification prevailing at that time which was built by the architect of construction.

Thus, according to the architectural evidences collected from the excavation, the portico included two rooms alongside the corridor while the passage wasn't located in main entrance of the main square domes.

This style of architecture might define the access to the second level fire for the pilgrims which were in the rooms alongside the corridor which is inferred from the time of walking in the corridor. There may be also a barrier between the contents of fire chamber and pilgrims outside the fire chamber and hence the corridor was not located in the axis in order to separate authorized and unauthorized people from holy fire, or to prevent people from looking through at the number one fire.

The north portico room entrance of square dome and exploration operations: Here are some spaces around the fire chamber or Ouddan. There are spaces around brazier.

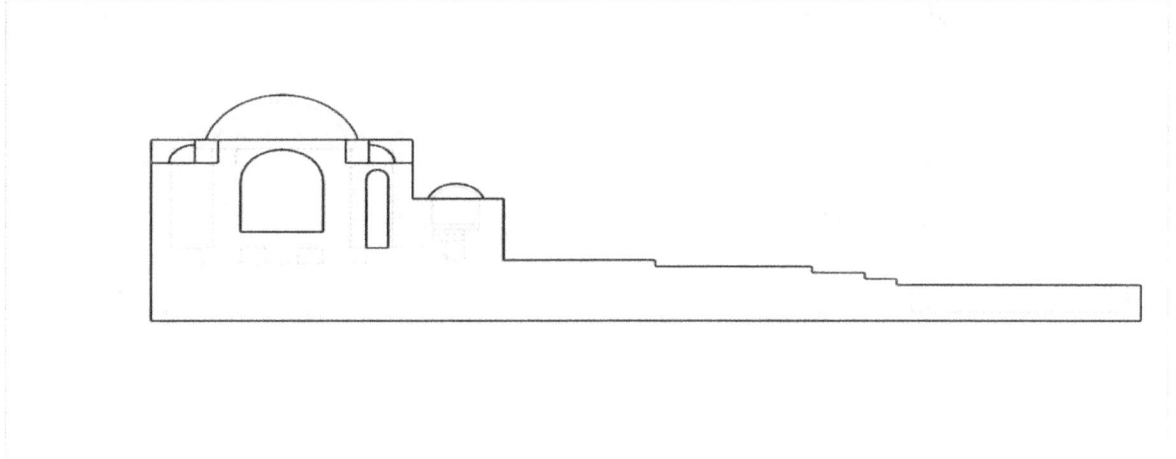

Figure 6: Cutting three dimensional of reconstruction plan of Rivand square dome

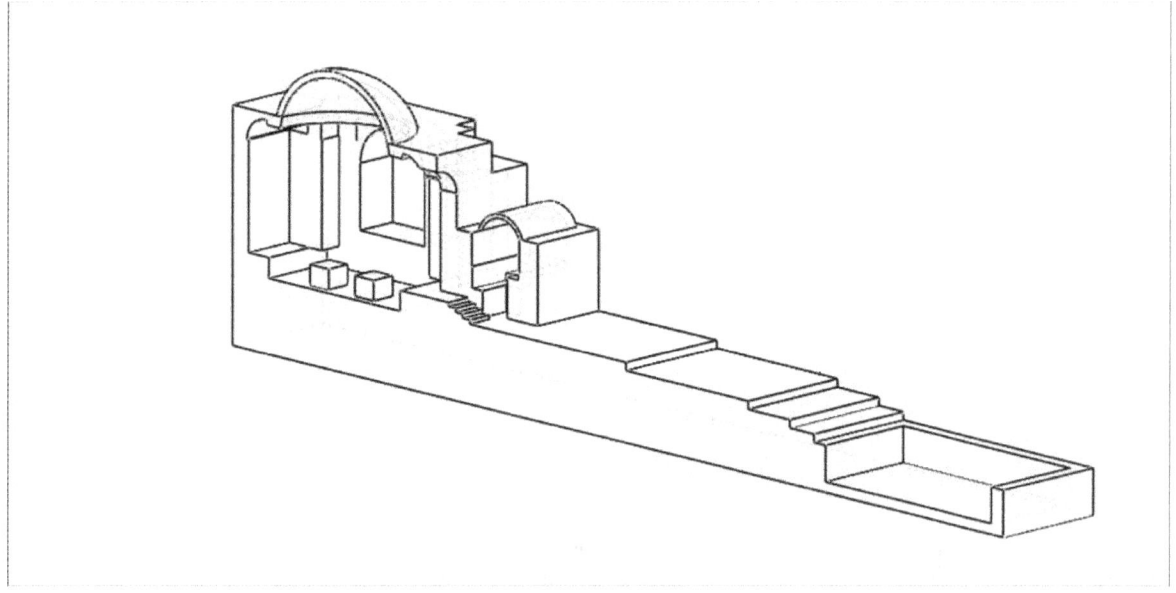

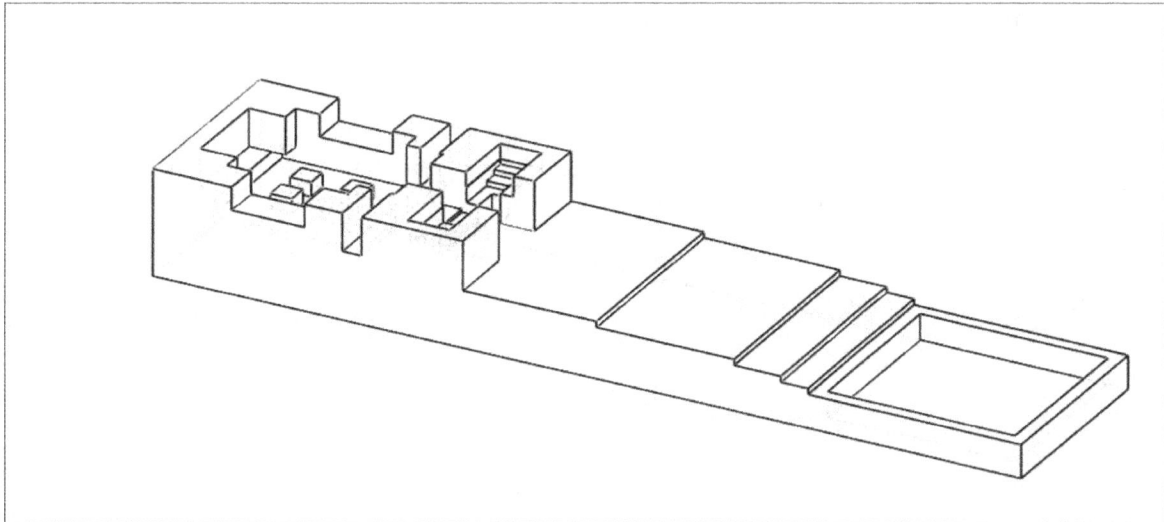

Figure 7: Level–three dimensional of reconstruction plan of Rivand square dome

The structural properties of these three sections of this area are as follows:

Outside and inside, the geometry of the square domes are square platforms which are rectangular but overall the building is square. However, the rectangular particles quantitatively dominate the same square.

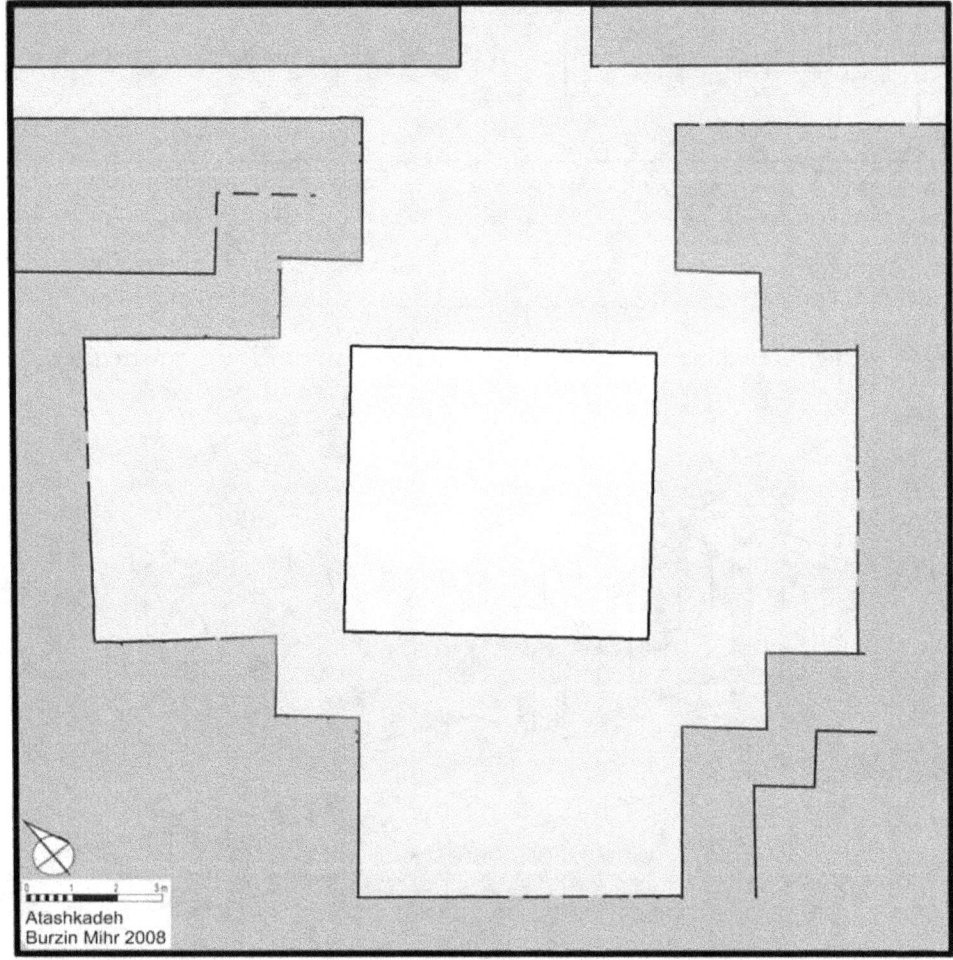

Figure 8: four sediment, blue, rectangular, yellow

Balance

Balance with some neglect in geometry and implementation has long and wide balance. The south platform has less depth than the other stairs (Fig 8).

Symmetry

Parallelism of the building in the floor and roof has wide and long balance (Fig 9).

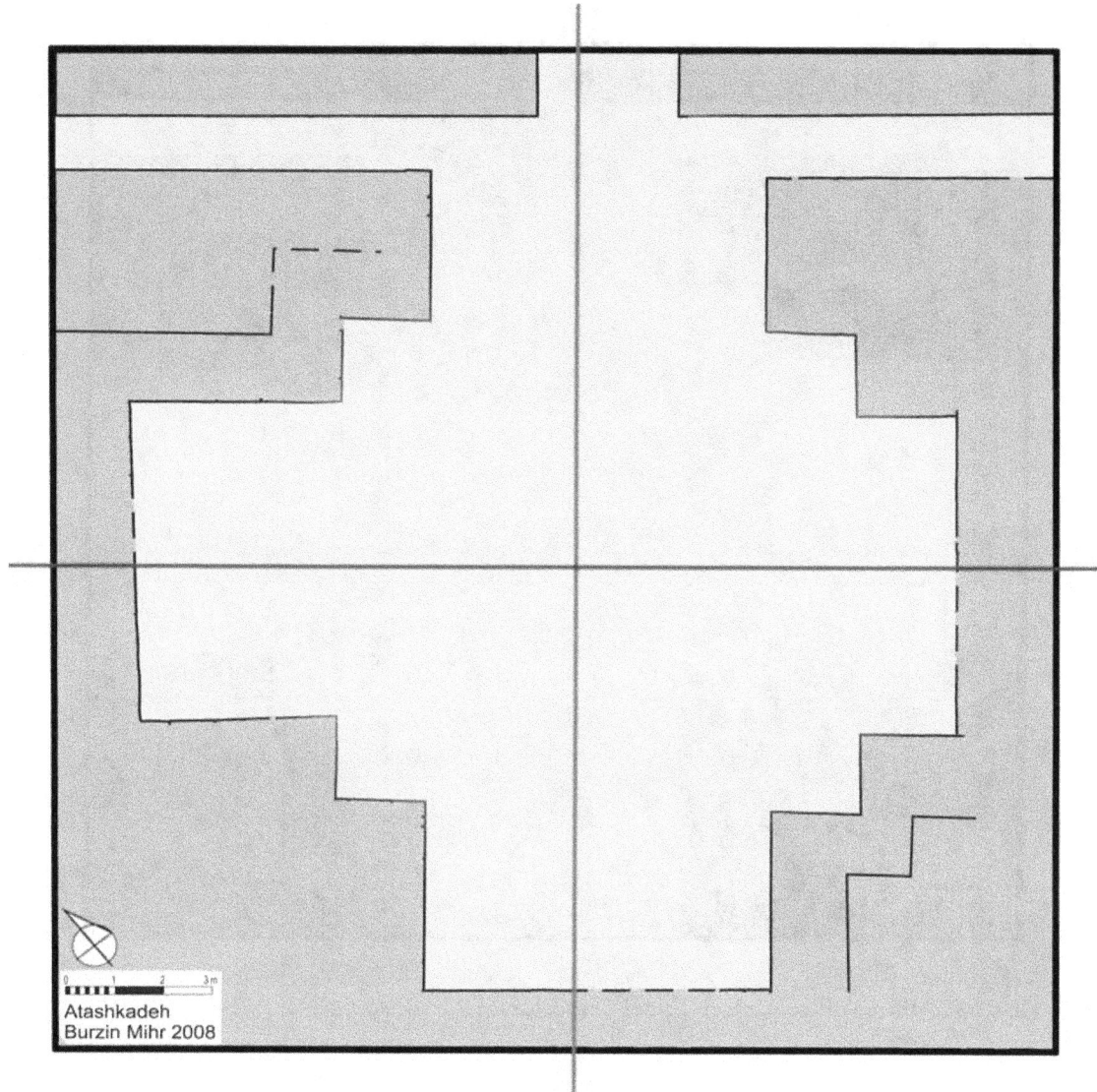

Figure 9: Balance and symmetry in square

Rhythm

The repeated rhythm of the rectangular shape of the platforms has given rhythm to the building.

Circulation

According to the available evidences and data presumption existed from entrance of the *Chahartaghy* from north east area with a portico.

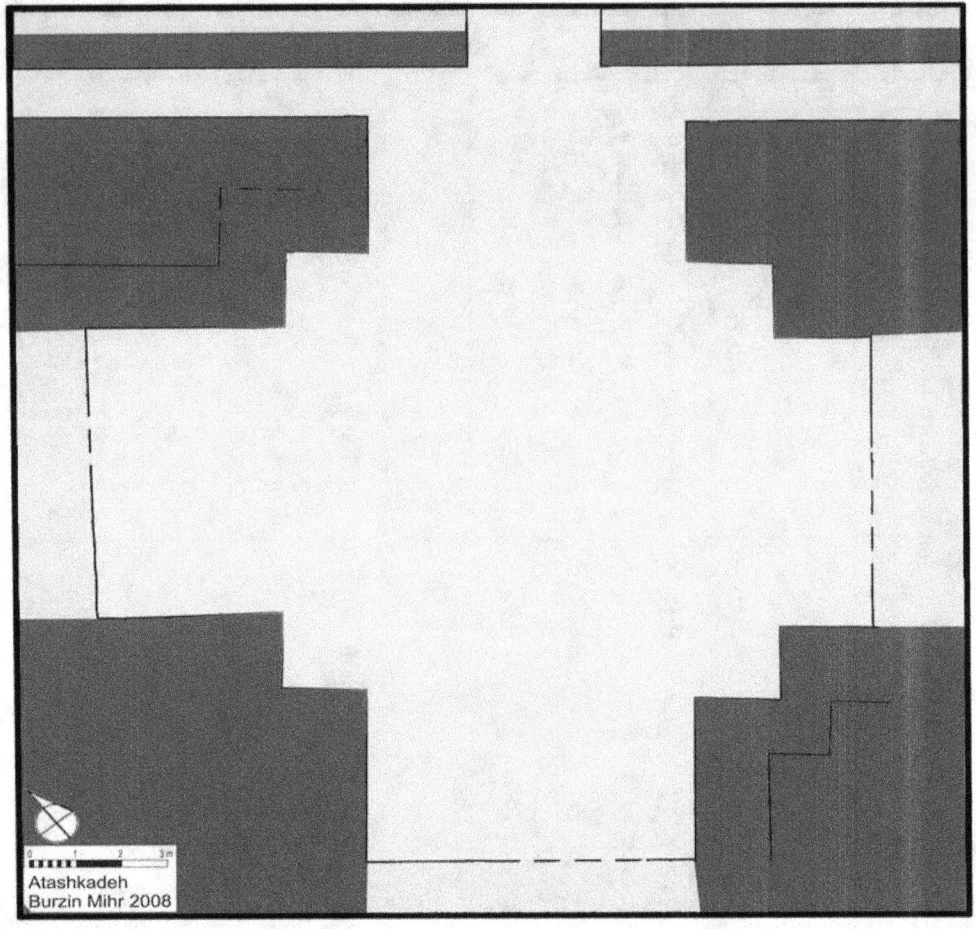

Figure 10: Circulation access: Yellow Level 1 and Level 2 blue access

Circulation of ventilation and light

Circulation of ventilation and light is the only evidence left from the light window and ventilation in the north east wall which is at the top of the arc. Despite this and the architectural evidences left all the arcs were blocked and consequently ventilation and light were done through entrance and air out let.

Full spaces in the *Chahartaghy* are divided in: A: Covered full spaces   B: loaded full and spaces.

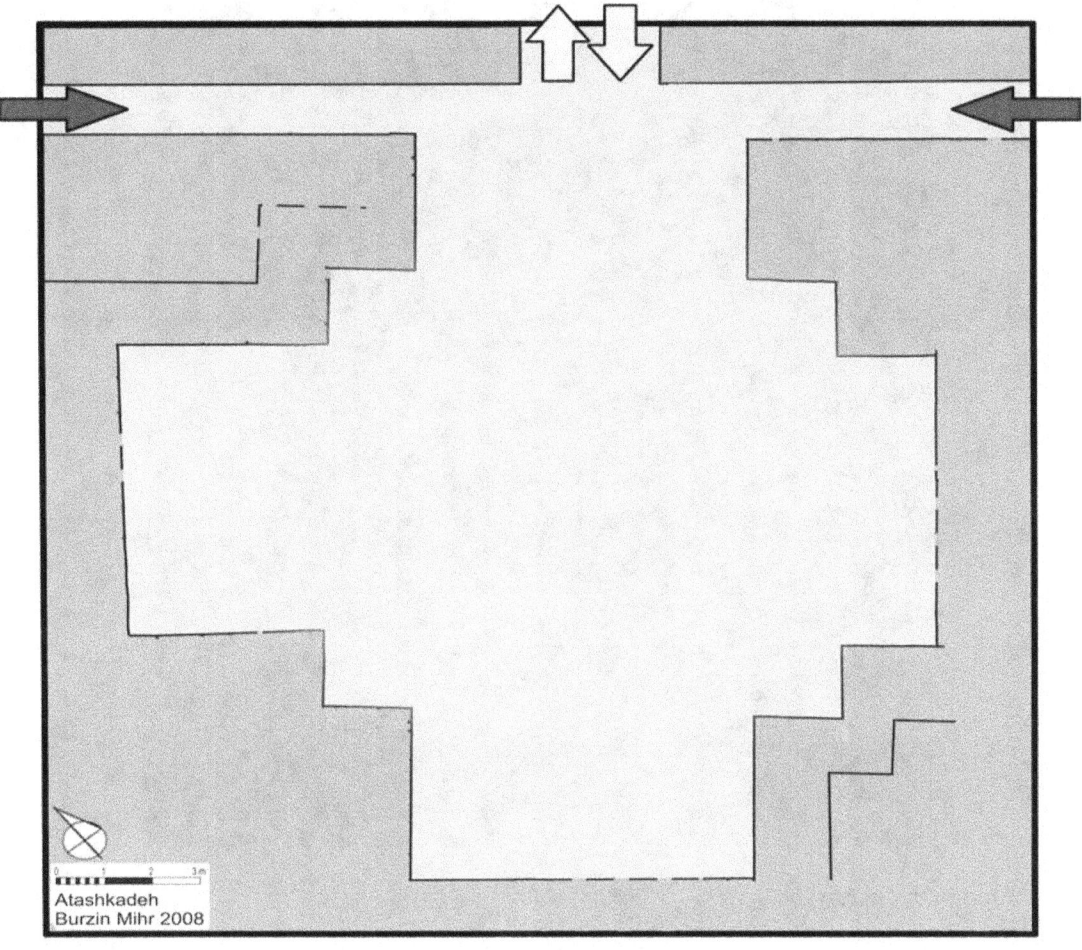

Figure 9: Space filled square dome: blue space filling space filling bearing non-bearing yellow.

The construction and implementation

First step: In the first place, platforms were made based on the topology of the site where they were pitted and filled by stone and cliff, which was used as a base. Nature conservancy was considered in footing of the construction and it didn't damage the nature at all.

Second step: basing of square domes by mortar consisting sand gravel clay and lime syrup. The stones are bigger and thicker at the base of the footing and the more we move up the less the thickness and length.

Third step: Construction of arcs was made by mortar and clay, with proportion of 3/1 (mortar to clay).

Pic 12 : One port chartaghy

Fourth step: construction of pillar in order to prevent the expulsion of the arcs by the same materials.

Pic 13: Construction of *Chahartaghy* pier to using stone rubble

Fifth step: construction of the zone of transition in internal squares of construction by carved barrel- roof stone to the center of square. In the center there are remainders of carved stones related to a sky light. It is placed at the top of the arc and other than light, is efficient for decreasing the load of old architecture.

Pic 14: zone of transition (squninch)

Sixth step: After turning the plan from *Chahartaghy* into eight columns, a circle to construct the dome is done. It shoud be mentioned that the whole *Chahartaghy* of are ruined and just some parts of it are left.This style of dome construction has been used for making Islamic settlements , especially in making tombs in the Khorasan Province (Murrie Clevenger,1968:57-64).

Decorations

Among the important findings of the excavation we may point out the inscription which was revealed in the second season in architectural places (trench 3) which probably is a waiting room or Estodan. These paintings are inscriptions consisting of human, animal, natural and geometrical motifs which were inscribed on the west and north walls of the mentioned room.

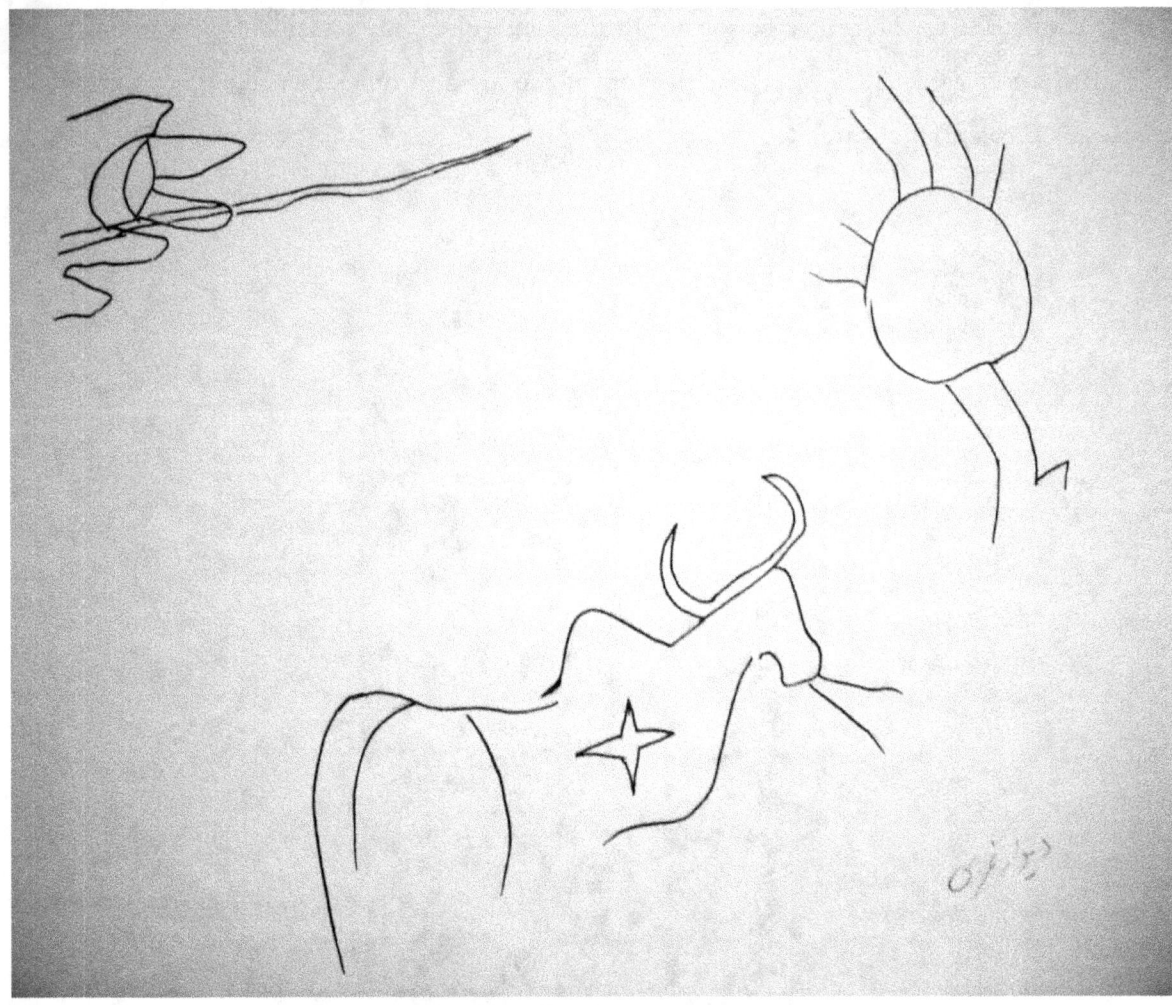

Pics 15- the discovered room, a waiting room and the renovation activities after the excavation - picture/design Buffalo

Buffalo is hunchbacked and has the drawing of swastika on its shoulder. The dimensions of the swastika are 1.5 ×1.5 cm. This cow has two horns which look like an arc, and probably has fodder in his mouth and the head is prone to right three faces. The picture of cow's legs and feet are incomplete. This drawing is incised and is drawn by a single move of the style/pen (Pics 15).

Pics 16 - motif of cow and swastika on the shoulder found in trench 3e

The Sun's diameter is 3.5 cm. 2 simple 5cm-long geometrical lines parallel to each other with 8mm distance, these had made the connection between the sun and the earth. This sun has radiance on the upper part. This sun is 7cm away from the cow and is on the north of the cow 8cm above the cow. This drawing had been incised.

Human hand - this hand is probably a left hand. The painter had a strong sketching skills and this hand is in front of the sun with open finger as if it's pointing to the sun and is showing it. This hand is comparable to the picture of the hand in stony bier of Birjand and Kangan in Afghanistan.

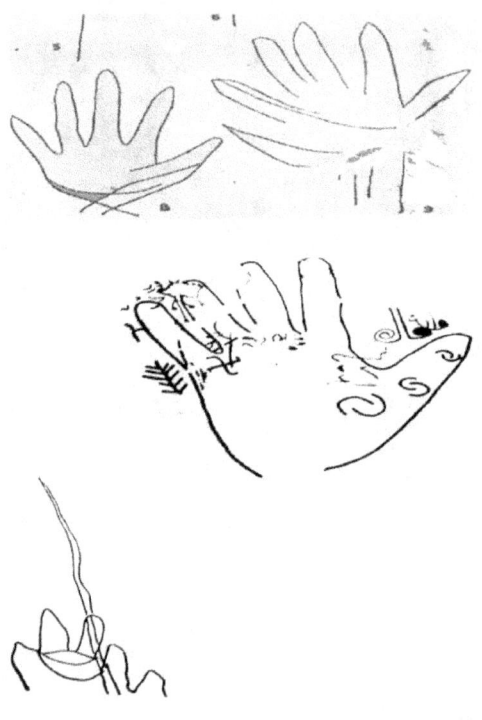

Pic 17: image of a human hand in Kangan in Afghanistan

Pic 18: The role of the human hand in the the Rivand square dome

- Picture/design of goat or Bezoar goat. This picture is incised and placed about 70 cm away from the cow drawing. Its face and stance are towards west. It's possible that it has some fodder in its mouth and has some kind of torque around its neck. The figure of the swastika cross is contour. On the torque of this goat it's more like a gazelle than a goat. The pictures/form of its leg and foot are incomplete.

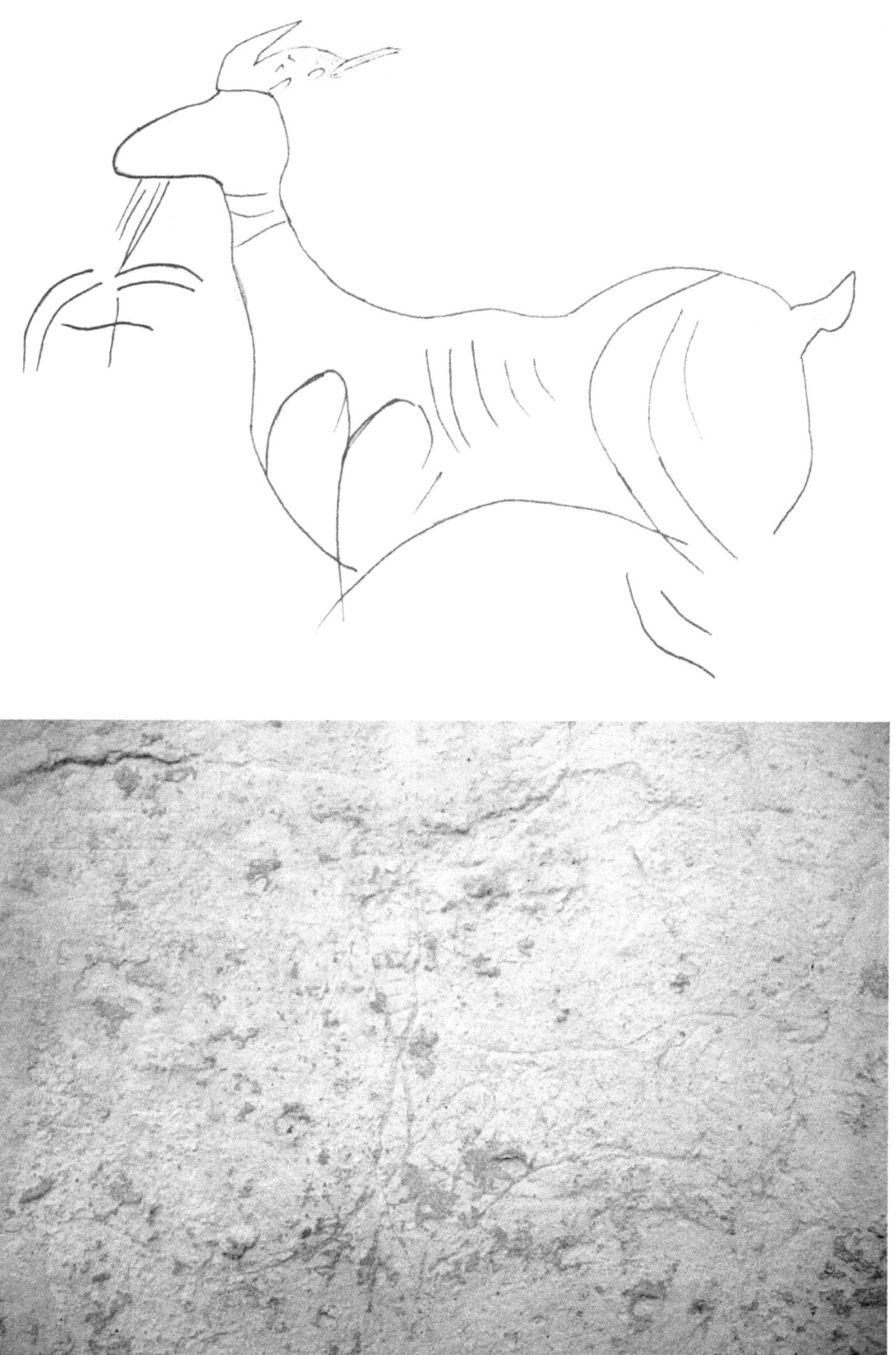

Pic 19 and 20: image of goat and Mehr's (Mithra) cross in Rivand square dome. Picture/design of a camel with the carriage under its mouth.

This drawing is incised. The mouth of the camel is out of the ordinary proportions. Its ears are sharp and just like the neck, the ears and faces of this animal are incised. The drawing is incomplete.

Picture of a donkey, this picture is incised and incomplete. The drawing of the donkey is side view/profile. Its tail is short and its mouth is open. The drawing is not complete and its stance is towards the north.

Picture of a Monkey, this picture is 2cm below the picture of the donkey and its stance is towards the north. This drawing is not strong, and picture of the eye and foot is incomplete.

Picture of an elephant. This picture is incised. The elephant moves towards the west and its head leans to right and it is pictured from behind and its right foot shows a sense of movemnent Picture of several crisscross lines, their general shape is like Mehr's cross. These lines are crossing each other and are erratic. They make shapes of different erratic design, both square and rectangular. It is most probable that these lines show the number of the dates. A guard or a magus guardian of Fire is present. Or it is possible that these were used for dating (Pic 21).

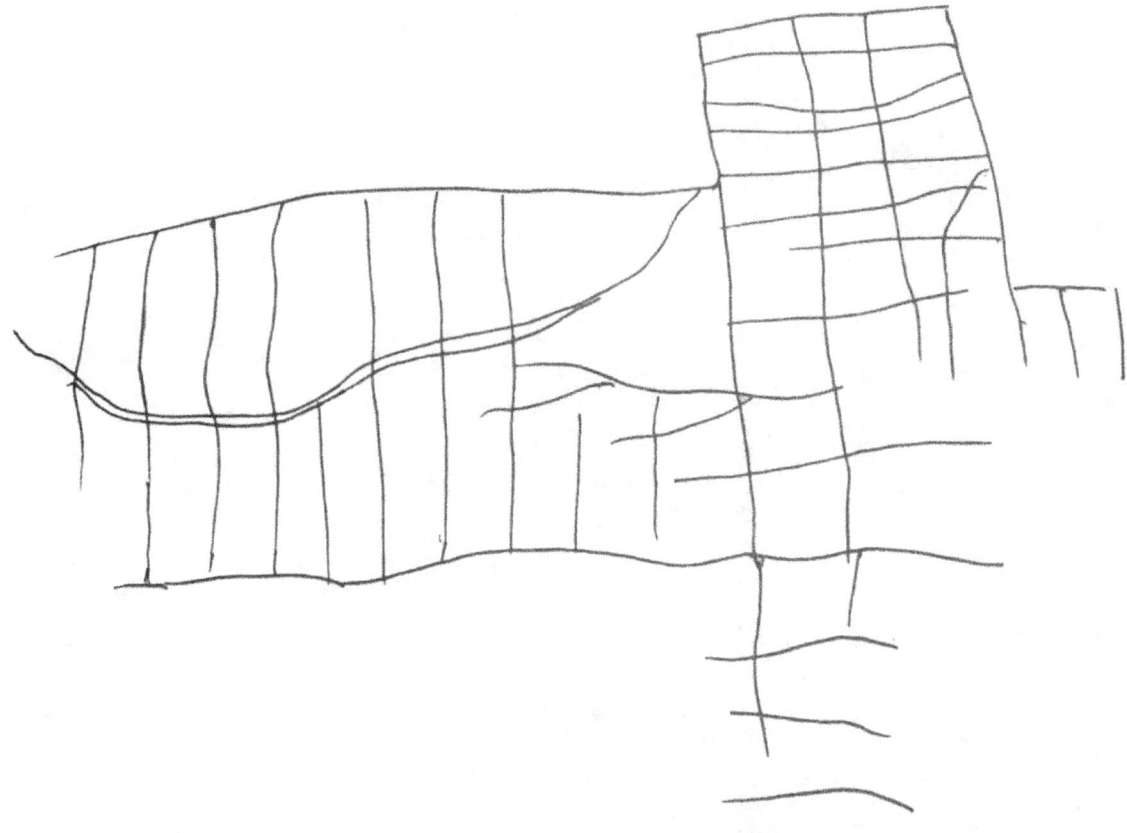

Pic 21: crisscrossed lines, probably a dating table

Conclusions

Before the archeological studies of Iran & Poland expedition, it was supposed that the square dome of Rivand was a single square dome, but the data obtained from the excavation showed that this construction is a fire temple and the holy fire was kept in it. It had porticos, an entrance portico, a reservoir of water, an ablution room, a waiting room or Estoodon, resting room and entrance stairs from the reservoir to the central place of the fire temple. According to the pattern represented for the four vaults by Gropp, it may be concluded that the Rivand square dome in Sabzevar is the first kind called Edgier. In this pattern, the square dome is a rectangular building through which there is a room with dome named Adriyan. This room is surrounded by a corridor. Discovered spaces of this construction show that the building has two architectural periods: the first one belongs to the Sassanian kingdom and the other spaces were built by extending them. Chalk works on the coin, the earth-wares, used materials and brick dimensions show that this is a construction of the Sassanian kingdom. The last era of the fire temple architecture belongs to the Islamic age. On the basis of the cultural evidence, the building belongs to Kharazmshahin's kingdom. During this era, a wall was built on the stairs and these two rooms were separated from each other by this wall. Also, the entrance to the fire is from the southern room. Historical evidence shows that the Zoroastrians left Khorasan and moved to the areas outside of Iran, particularly India. By comparing the plan of the square domes with each other, the Sassanian square domes such as Azar Goshnasb and the Bandian fire temple in Iran, it may be concluded that despite having a cross-like plan and similar structures, this square dome has very thick pillars and ratio of its interior space to the structure is not symmetrical and hence, it is similar to the Sassanian square dome called Bzehur in Khorasan.

The following hints indicate that the architecture of the Rivand square dome was Sassanian: cruciferous architectural space, which is the common form of Sassanian fire temples (Huff, 1975: pp243-354), style of the arches, plaster type mortar (which was recognized by testing), carved stone and façade working of the walls with plaster, specially the zone of transition (squninch) technique in transforming a circular base in building a dome - which is a Sassanian architectural innovation and was used for the first time in Ardeshir's building in Firozabad Fars and is mentioned by Reuther (*Reuther, 1977: 498*) and Schlomberger (*Schlomberger, 1974: 217*) as an important signs in recognizing the source of Sassanian buildings. Moreover, the discoveries of important cultural materials too underline the fact that the building is Sassanian. For instance, mention may be made of a beautiful arcograph with meander designs which is comparable to the arcograph of the Sassanian building in Bandian Dargaz which was discovered in the excavation of Bishapur palaces. Also, one may mention the discovery of a coin which belongs to Khosrow II, the renowned Sassanian king. These are very valid and reliable documents supporting the idea that the square dome in Rivand is a Sassanian building.

Although some researchers maintain that the construction is the Azar Barzin Mehr fire temple, due to the above arguments one can't say for sure that it is the Azar Barzin Mehr fire temple. More extended excavations and archaeological studies in other areas of the Rivand Mountains are needed to prove this assumption. It is hoped that the third season of excavations will shed light on other aspects of the building.

Appendix

Laboratorial studies: some samples of the mortar used in the temple were taken from the mortar of the building and sent to laboratory. The mortar was studied with the help of the SEM method. The results obtained through the SEM test are not reliable with regard to the quantity aspect but it was useful in specifying the fundamental elements of the sample structure. Main and Index phase of the unknown sample are: calcium, sulfate with ions of potassium, sodium and magnesium, which in the process of sedimentation (CaSO4) forms calcium sulfate which is plaster. Therefore one may conclude that plaster was one of the fundamental elements of mortar used in the structure of Rivand square dome. (pic 22)

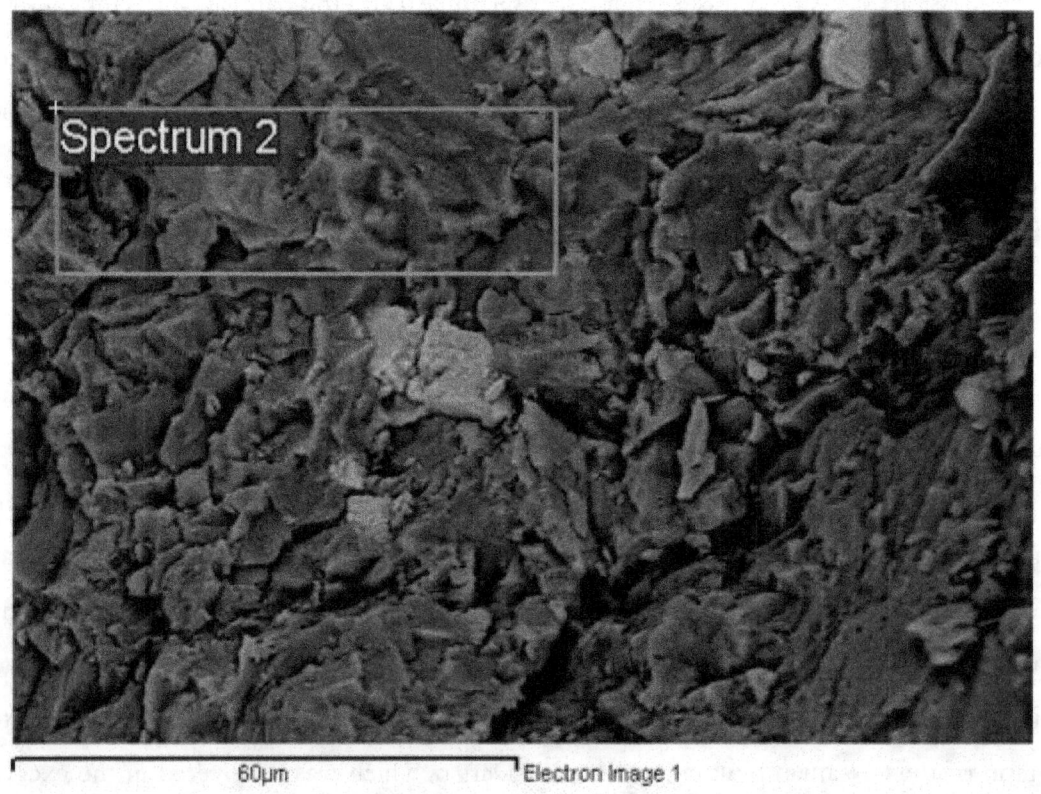

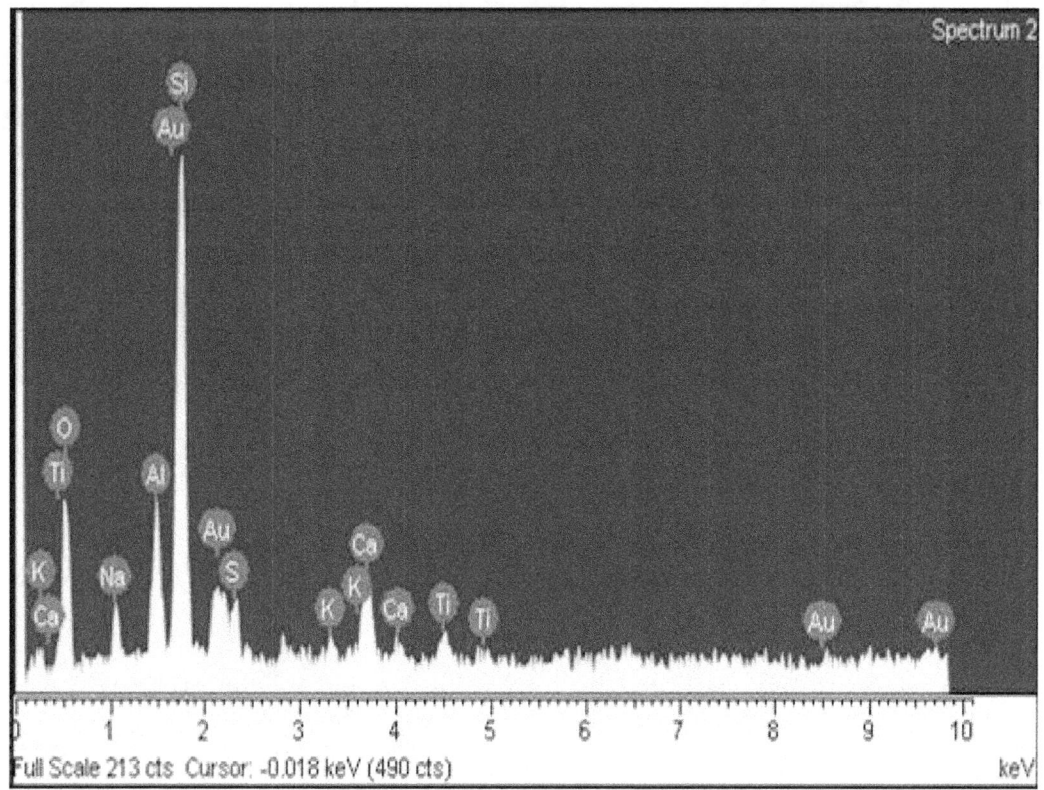

Pic 22 shows the use of SEM and AlSi phases, Pb, Na, Ti, K, in the chalk composition.

Acknowledgment:

My grateful thanks are due to those who have directly or indirectly contributed to the completion of this paper. My special thanks go to Ms Barbara Kaim, leader of the group from Warsaw University, and her group and other co-workers/colleagues as well as to Ali Zarey, Mohammad Abdolzadeh, Siamak Sharifi, Majid Hatami, Hossein-E Ghadi, Alireza Parvaneh Aval, Amir Sheikh (archaeologist), Ali Salehi and Mahnaz Moghadasy.

Post script:

1) Foshtongh is small village 35 km North West Sabzevar and 10 km of Rivand River

2) During these two excavation seasons the group probed seven Sondage (bore hole) 3 in the first season and 4 in the second season in the interior and exterior parts of square dome Taghy.

3) The excavation in Damghany hill of Sabzevar was conducted in 2009, supervisor of this excavation was Henry Frankfort and Ali Asghar Vahdaty.

4) Bandian site is placed 2 km northwest of Dargaz country which is 20 km away from border. Excavation in this site which was led by Iranian archaeologist Mahdi Rahbar led to the revelation of important architectural structures like a big hypostyle, a room for keeping the votives fire

temple Ivan/veranda, around structure and a room for ossuaries. The excavator of Bandian calls this complex a devout/ hieratic place which belongs to the Sassanian period.

5) The historical complex of Takhte Suleiman is located 43 km north of Takab and 3 km east of Takht-e Suleiman in west Azerbaijan province Takhte Suleiman fire temple as one of the 3 important fire temples of Sassanian period. It belongs to the royal family and is known as Azar Goshnasb fire temple in Pahlavi script.

6) Baze-Hur is the famous square dome of Sassanian period which is located on the way of Mashhad to Torbat Heydarye near a place called Robat Sefid a vary thick pier and squinch of the dome built by wood are the special features of this building.

Bibliography:

1) Ebne Hughel, Soratolarz, translated by Jafar e Shoar, IInd edition, Tehran, Amir Kabir publication. In Persian.

2) Akbary, Amir, 1382, Tarikh-e ejtemaye Iran dar asr e Sassanian, Ist edition, Mashhad, Mohaghegh publication, in Persian

3) Jamasb Jey (editor) 1371, Motune Pahlavi, Reported by Saeed Oryan, Translated, Tehran National library: in Persian.

4) Boyce. M., 1375, Tarikh e Kish e zartosht, translated by Homayon Sanity zadeh, second edition Tehran, in Persian

5) Christiansen, A., 1385, (Persian translation) Iran dar Zaman Sassanian, translated by Rashid Yasamy, 5th edition, Tehran, sedaye Moaser publication in Persian.

6) Mashkur, M.J., 1347, Tarikhe ejtemaye Iran dar bastan, Tehran university press: in Persian.

7) Moein, M., 1355, Mazdiasna va adab Parsy, Tehran, Tehran university press in Persian

8) Bahar, M., 1375, Pajuheshy dar asatire Irani, Tehran, Nashre cheshme publication, in Persian.

9) Pope, A, 1338. Honarre Iran, Translated by Parviz Khanlary, Tehran, Safy Alishah publication in Persian

10) Tohidi, F., 1067, Unreported of archaeological survey of Sabzevar, Archive of cultural Heritage, Sabzevar unit.

11) Ghare Khany, H., 1363, the historical Asare bastany va boghae motebarekey atrafe shahrestane Sabzevar va Asfaryan, Tehran, Yasavoly publication in Persian

12) Beyhaghi. Ebne Fangh., 1317, Tarikh Beyhaghi, edited by Bahmanyar IInd edition Tehran, furughy bookstore publication in Persian.

13) Purdavood.A., Yashtha, vol IInd, Bombay, 1931.

14) Kazemy , Y., 1386, Atashgah e Esfahan, Ist edition Esfahan, Sazmane farhangy shardarya Esfahan publication, in Persian.

15) Schippmann, K., 1972, the development of Iranian fire temple international congress of Iranian art and archeology, Tehran.

16) Gropp ., 1969, die function des fuertemles der Ziriaster aminf 2 , pp166-173.

18) schlumberger, D., 1974, Sassanian architecture, memorialjean de foundakian part 215-225

19) Kwal , E., 1979, Galeh yazdigird , Iran, vol xvll.

The Zoroastrian Holyland of Haetumant by Reza MehrAfarin,[326] Seyyed Rasool Mousavi Haji,[327] and Javad Neyestani[328]

Abstract.

Haetumant Rāyvmand is the eleventh wonderful and exceptional piece of land or country created by Ahura Mazda, hence this is the most ancient name that still remains in the literatures of Sistan. *Haetumant*, apart from the fact that it is paralleled to Hirmand River, is also known as the land of Sistan. This river has been praised quite often in the holy Avesta and considered one of the holiest rivers in the Zoroastrian religion. One of the reasons for this river being holy is its charisma or the presence of Xwarnah (Divine Grace) within it. This Divine Grace or charisma illuminates the heart anyone who gets to place their hand into it; he will not only be pious and great, but will also achieve his aspirations.

As such, based on the Avesta and Sassanid-Pahlavi texts, the Zoroastrian religion took shape in the land of *Haetumant*. Messiahs of this religion, too, would set their feet on this piece of land. A large number of religious dignitaries also emerged on this land and that could have been possible with the blessing of charismatic presence of divine light in the Haetumant River. Apart from *Haetumant*, eight other tributaries on this land have been mentioned in the holy Avesta, most of them conform with the present names of Sistan River. *Kiansiyeh (Hamun)* Lake and *Ošidam Ošida* (Kuh-e—*Khwajeh*) are other natural phenomena that exist on the land of Haetumant and have been remembered many times in the Avesta.

We have studied passages in the Avesta, and analysed each of its paragraphs that have either a direct or indirect relation to Sistan. In addition, we have compared them to the Pahlavi texts, as the purpose of this manuscript is to show that Zoroaster, the Iranian prophet had emigrated from his original land to Sistan. He received Manthra (afflatus) on Khwaja Mount (Ušidam Ušida) by protection of Goštaspa, the governor, who accepted the Zoroastrian religion in this country. After stabilization of the faith, the Zoroastrian clergymen proclaimed the new religion to other Aryan lands, including the west of Iran.

Keywords: *Haetumant*, Sistan, Zoroastrian religion, *Hamun* Lake, *Ošida* Mountain.

---

[326] Assistant Professor, Department of Archaeology, University of Sistan and Baluchestan, Iran.
[327] Assistant Professor, Department of Archaeology, University of Sistan and Baluchestan, Iran.

Haetumant and other Tributaries

"The eleventh piece of land and the outstanding country that Thy –Ahura Mazda –created is *Haetumant Rayvmand Farahmand*. Then on, Ahriman or Devil would cause death and originate damaging and harmful magic and spirits. [Vandidad, Chapter 1]. Apart from being known as Hirmand River, *Haetumant* was the name of the land of Sistan. Therefore, this is the most ancient name that is still prevalent in Sistan. *Haetumant*, as is mentioned quite often in the Avesta, is the compound of *haetu* and *mant* (mand). The first part means dam or sheet; that is equivalent to 'setu' in Sanskrit, which means bridge or dam. The second part, 'mant or mand' means possessor or holder, and is also seen in a number of Pahlavi and Persian terminologies such as 'arezumand' (desirous) or 'aberumand' (respectful). Consequently, *Haetumant* means possessor of the dam or barrier. The part of the land that is irrigated through this river and those lands wherever this river flows has been named as Hirmand" [Mostafavi, 1982:61 -3].

In Islamic texts, *Haetumant* has been recorded differently, for example 'Milmand', 'Hindmand', 'Hirmand', and 'Hirmid'; whereas in the Greek texts names such as 'Atimandrous', 'Atimander', 'Arimantous' and 'Arimandrous' have been used[Azarneyusheh, 1995:106-7]. The source of this long and meandering river that has a length of about 135 parasangs (810 kilometers) is the Ghaur Mountains in Afghanistan [Mostaufi, 1982:22]. The river that flows from different provinces and creates a large population on its fringes irrigates large stretch of land in Sistan and finally pours into the Hamun Lake. According to Herodotus, if Egypt is considered a gift of Nile, Sistan is a gift of Hirmand [Bosworth, 1991:70-71]. This seasonal river, where the water levels increase and decrease at different periods of time, has often been praised in the Avesta; hence, it is counted as one of the holiest rivers in Mazdaism. In Vandidad, Chapter 19, Passage 30, after eulogizing on the six-folded countries, the verse praises illuminating Khuniras and consequently Hirmand-e Farahmand.

Hirmand has is also referred to twice in the Zamyad Yasht (Hymn to the Earth), Plot 9, Passages 65-8. After praising the glorious and powerful Mazda, it says:

"This glory is from the one whose sovereignty is the place forms the meeting point of Hirmand River and Kiansiyeh (Hamun) Lake or a place where Ošidam Mountain exists".

Following the above passage, eight other tributaries have been remembered after *Haetumant* that finally fall into Kiansiyeh. Here, Hirmand is called as a magnificent river with white and rebellious waves, as well as a powerful force that could submerge non-Iranian nations. Also at this point there is narration about the aegis of the king that existed in this river.

---

[328] Assistant Professor, Department of Archaeology, University of Tarbiat Modarres, Iran.

In the Avesta, Hirmand is remembered as a river where the aegis of the king existed (Zamyad Yasht, Plot 9; Passage 65-68). A halo or light that illuminates any heart or gets into ones hand, he becomes dexterous, a hero, pious, a great man; a light that is greater than rest of the Creator. The light or aegis is where both materialism and divinity exist . The royal aegis brought a particular sanctity to Hirmand; hence, its presence caused that a many would strive to touch it with their hands because:

"The divine light becomes friend to the one whose dominance starts from the place where Kansaoyeh was formed from *Haetumant*"

The dominance of Zoroaster (Zarathuštra) upon demons began from the land of *Haetumant*. The dominance of Guštaspa upon his enemies began on Frazdānu Lake and the dominance of Soshyant upon Ahriman begins from the land of *Haetumant*. By this way, the aegis of the king became friendly to them, making them victorious and successful.

Undoubtedly, the sanctity of this river began during the pre-Zoroastrian era [Christensen, 1368:30-31]. The reasons for this sanctity have been distinguished. The presence of a river in Sistan has been the source of life and culture, and, draught there is just synonym for the destruction of life and the migration of people to other regions. On this land, considering its salty soil, one could not resort to a well or an aqueduct, therefore, population is not sustainable without a river. In reality, dryness of the Hirmand transforms the land of Sistan into a desert. Some of the sculptures acquired from *Shahr-e Sukhteh* (the burnt city), particularly the one on blue vessel is reminiscenct of divine water, thus it shows sanctity of this lake during antiquity.

As a matter of fact, a number of glorious cultures emerged on the fringes of Hirmand and its tributaries. This river transformed Sistan into the granary of Iran. Also, flocks of goast, sheep, and cows made the people rich. In Vištasp Yasht (Fargerd 1), Zarathuštra prayed for Guštaspa:

"….May you become pious like Zarathuštra, may you become like Abtin family that possessed strong hoards of animals and grain…may you enjoy horses like Puroshaspa…"

Referring to Dinkard (Book7), Christensen also writes: Vištaspa, a successor and son of Lohraspa possessed a large number of domesticated animals and his reputation had gone to the far-flung countries [Christensen, 1989:137]. Hoards of cows and sheep were the outcome of *Haetumant* River that makes the families with animal husbandry famous and rich like the one Guštaspa. According to Professor Bahar, Urvasa in the Avesta is named as Urwes in the language of Pahlavi, is another name of Haetumant River because in the Avesta, the Urwes falls into Kiansiyeh Lake [Bahar, 1996:163].

Haetumant or *Urwes* River that was the source of happiness, life, culture and divinity, encountered all kind of death and destruction sent by Ahriman; for example, he sent locusts and spiders to the land of Haetumant [Bahar, 1990:134]. Afrasiyab too, after conquering the Haetumant River, made its water dirty and sluggish and expelled the population around it. However, with the offerings of Hūm and Zohr, the river regained its sanctity [Bahar, 1990:76-7]. Zamyad Yasht, apart from Haetumant, names eight other tributaries that fall into Kiansiyeh Lake, as well.

"65....we praise powerful created light that is unexpected to be acquired, the most praiseworthy, pious and agile that is superior to rest of the creation".

"66... to one whose glory rises at a place forming Haetumant River and Kiansiyeh Lake and the place where Ošidam Mountain exists and water coming from the surrounding mountains overflow".

"67.... To one (Kiansiyeh Lake) that falls and flows towards it: Khvāstra, Hvaspa, Fradatha, Khvarenahvaiti fall into it and flows toward the magnificent and powerful Haetumant with white inundated waves" [Zamyad Yasht, Plot 9, Passages 65-68].

Due to flat surface and soil quality, rivers in Sistan usually change their courses. Consequently, the name of old beds could have possibly been applied to the new ones. Despite time elapsing few millennia since the time of the Avesta, most of names given to this river corresponded with the present names. For instance, the Xastra River is corresponded to Khāshrud. The word is an attribute meaning possessor of a garden or fine pasture. According to Gnoli, this river is conformed to 'Wadi-e-Nasl' or Nahr-e Nishk' from Islamic sources [Azarneyusheh, 1995:109]. Hvaspa means one who owns a fine horse. In the 2nd century AD, Ptolemy, a Greek geographer recorded it as Xoaspa and presently it is named as Khuspas. This is one that emerges from the east and falls into Hamun [Pourdavoud, Yashtha 2:344].

Fradatha means increasing and bolstering or progress and development. Or with a similar testimony by Pliny, Afradous is the same as Farahrud that passes through big cities [Pourdavoud, Yashtha 2:344].

Xvarenanhaiti means overflow with glory. Plinius from Rome (23-79 AD) recorded it as Frankotis. Today, it is known as Harirud or Harut [Pourdavoud, Yashtha2:344]. Urvatha with an attribute mostly encountered with pasture or pastures and this also falls into Hamun [Mostafavi, 1982:81-2].

According to Gnoli, Erezi is probably the name of a river derived from Erezi meaning slope. According to Markwart, the Xar River existed between Khāshrud and Khuspas. Zarenumaiti means golden. Describing lack of identification, Hartsfield believes that the Zarenumaiti might be the same the Xar [Azarneyosheh, 1995:112-3].

One of the rivers mentioned in Bondahesh and its location has been identified somewhere in Sistan is Vataini. According to Bondahesh this river emerges from Kiansiyeh and flowed through Sistan [Bahar, 1990:76].

After entering into Sistan, the Hirmand and other tributaries form three segregated lakes. During the high season, with an abundance of water, these three transform into one, the Great Hamunis is formed. Overflowing water returns to soil of Afghanistan through the Shileh River that is actually part of Sistan and fall into Gowd-e Zerreh Lake. However, the source of the Shileh is the Hamun, because after emerging from this lake and flowing through Sistan, this falls into the same land. Therefore, the Vataini River probably is the sameas the present day Shileh.

As has been mentioned before, rivers in Sistan change their courses continuously due to flatness of surface and its alluvium soil. Consequently, some of them whichflowed and existed during pre-historic Sistan like the Shahr-e Sukhteh were completely dried up. On the other hand, other rivers in the area could open their ways towards the lake and gave rise to new cities. Therefore, the present river cannot either be considered the same the Avestan rivers, nor can they be identified completely unless we believe the deserted rivers gave new way to a new estuary. In all, efforts of researchers are praiseworthy with respect to conformity of the Avestan rivers in Sistan with the present ones.

The problems that have been discussed here can reach a positive and sensible conclusion are that since a person may not have observed a particular geographical condition of a region closely, the exact description of that region is not possibly not clearly defined for him. From the study of the Avesta, it is deduced that the composer himself observed and knew the region very well so he could present a precise and beautiful account in a religious text, with accuracy and delicacy. Presenting different witnesses and the acquired result, we can thus assert that if Zoroaster did not hail from Sistan, he actually lived there for a period of time.

The Kiansiyeh Lake

The Zamyad Yasht (Keyan Yasht) discusses the physical characteristics as well as geographical history of Sistan. Courageously, this Yasht (Hymn) can be named as the Sistan Yasht, because it contains most of the instances related to this land. Kiansiyeh, that is referred to three times in the Avesta has been mentioned twice in the Zamyad. The Avesta itself suffices in order to distinguish and identify this geographical location. Likewise, the Pahlavi texts also contain stories related to Kiansiyeh in Sistan. Before it, we found that Haetumant is a place of divine light and thus this Yasht refers:

..... [A light] is one who sovereign of a meeting point between Hirmand to Hamun. The place consisting Ošidam Mountain and that overflows with abundant of water from the surrounding mountains [Zamyad Yasht, Plot 9, Passage 66].

The Hirmand is the only important river that falls into the Hamun Lake on the soil of Iran. This is one of the biggest fresh water lakes in Iranian plateau. Hirmand forms from the Baba Yaghma River, west of Kabul and enters into Iran after passing about 1200 kilometers and finally it falls into Hamun [Badiee, 1983:145].

The Avestan name of the Hamun Lake is *Kansaoya* or *Kensu*. In the Pahlavi or Pazand texts, it is called as Kiansiyeh or Kianseh. In Persian books like '*Sad Dar-e Bondahesh*', *Ravāyat-e Darab Hormuzdyar*' it is named as 'Kanfseh'. In the Avesta, it has occasionally been remembered with Zariyeh (river) or Aap (water). Kiansiyeh (Hamun) in Iranian legends is one of the most respected waters on the earth [Doostkhah, Avesta, Vol 2:1037-8].

Afrasiyab, who was striving for the divine light, paid attention to Haetumant once he knew its exact location. Consequently, he embarked upon creating streams in Sistan towards Hamun and constructed one thousand streams, the *Haetumant* River and seven other rivers were viable for shipping and provided an abode for the people on their fringes [Christensen, 1989:128-9]. Despite his services and efforts, Afrasiyab remained unsuccessful in acquiring the divine light. Zamyad Yasht, Plot 8 discusses Afrasiyab's efforts and their consequences.

From the above verse, we come to know that Afrasiyab hastened three times, naked, towards the Farakhkert River for the king's aegis, not knowing that it belonged to the Iranians sects and Zoroaster. After full the moon, at his third attempt, a branch 'Ūzhdanvan' emerged from the Farakhkert. Thereafter, Afrasiyab of Turani became despairing of the aegis and abandoned his efforts. But, he now embarked upon taking revenge. In the verse 9 that follows the above aspect, the Kianseh Lake has been identified at the place of aegis where the Hirmand falls. Possibly, the branch where the aegis appeared the last time, which is remembered as Ūzhdanvan is the same the Frazdanu River, that is the name of the same lake but with a different form.

Based on a passage from Zamyad, once Afrasiyab became disappointed, he turned to revenge. But every time he returned from the Farakhkert River with an empty hand, cursers uttered:

"ایث، ایث، یثن، اهمایی، اوث، ایث، یثن، کهمایی!"

Although the exact meaning of any idle talk of Afrasiyab is not clear, they warn, " ...now I would break all wet, dry, big, pious and beautiful so that Ahura Mazda would be brought at bay " [Zamyad Yasht, Passage 8].

According to the definition of Bondehesh, Afrasiyab took his revenge by destroying a thousand of the small and big streams including Haetumant and Vataini and six rivers suitable for shipping [Rashed Mohassel, 1990:83].

In Mazdaism, the Kianseh Lake enjoys special status with regard to its length and divinity. Also, because Soshyant of the Zoroastrians was born in this lake. "At the same time Astvaṭ ərəta, an ambassador of Ahura, son of Vespa Turveiri emerged from Kianseh water, and a victorious maul came up---the same maul that courageous Fereydūn possessed at the time of killing Azhi" [Zamyad Yasht, Passage 15].

Zarathuštra replied to Ahriman: O wicked Ahriman...I will defeat the devil...defeat eunuch devil until Soshyant is victorious, emerges from Kianseh and lives on the wide arena of Nimruz [Vandidad, Fargard 19, and Section 1].

Astvaṭ ərəta or Soshyant and his brother would be born on Kianseh. Based on the Avesta and Pahlavi-Sassanid, 99999 guards were to protect the seed of Zoroaster the Spitaman on Kianseh Lake. Apart from names mentioned before, Hamun Lake was also known as Frazdanu, Seh Tukhmeh, Varoksha, Vezrat [Aban Yasht, Passage 25].

"One who offered Guštaspa 100 horses, 1000 cows, 100000 sheep on Frazdanu [Aban Yasht, Passage 25].

In the Bahman Yasht, we come across Uxšyaṭ.ərəta (Hoshidar) being born in Frazdanu [Doostkhah, Avesta Vol2:1021]. Bondahesh has also mentioned this lake and says Frazdanu is in Sistan. It says a man who accepts bad and destroys things is not virtuous at all [Bahar, 1990:77]. Zand and Hooman Yasn also mention that Hooshidar, the son of Zoroaster will be born at the Frazdanu Lake [Hedayat, 1961:57]. However, Seh Tukhmeh has been named in such a way that the seed of Zoroaster that would give birth to his three sons of Hooshidar, Ušēdarnah and Sošyant, and they would be brought up at this lake [Rashed Mohassel, 1990:87].

With reference to Vorokša, Azarneyosheh quotes Christensen, saying that this cannot be any other than Hamun and he further confirms: With little care about the word, it can possibly be said that Vorokša is another distortion of the name 'Varkasaoya' is Kianseh. In other words, this is the same Kasaoiyeh [Azarneyosheh, 1994:1012].

In the Avesta and Pahlavi-Sassanid texts, the Hirmand River has been named as the Zereh. One researcher thus writes "the Zereh is a tiny river where water increases and decreases depending upon the seasons. Its length is about 30 parsangs i.e. from Kuwein region of Qohestan to Kerman Bridge in Fars and its breadth is a water lodge with abundant of fish, bamboos and crocodiles of a particular type [Jeyhani, 1989:163]. Apart from this, most of the writers reach commonality on the point that the Hamun Lake has always been the only fresh water lake in the region. For that matter, Bondahesh indicates: In the beginning, the water was fresh with traces of aquatic cretures such snakes and frogs in it. Other small rivers with salty and polluted waters too became fresh due their proximity [Bahar, 1990:74].

Probably, the belief about the Zereh Lake, apart from the destruction by Afrasiyab, allowed other narratives to emerge in the Pahlavi texts. Based on the legends, once Jamshid lost the aegis of the kingship, he along with his sister Jamak accidentally took refuge in the Zereh Lake, but Ahriman found out their refuge. Thereafter, a devil and a fairy appeared in human form and offered matrimony with them. Jam accepted the offer and selected the fairy as his wife and gave his sister to the devil. With these marriages, a number of mischievous and dangerous beings were created. According to the legend, a number of turtles, poisonous lizards, greyhounds as well as various others aquatic creatures were born from the marriage of Jamak and this devil, hence, the Zereh Lake turned stagnant and dark due to stinking devil [Mirfakhraee, 1988:7].

Uši.darəna Mountain

TheUši.darəna is a mountain that, after the Alborz Mountain, has been remembered more than others in the Avesta. We come across this name 12 times in the Avesta. If we may count Uši.darəna with equivalent names, then this has appeared 15 times. In the meantime, some mountains other than Hokkar have been mentioned approximately twice, although they must be counted as the peak of Alborz. Based on the Avesta, the Pahlavi texts and Avestalogists, Uši.darəna is located in Sistan and its location has been distinguished in the Zamyad Yasht, Plot 9:

.....[a light] is one who sovereign of a meeting point between Hirmand to Hamun. The place consisting Ošidam Mountain and that overflows with abundant of water from the surrounding mountains [Zamyad Yasht, Plot 9, Passage 66].

At least three aspects can be determined from the above passage. First, the light is linked to one whose desire of sovereignty is at the meeting-point of Hirmand River and Kianseh Lake, and that is covered by Uši.darəna.

Here, one must place emphasis on 'meeting place' and 'there'. As we know, the falling point of the Hirmand is the Hamun Lake; there is an isolated cliff that in reality is counted as the only mountain inside Sistan and presently famous as Kuh-e-Khwajeh. The word 'there' points to 'the place of disintegration'. Therefore, other than the falling point of Hirmand, the place cannot be traced for Uši.darəna (Kianseh).

Another aspect is the last sentence of this passage. 'And the surrounding mountains make the water available abundantly and overflow'. It means surrounding mountains of Uši.darəna—that make water available and which then falls into Hamun i.e. Uši.darəna is like an island, which existed in between. Uši.darəna is the only mountain and with regard to its width and height cannot be the source of a river or rivers.

Suppose, we don't identify Uši.darəna as Kuh-e-Khawajeh then the above sentence could be interpreted as: 'from this mountain, an abundance of water comes and overflows'. Since the discussion is about the surrounding mountains with waters, therefore, Uši.darəna itself had no water available rather acquired it from others. Kuh-e-Khwajeh also lacks water itself and acquired it from other mountains.

The last aspect that can be pointed out: there is Uši.darəna Mountain that is stretched out'. At the heart of Hamun Lake, there is an isolated projection of a black cliff of about 120 meters height. Since there is hardly any visible projection in the wide Sistan Plain which is flat like the palm of a hand, a small projection like Kuh-e-Khawajeh is not only strange, but could be seen as a high peak for local people, because it is distinguishable from each part of Sistan and there exist no other mountains.

Oshidam is also known with other names 'Ošidarena' [Pourdavoud, Yashtha1:64-5], which can be studied through Avestan texts: "... we praise that mountain of Ošidam Uši.darəna for its gracious needs day and night [Hormuzd Yasht, Passage 28].

In this sentence, Oshidam and Uši.darəna appear synonymous with each other and there is no sign that they are separated. "O', Zartosht the Spitaman, the foremost mountain emerged on this land is the tall Alborz linking eastern and western landscape. Oshidam Uši.darəna and Erezifyeh emerged from these mountains"….. [Zamyad Yasht, Passage 20].

According to this hymn, there are 2244 mountains around the world, the 12 foremost occur systematically in Zamyad Yasht. The first and second mountains as well as sixth to twelfth have come systematically but order is lacking between the third and the fifth mountains. However, a systematic order can be distinguished on the basis of available texts. The Manousheh Mountain is located in Khurasan bordering with Turkmenistan [Bahar, 1990:72]. Thus, the third mountain after Xerxes is Manousheh and before Arzure, there is the sixth Erezifyeh Mountain, hence this comes fifth in the order. Between the third and the fifth i.e. Manousheh and Erezifyeh, there is

Ošidam Uši.darəna. Thus the two names are one and can be counted as fourth in the given order. The Pahlavi text also precisely points to Ošidam Uši.darəna in Sistan and says the mountain that is names in Pahlavi as Osh Rashtar (Oshida) is in Sistan based on Bondahesh Chapter 12, Paragraph 15.

An attribute in the Avesta for Ošidam Uši.darəna is the provider of comfort or ease. This attribute has been repeated in 11 of 12 cases where the names of this mountain appears and is followed by the name of Mazda. The attachment of the aegis of the king to the name of Ošidam Uši.darəna is another testimony of the presence of this mountain in Sistan.

The sanctity of the Uši.darəna Mountain is to the extant that it has been presented as pious thought, speech and character in religion. Describing Uši.darəna, Pourdavoud writes: the first part of the word Uši.darəna may have come from Uši means 'daybreak' or 'early morning' and in Sanskrit it is Vsas. In reality, it means shiny and bright, which Bartholomew refers to as early morning, daybreak and the same dictum is Osh.hangah, which in Mazdaism is one of the five-folded days and nights and that denotes from mid-night to sun rise [Pourdavoud, Yeshta2:321]. He believes that Zoroaster was revealed on the top of this mountain [Pourdavoud, Yeshta2:64]. The problem of transferring the revelation from Ahura Mazda to Zoroaster on top of the mountain can be extracted from Hormuzd Yasht, Passage 27 which says:

…….praise be upon the power of memorization of Ahura Mazda…..praise be on the power of speech of Ahura Mazda…..praise be upon Ošidam Uši.darəna with its gracious need days and night'.

Here the revealed words have been praised due to their utterance by the tongue. Ošidam Uši.darəna Mountain has also been praised likewise. In this passage, there is close direct connection between the revealed words and Ošidam Mountain. It can be inferred that the time Zoroaster stayed in Sistan; he possibly acquired part of the Avesta on the top of this mountain, in the same way as Prophet Moses and Prophet Mohammad received their divine revelations on Tur and Nur Mountains, respectively; both the mountains too are holy to these religions as well as their followers. Principally, mountain has special status in the revealed religion because it provides a secluded and quiet place for thinking and secret exchange with Almighty, the Creator.

The sanctity of Ošidam Mountain has turned it to the abode of pious people [Pourdavoud, 1972:23] and during Nowruz (the Zoroastrian New Year) or the autumnal equinox; thousands of Zoroastrians from across Iran make pilgrimage to it. This is a tradition that has not been forgotten and continues as before in a different form, even with the passage of thousands of years as well as changes in the faith of people in Sistan.

It is worth mentioning that this mountain, apart from the Zoroastrian religion, also enjoys sanctity in Christianity and Islam. Some of the Christians believe that a star that appeared in the east that was followed by three Persian Magi who encountered with the birth of Jesus Christ appeared from the Kuh-e- Khwajeh.

The Khwajeh is the name given to this mountain in the later Islamic period. Before, it was famous as Kuhe-e-Khuda (the Mountain of God). Khwajeh Kuh probably became famous with the change of name of god to Khwajeh. On the top of this mountain, there is a mausoleum of Khwajeh Ghaltan who is known as the successor of Ali (AS). Thus, a large number of Muslims from Sistan make annual pilgrimage to this place (especially at the time of Nowruz) and offer animals for sacrifice. On southwestern part of this mountain, another tomb with the name, 'Pir Gandom Beryan' exists. The name seems to be synonymous to one of the offerings made to this tomb [Mostafavi, 1982:115].

Consequently, one can say that the sanctity on Kuh-e-Khawajeh has roots in the ancient religious practices of local people. Accordingly they celebrate the auspicious events based on their ancient traditions remembering the actual aim of the pilgrimage or remembering the associated mystic meaning.

Conclusion

The Avesta, a holy book of the Zoroastrians is an ancient document, the study of which could draw us to the part of historical geography of ancient Iran. However, it is worth mentioning that the later religious texts, especially the Sassanid-Pahlavi that play an important role in describing and paraphrasing this holy book, are needed at in comparison witht the Avesta in order to complete the hidden knowledge.

The land of Haetumant that is remembered so many times in Avesta, as described by Vandidad, is the eleventh outstanding country created by Ahura Mazda.

Haetumant, with a little change in dictum, is the present name of the Hirmand River that flows in eastern Iran and falls into the Hamun Lake in the Sistan province. As such, at the time of the the Avesta, a wider area covered by the course of Hirmand was called the land of Haetumant and it is the most ancient name that is still prevalent among people of this land.

The land of Haetumant, in the faith of ancient Iranians, enjoyed religious and divine importance due to possessing the aegis of the king. In the Zoroastrian faith, that aegis or light was bestowed upon the one whose sovereignty was at the termination of Haetumant River into Kiansiyeh (Hamun) Lake. By this way, the land became a seat of various godly men, kings and

Zoroaster himself who endeavored to acquire that divine aegis. The Kiansiyeh Lake that is identical to Hamun has been praised many times in the Avesta due to the preservation of Zoroaster's semen in it, allowing the birth of the Soshians (messiahs of religion) on its shore along with Ušidam Ušida, the dissention point of afflatus on it.

One of the other sanctities of the Haetomant land is the immigration of the Prophet Zoroaster to this region. Zoroaster, who was faced with the animosity of his townsmen, immigrated to Sistan, where the Kianid king, Goštaspa ruled. The prophet, with the advocating of Goštaspa succeeded to develop the new faith not only in this region but also spread it to other Iranian lands. After marriage with Hvōvi, a member of a great family and akin to the court of Goštaspa, Zoroaster copulated with her three times on the shore of Kiansiyeh Lake and every time his semen effused in the lake in order to give birth to the Soshians (behests of Zoroaster religion) at the end of each three millennium in his land. Copulation of Zoroaster with Hvōvi on the shore of Kiansiyeh Lake, the nativity of Soshians in this region, obtaining Xwarnah (charisma or Divine Glory) from Haetomant river by Zoroaster and the other great men of the faith as well as patronage of Goštaspa of Kianid from the prophet, all shows the presence of Zoroaster in the east of Iran (the land of Haetomant). From the other side, the clear description in the Avesta about the land of Haetomant (Hirmand River, canals, Hamun lake, Ušidam Mount, ...) shows that the composer of the Avesta has seen this region in great detail and knew it very well.

The land of Haetumant, due to hundreds of water streams and a number of tributaries is counted as the most populated and fertile place in Iran, but Ahriman (Devil) caused death and originated damaging and harmful magic and spirits in it and also, Afrasiyab, who is known as an enemy of Iranian religion, deviated the course of these rivers in order to get revenge from Iran Shahr, hence, Sistan encountered severe droughts. But, finally this region will get achieve grandeur and terminate the period of its affliction and drought at the time of the arrival of the Saviour-Soshians, epiphany promised by the Avesta once again.

References

- Azarneyosheh, AbbasAli [1995], 'Nomenclature of historical names of Hirmand', *Journal of Humanities*, Zahedan: University of Sistan and Baluchestan, no.1, vol.1
- Bosworth, Edmond Clifford [1991], *History of Sistan*, trans. Hassan Anousheh, Tehran: Amir Kabir Publications.
- Badiee, Rabie [1983], *Detailed Geography of Iran*, vol.1, Tehran: Iqbal Publications.
- Bahar, Mehrdad [1990], *Bondahesh, Franbagh Dadegi*, vol1, Tehran: Toos Publications.
- Bahar, Mehrdad [1375] *A Research on Iranian Legends*, Tehran: Aagah Publications.

- Pourdavoud, Ibrahim [1996], *Yashtha 1*, with the cooperation of Bahram Farahvashi, Third edition, Tehran: University of Tehran
- Pourdavoud, Ibrahim [1986], *Yashtha 2*, Third edition, Tehran: University of Tehran
- Pourdavoud, Ibrahim [1927], *Predestined Sushiyanet of Mazdaism,* Bombay: Hur Publication of Gwalior Tank
- Pourdavoud, Ibrahim [1978], *Visperad*, with the cooperation of Bahram Farahvashi, Second edition, Tehran: University of Tehran
- Jeyhani, Abolqasem Ibn-e Ahmad [1989], *Shapes of the World*, (ed) Ali Bin Abdus Salam, Astan Qods Publication.
- Doostkhah, Jalil [1996], *Avesta*, Vol.1, Third Edition, Tehran: Morvarid Publications.
- Rashed Mohassel, Mohammadtaghi [1990], *Salvations in Religions* Tehran: Institute of Cultural Studies and Researches.
- Christensen, Arthur [1989], *the Kiyan Dynasty*, Trans. Zabih Ullah Safa, Fifth Edition, Tehran: Scientific and Cultural Publications.
- Mostafavi, Aliasghar [1982], *Predestined Land*, Tehran: Neda Publications.
- Mirfakhraei, Mahshid [1988], Pahlavi Traditions, Tehran: Institute of Cultural Studies and Researches.
- Hedayat, Sadegh [1961], Zand and Hooman Yasn (Bahman Yasht), Third Edition, Tehran: Amir Kabir Publications.

Haetomant (Hirmand)

Kiansiyeh (Hamun) Lake

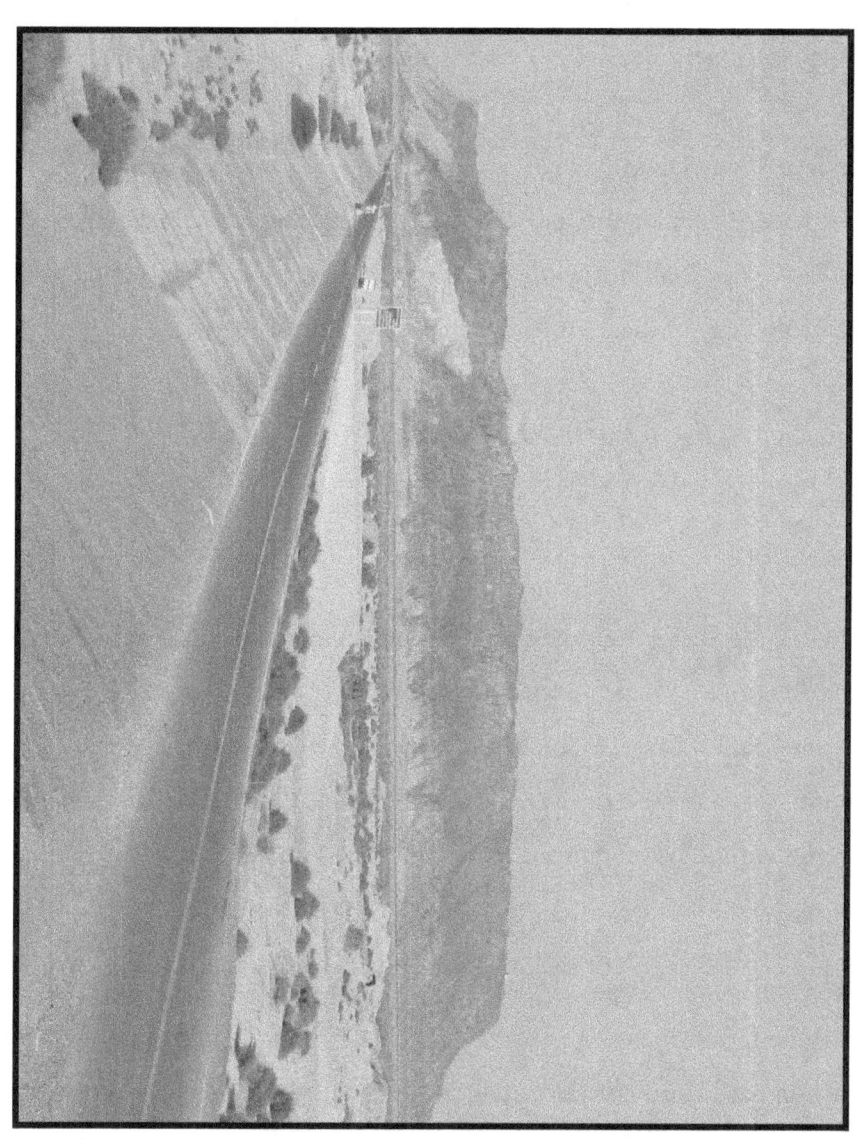

Ošidam Ošida (Kuh-e—Khwajeh)

The Archaeological Evidence in Tarik Dareh (Dark Valley), in Hamadan, Iran, by Masoud Rashidi Nejad[329] and Amirhossein Salehi[330]

Abstract.

Pursuing the report of Dare Divin (Divijin) engravings in south west Hamadan by Sarraf (1997), (fig 4), the writer succeeded in identifying some in this area. They are divided into two categories; zoomorphic and ideogram. Referring to the results of studying other archaeological findings, we are able to estimate the date of these engravings.

Keywords: Engraving, prehistory art, Parthian, Tarik Dareh

Introduction

Following a glance to the ecological system and cultural study of the inhabitants that established themselves in these regions of Zagros, it seems necessary to follow the same routine methods of studies in the surrounding valley of Hamadan region, in order to gain a clear perception. In this article we attempt to reach to a better understanding of archaeological findings such as engravings, potteries and nomadic camps in the feet of Alvand range of mountains (Map 1).

Engravings

The first group of the motifs includes an animal figure, 1.5 m long, in 3-4cm width lines which have been created on hard Cordierite Hornfels and covered all the stone, petrological and paleontological facts show the creation of fossil in sedimentary rocks such as Horenfels stones with high grade metamorphism seems impossible.

This sample has been created by a hard object (probably by one type of chip), in two steps, since there is a clear inconsistency between the width and continuity of lines in head and body. The image is considered of badger family (Rudak), or otter which usually live on steppes, forests and mountain areas.Visual features, such as profiles and parallel and scrambled grooves on the foot and head of the image remind us of engraved horse panel in Chauvet cave of solutreen period.[331]

---

[329] Is a MA. of achaeology, Department of Archaeology, Faculty of Humanities, Tarbiat Modares University and instructor of the Islamic Azad university of Hamadan Branch, Mail: mrashidinejad7@gmail.com.

[330] Is an instructor at Semnan University of Tourism & is currently a PHD student at Tarbiat Modares University in Tehran.

[331] For details see: http://www.culture.gouv.fr/culture/arcnat/chauvet/en

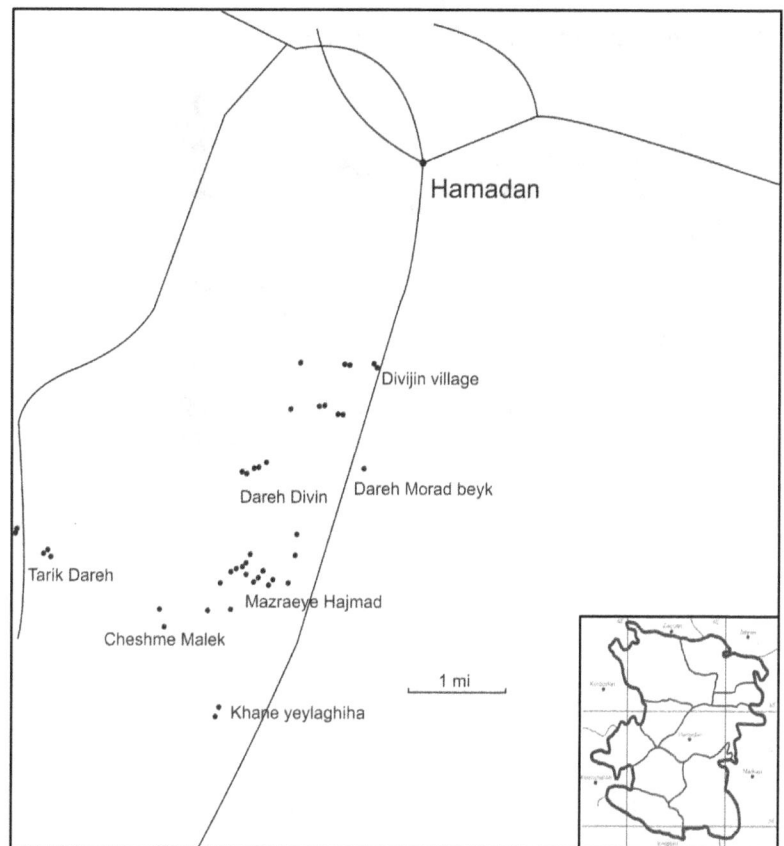

Map 1: Dispersion of Tarik Dareh, Cheshme Malek, Dareh Divin and Dareh Morad beak engravings, Hamadan province

 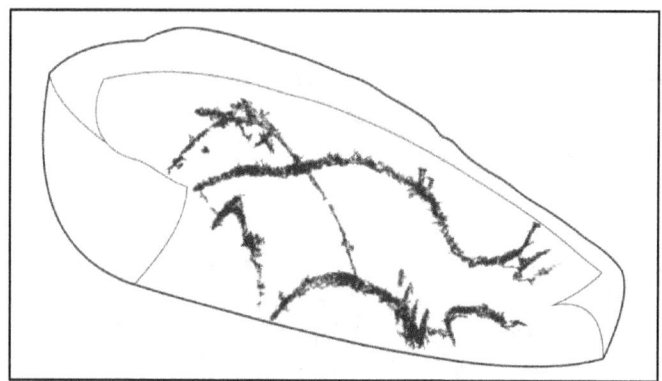

Figure 1: Tarik dareh, zoomorphs, site: N34° 44' 09.8" E48° 26' 40.6"

In this sample we come across a metamorphosis, because it has not used the trace of usual rock art in Iran. It's iconography shows the image of this sample seems much older than other findings in this area, because the artists attempting to display animals in actual size are one of the steps of human being evolution (see Goldhahn, 2004, 55 , this knowledge is supported when we take into consideration the art history and also the realistic type of Paleolithic to Neolithic period (Hauser, 1998, 8).

This similarity is well shown in the paintings of hand stencils and Gazelles of Eshgafte Ahoii in the Bastak region from epipaleolithic and Neolithic periods (?).

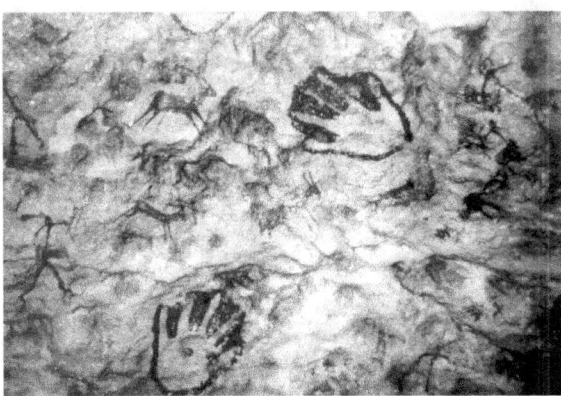

Plate 2: Bastak district in Hormozgan province, hand stencils, hunters and Gazelles paintings (Asadi, 2007, 65-70)

Like indigenous art of Africa and Australia[332], probably the similarity of this sample of comparison with Paleolithic samples in Europe is derived from the same structure of the human neural system, not from simultaneous events.[333] We can evaluate this similarity in the scope of time and place. However, the presence of Homo erectus in south west Asia (Rightmire, 2009, 16046), and evidence of upper and lower Paleolithic in Iran (Ariai, 1975, Sdek-Kooros, 1974, 53-65 & M.Otte, F.Biglari, 2007, 84), have made us hopeful to find signs in regard to this period. Near this finding, symmetrical lines that are likely to be engraved by man can be seen.

 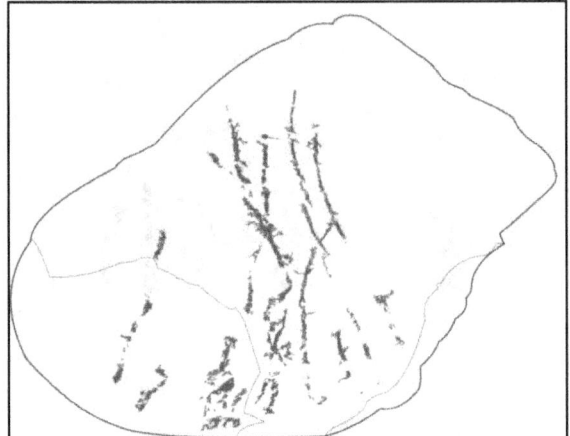

Figure 2: Tarik Dareh, Symmetrical lines.

---

[332] The Asian material shows several distinctive similarities with that from Africa, and even with the Australian corpus (Bednarik, 2010, 10). It is the cave art of France at Spain that is the oddity, the anomaly (Bednarik 1993). such association are repeated in several caves, relationships that contrast strikingly with prehistoric rock art systems elsewhere the world (see Chazine, 2005, 219-230).

[333] Such as the shamanic paradigm involves basic brain processes, neurognostic structures, and innate brain modules (Winkelman, 2004, 193).

From petrological and paleontological point of view, the creation of fossils in sedimentary rocks such as Horenfels stones with high grade metamorphism seems impossible. The second group of Tarik Dareh engravings seems to be zoomorphic types which are mostly shown as a customary rock art in Iran (fig 3). These could be compared with the finding in Dareh Divin and Dareh Morad-Beyk (fig 4, 5 & 6). Their schematic style could at least be seen since 3rd millennium BC. Thus, terms of time and typology in one location seems to be a natural phenomenon.

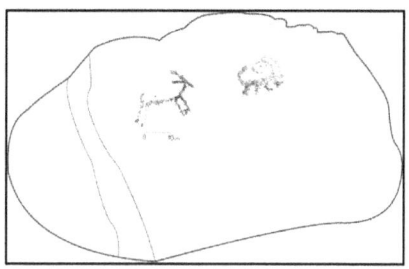 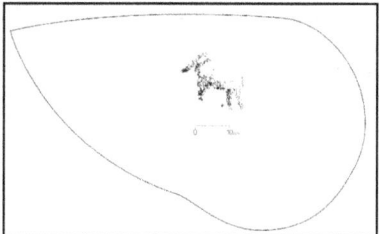 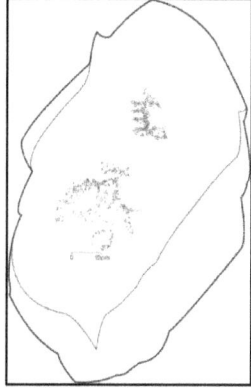

Figure 3: Tarik Dareh, zoomorphs

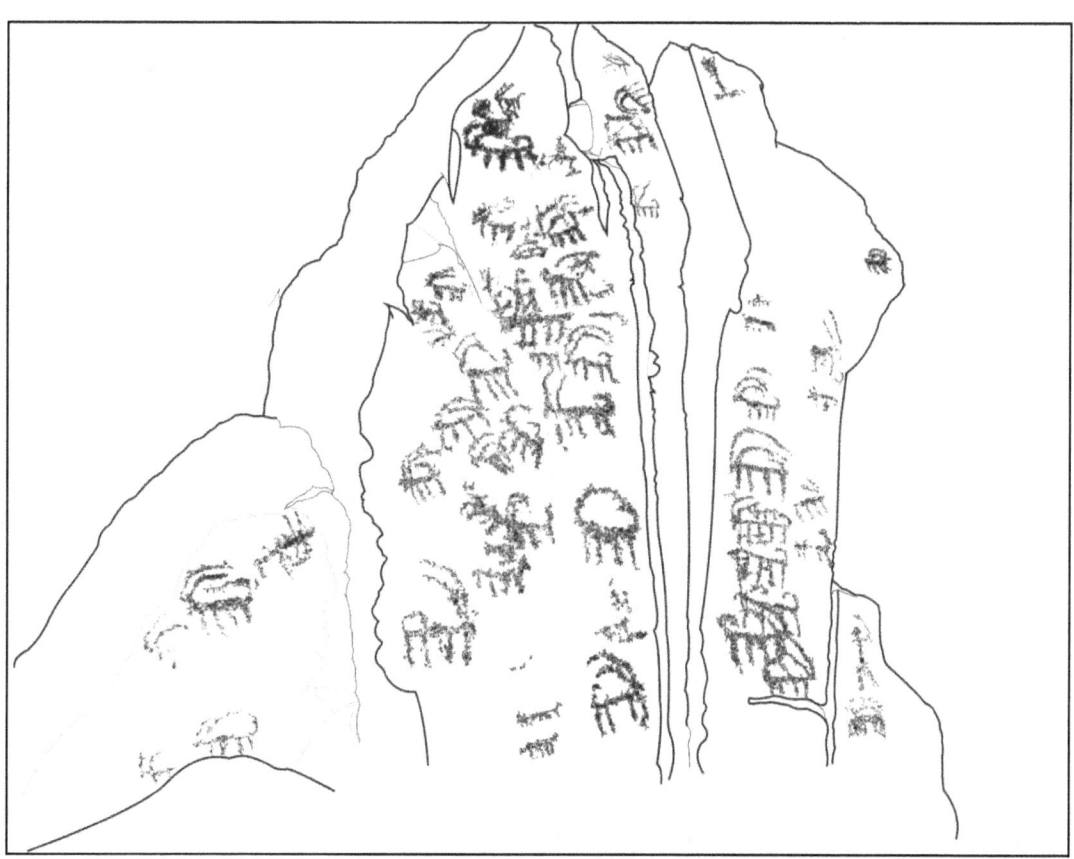

Figure 4: Dareh Divin, Sarraf, 1997, zoomorphs and anthropomorphic

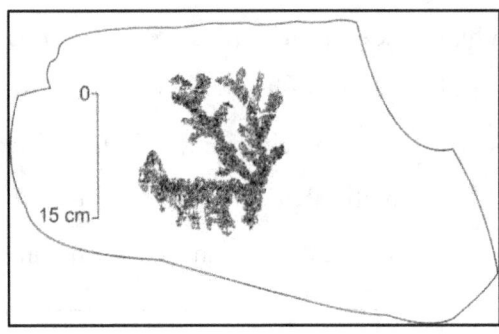

Figure 5: Mazraeye Hajmad, Dareh Morad beyk, zoomorphs

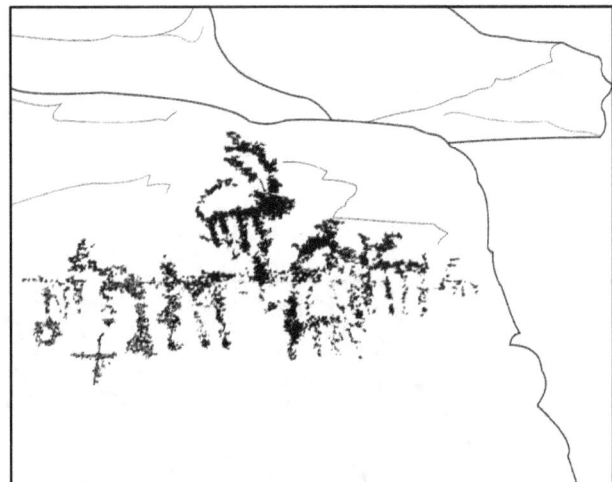

Figure 6: Dareh Morad Beyk, zoomorphs and symbolic

Seasonal camps (semi permanent camp)

More archaeological evidence in Tarik Dareh includes seasonal camps of nomadic communities which are made of fluviatile slabs. These camps were made using the dry stone method and oval shape. Since they are located in isolated locations, they are still remained intact (fig 7). Some of the camps are adjacent to main spring of Tarik Dareh, like the left sample, and, some of them are built on higher levels with larger stones (eg. right sample).

They are different from the modern camps in geometrical plan, utilizing mortar and nich, however, they use the same platform and materials. In some camps which have been used as dwellings, new walls were laid either along the lower rows or were made with a little tilt.

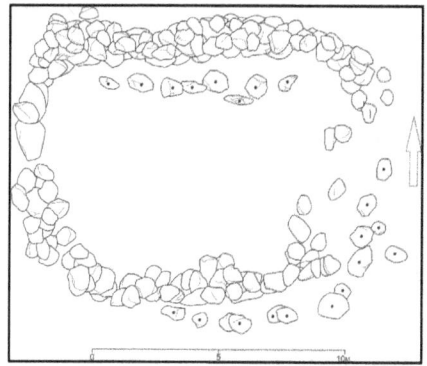 

Figure 7: Tarik Dareh Camps, in some camps which have been used and dwelled, new walls were laid either along the lower rows or were made with a little tilt, (the marked stones belongs to the earliest period).

Nowadays, many camps are put up near the sale centers of Dareh Abasabad. Nomadic pastoralists were dependent on urban and village markets and they continue to play a key role in near east's economy (Betts, 2001, 615- 620). So potshards, textures related to late chalcolithic period and some samples related to Parthian period can clearly show the same continual routine of living style in Tarik Dareh. Additionally, data obtained from potshards and study from the similar seasonal camps in Gave Tapeh (Taj Bakhsh, 2009), show settlers having access to water sources and being close to city dwellers' culture in Ecbatan Parthian period acts as evidence to show the cultural relationship between societies, which had different social structures from the past time to present day.

Pottery

Most of the potteries found in Tarik Dareh probably belong to the Parthian and the chalcolithic (4300–3300 BC) period and can offer a valuable basis for dating second type engravings (fig 8).

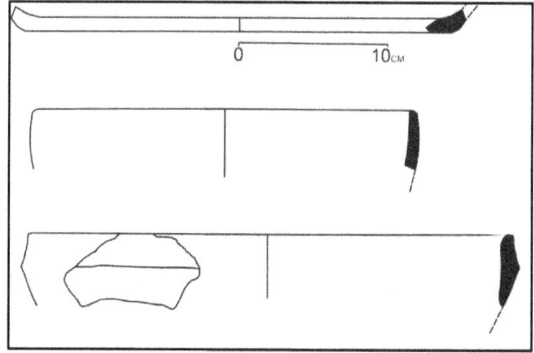 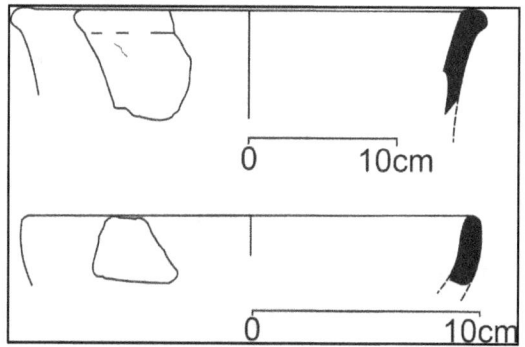

Figure 8: Tarik Darreh, potsherds, (that which is chalcolithic period, left-up).

201

References

1- Ariai. A. & C. Thibault, 1975. Nouvell Precision a propos de L'outillage Paleolithque ancient sur galet de Khorassan (Iran), Paleorient, Vol. 3, 101-108.

2- Asadi, Ali, 2007. Eshkaft-e-Aahou: A Rock Art Shelter in Bastac District, Hormozgan, Bastanpazhuhi, Vol. 2, No. 3, 65-70.

3- Bednarrik, R. G., 1993. "European Palaeolithic art: Typical or exceptional?". Oxford Journal of Archaeology 12(1): 1-8.

4- Bednaik, R. G. 2010. An overview of Asian palaeoart of the Pleistocene, IFRAO Congress, Symposium: Pleistocene art of Asia (Pre-Acts): 1-10.

5- Betts, A.V.G. 2001. Pastoralism. Pp. 615-620 in B. Macdonald, R. Adams and P. Bienkowski (Eds) The Archaeology of Jordan, Sheffield Academic Press

6- Chazine. Jean. C. 2005. Rock Art, Burials, and Habitations: Caves in East Kalimantan, Asian Perspectives, Vol. 44, No. 1 (by the University of Hawai'i Press).

7-Goldhahn, J. 2005. Kosmologiska mantlarstrodda tanker kring hall bilds for skingens primitiva arv och epistemologi Jamte bron salderns kosmologi in situ 2003¬, 9-42.

8- Hauser. Arnold. 1990. The social history of art from prehistory times to the middle age, London, Routledge, p. 8.

9- Rightmire. G. Philip. 2009. PNAS, September 22, vol. 106, no. 38, 16046-16050.

10- Sadek-Kooros, Hind, 1974, Paleolithic culture in Iran, Proceedings of the II nd Annual Symposium on Archaeological Research in Iran, Tehran 1975, F. Bagherzadeh (ed.), Iran Center for archaeological Research, Tehran, 53-56.

11- Sarraf, Mohammad Rahim. 1997. Sang-Negarhaye Dare Divine Alvande Hamadan, gozareshhaye bastanshnasi, Vol. 1, 16-24.

12- Taj Bakhsh. Roya. 2009. The Reporting of didactic excavation Department of Archaeology, the Islamic Azad university of Hamadan Branch in ancient Gav Tape, the Cultural Heritage, Handicrafts and Tourism organization of Hamadan province (not yet published).

13- M. otte, F. Biglari, D.Flas , Shidrang, N. zwyns, M. Mashkour, R. Naderi, A. Mohaseb, N. Hashemi, J. Darvish & V. Radu. 2007. The Aurignacian in the Zagros region: new research at Yahfteh cave, Lorestran, Iran, AntiQuity 81: 82 – 96.

14- Winkelman. Michael. 2004. Shamanism as the original neurotheology, Zygon, vol. 39, no. 1: 193-217.

Part 2: Arts

Hagar Qim Stone Age Megalithic in Malta, photo by Payam Nabarz.

Kephra by Akashanath

Figure 1: *Kephra* by Akashanath.

a. Historical background

It is possible that the once inaccessible nature of the ancient Egyptian religion might have indirectly led to its near ubiquity amongst 20th century occultists. It seems the cultures most remote in time and space are often those most likely to excite the imagination. Like many children of the 1960s, I queued for hours outside the British Museum for the chance to glimpse the death mask of Tutankhamen when it was first brought to this country. My first proper introduction to the gods of ancient Egypt, though, was through the rituals of the Hermetic Order of the Golden Dawn and Aleister Crowley's offshoot, the A∴A∴. During the late 19th century, the occult revival rapidly devoured any esoteric philosophy known to history or fantasy. This often took the form of re-working masonic rituals or degrees to incorporate the symbols of the desired mythos. It is to this class that the early Golden Dawn rituals belong, although they rapidly evolved beyond imitation into something truly original.

The Golden Dawn wasn't the first Order to incorporate Egyptian symbolism into its rituals – the masonic Rite of Misraïm (later reformulated as the Ancient and Primitive Rite of Memphis and Mizraïm) is one example with which the founders of the Golden Dawn would have been well aware. It's an example of what is called 'high grade' masonry; it is 92 rituals being performed sequentially. The rituals, though, were dry and formal, with no obvious intention to transform consciousness. The Golden Dawn, on the other hand, was very aware of the capacity of ritual to genuinely initiate, to raise consciousness to a higher level. Many members of the Golden Dawn, such as the poet W.B. Yeats., were intimate with Theatre, and the Order used a great deal of theatricality to inspire participants in its rituals. But the real secret of the Order was the syllabus of study, initially theoretical and then practical, which 'primed' initiates to ritual symbolism before 'detonating' during the actual event.

The formation of the Golden Dawn in the late 1880s was straddled by two pivotal moments in the development of English Egyptology – the first English translation of the Rosetta Stone in 1858, and Wallis Budge's translation of 'The Book of the Dead' in 1895. The impact of these events on contemporary occultists must have been enormous - finally it would be possible to gain some factual understanding of the great civilisation that stood at the base of the classical world. Samuel Samuel Liddell MacGregor Mathers was a Freemason and co-founder of the Golden Dawn. Like Budge, he spent a great deal of time in the British Museum, though his focus was magickal rather than academic. Some of the later rituals of the Golden Dawn and Crowley's A∴A∴ derive directly from Budge's Book of the Dead, but it's more common to find passages that are merely strongly reminiscent.

b. Ritual

On completing the ceremonial 'Outer' degrees of the Golden Dawn, the initiate has to cross the 'Veil of Paroketh' before beginning her or his instruction as an artisan magician. At this point, he or she may begin to perform rituals to bring about change in the phsyical world, a branch of magick commonly known to modern initiates as 'sorcery'. Magicians achieving these grades could also ask for charters to found their own 'Temples' to carry out the group rituals of the Golden Dawn and it's 'secret' Inner Order, the R.R. et A.C.. Perhaps unsurprisingly people holding these degrees often had ideas of their own, and sometimes preferred to start Temples in their own independent Orders. This eventually led to the factionalism and schism that still dogs the Golden Dawn and its successors, and which coincidentally prevents us from including here the full text of *Liber Resh* (which is, however, freely available on the web).

Cambridge undergraduate and dandy Aleister Crowley was one of the less reputable members of the Golden Dawn's Isis Urania temple in London. Probably because of the l,ow esteem in which he was held there, he had been unable to obtain admission to the Inner Order. So he relocated to Paris and ingratiated himself with the 'Outer Head' of the Order, Mathers. After initially taking Mathers' part in a dispute with his co-founder William Wynn Wescott, Crowley and Mathers fell out badly. A humorous skit based on the magickal battle between them is reproduced in Crowley's novel *Moonchild*. It seemed for a short while as though Crowley had finished with magick altogether, but according to his own (pathologically inaccurate) account, the gods would not let him retire. After eloping to Cairo with a friend's sister, he 'received' three prophetic soliloquies he would later place at the heart of his new magickal system, which he called 'Thelema'. All three Chapters of *The Book of The Law* are shot through with references to the Egyptian gods and their Priests, and the language is strongly evocative of Budge's *Book of the Dead*.

Several years later Crowley founded his own organisation, which he called the *Argentium Astrum* or Silver Star. On the surface of things, Crowley's A∴A∴ could be thought of as an attempt to out-do both the Golden Dawn and the R.R. et A.C. by creating an 'inner inner' order. Whether Crowley's intentions were sincere, sarcastic or both, his output was prolific and sustained. Between 1909 and 1913 he privately published 10 issues of his Journal *The Equinox*. Volume 1 Number 6 contains *Liber Resh vel Helios,* an adoration of the Sun to be performed at sunrise, midday, sunset and midnight. The rubric is very short, and follows the same basic formula at all four times of day. The four rituals are dedicated respectively to four forms of the sun-god, Ra, Ahathoor, Tum and Kephra. The text of the evening adoration reads:

> *Hail unto thee who art Khephra in Thy hiding, even unto Thee who art Khephra in Thy silence, who travellest over the heavens in Thy bark at the Midnight Hour of the Sun.*
> *Tahuti standeth in His splendour at the prow, and Ra-Hoor abideth at the helm.*
> *Hail unto Thee from the Abodes of Evening .*

Crowley has been repeatedly accused of breaking his oath to the G.D. and publishing their rituals in The Equinox, and the second part of the accusation is incontrovertible. However, Crowley's take on ritual magick was innovative and distinct from that of the Golden Dawn in several important ways. The A∴A∴ Motto "The Method of Science, The Aim of Religion" implies a rejection of the hierarchy of magickal 'authority' of the Golden Dawn system, a rejection Crowley makes very explicit in many other places. Instead, the thelemic magician must rely on contact (and eventually unity) with her or his 'True Will'. In common with the Golden Dawn, the A∴A∴ identifies the True Will of the magician with Tiphareth on the Qabalistic Tree of Life, at the mid-point between Kether (supreme godhead) and Malkuth (the physical world). Interestingly, this point is represented by The Sun, and Solar imagery is frequently employed in thelemic rituals associated with making contact with the True Will. *Liber Resh* clearly belongs to this category.

It is likely that *Liber Resh* was written as a 'daily practice' such as modern initiates of the Golden Dawn and its successors are still required to perform for sustained periods during the early stages of their initiation. However, it seemed to come into its own during the 1920s, when Crowley founded his Abbey of Thelema in Sicily (see Chapter XVI of John Symonds' biography, *The Great Beast*). This marked an interesting and important development from the elaborate but occasional Temple rituals of masonry and the early Golden Dawn towards a monastic ethic of total daily immersion.

c. My Image

I've been performing Liber Resh for over 25 years, now, although not on a daily basis. Typically my own adorations of the sun tend to occur at the solstices and equinoxes, often in the company of my Brothers and Sisters of the Morning Sun. Attentive readers will deduce from my earlier reference to King Tut that I must be into my 40s, and may infer that I am at that time of life when the inevitability of death begins to dawn on one. A few years ago I awoke from a lucid dream in which I looked below the kitchen table to see a disproportionately large black beetle clinging to the underside. Though I am not normally phobic of beetles, the sight of this one filled me with nausea and fear. It didn't take me long to work out the symbolism, and only slightly longer to equate this with the midnight sun and the winter solstice. The beetle in the image is loosely stylised on the giant black stone Scarab still housed in the British Museum. The blue sun is the midnight sun, hidden beneath the northern horizon and incapable of shedding light on the physical world, but not the underworld through which the soul must pass (the *Duat*). As it says in *The Book of The Law* "*My colour is black to the blind, but the blue & gold are seen of the seeing. Also I have a secret glory for them that love me.*" The secret relates to the Formula of the Beast as contained in the gnostic Revelation of Saint John. The two tiers of six rays represent the number of Tiphareth (6), and also the first two sixes of 666, the Great Wanedring Beast beneath which all living beings reside. The third is contained in the circle, the three representing the Unity of Body, Spirit and Goldhead (Malkuth, Tiphareth and Kether). 666 is produced by multiplying the number of the Sun (6) with that of Aleph, the first letter of the Hebrew alphabet whose enumeration is 1 (Aleph) or 111 (Aleph=1 + Lamed =30 + Pe =80).

d. Egyptian Magick and the Academy

Whereas the Ancient and Primitive Rite has only fantasy and Greek and medieval Hermetica on which to base itself, Crowley and the G.D. had Budge. Compare the following adoration of Ra from Budge's 1895 version of *The Book of the Dead* with Crowley's *Liber Resh*.

> *"All the beautified dead (Aakhu) in the Tuat receive him in the horizon of Amentt. They shout praises of him in his form of Tem (i.e., the setting sun). Thou didst rise and put on strength, and thou settest, a living being, and thy glories are in Amentt. The gods of Amentt rejoice in thy beauties (or beneficence). The hidden ones worship thee, the aged ones bring thee offerings and protect thee. The Souls of Amentt cry out, and when they meet thy Majesty (Life, Strength, Health be to thee!) they shout 'Hail! Hail!' The lords of the mansions of the Tuat stretch out their hands to thee from their abodes, and they cry to thee, and they follow in thy bright train, and the hearts of the lords of the Tuat rejoice when thou sendest thy light into Amentt."* - From Chapter V, <u>Osiris as Judge of the Dead and King of the Under World</u>

In the intrduction to this passage, Budge mentions '*...Chapter XV, which contains a long Hymn to Rā at his rising, or Amen-Rā, or Rā united to other solar gods, e.g., Horus and Khepera, and a short Hymn to Rā at his setting.*' It is just possible that Crowley had access to Budge's translation of the mysterious Chapter XV, but the experienced occultist was more likely to have garnered the material directly, through ritual or trance. Many occultists cut their magickal teeth by reading (and later reciting) passages from earlier texts – with me it was frequently Crowley's Book of the Law. In his *A History of Prophesy in Israel* (1983), Professor Joseph Blenkinsopp postulates that the same approach was used in the schools from which biblical prophets emerged, explaining the frequent repetition of stanzas or phrases from earlier prophecies in later texts. In my experience ceremonial trance, when it emerges, is usually accompanied by a linguistic shift into the style of the deity or prophet as phrased in the texts with which the magician is familiar.

It is now common for historians or academics to recreate bygone lifestyles as 'experiments', often accompanied by TV crews. The additional insights to be gained by living as the ancients did are usually considered as valid historical investigation so long as they are consistent with the other evidence. In the case of ceremonial magick, though, this approach is problematic. For one thing there is the conflict between the required objectivity of the academic and the impassioned imagination the magician needs to produce a real trance. For their experiments, then, the historians of the ancient world must look to the occultists of today. This is a powerful argument for the necessity of journals such as this.

The mutual advantages are obvious, but not without difficulties and even the occasional paradox. For example, the view of the Egyptian underworld espoused by Budge and absorbed hungrily by Crowley is seen as too simplistic by modern Egyptologists. As one said to me when I told him of my intention to write this piece; 'You know Crowley got it wrong, don't you?'. Well, maybe. But on the other hand, generations of modern magicians have used his rituals to form their own contacts with the gods. And Crowley's grasp of many of the aspects of Egyptian ritual was clearly well ahead of his contemporaries. For example he had a firm grasp of the sexual nature of Egyptian ritual, referring to one of his magical (and sexual) partners as 'The Ape of Thoth', at a time when his academic contemporaries were glossing over the obvious sexual references with typical Victorian prurience (see, for example, the representation of the Chapel of Sokar in the Tomb of Seti I that omits the erect phallus of Osiris). If Crowley had waited for more definitive translations to emerge, he may never have undertaken the rituals that gave us this insight. This dilemma is a real one for all modern occultoists working in ancient traditions who are not themselves academics; we know our own theoretical knowledge must inevitably lag behind academia, but cannot allow that to become a barrier to our actual spiritual practices. These must be given a primary significance, and cannot be validated or invalidated by new translations or excavations.

My own connection with the midnight sun is certainly stronger as a result of my own visions and dreams than it could ever have been if it were totally dependent on academic sources. But at the same time I'm hugely grateful to Budge and his successors both for inspiring my imagination directly and for laying the ground for the 20th century revival of modern Egyptian magick.

Modern Altars by Ana C Jones

Sculptures created by Ana C Jones and used in for modern practise.

Part 3: Religious Articles, Poems, and Stories

Nowruz, Spring Equinox the Persian New Year; a shop in London, photo by Payam Nabarz.

Into The Looking Glass Tragic Reflections of Life by Lesley Madytinou

Prayer to the Muses

Hail, children of Zeus, Grant lovely song and celebrate the holy race of the deathless gods who are for ever.

Hesiod 'Theogeny'

Like no other civilisation, either past or present, the ancient Hellenes institutionalised and refined their expressions and understandings of the ineffable Mystery of the Gods throughout every facet of human life. The Kosmos, the environment and the sophistication of human society all expressed and refined the complex interactions between the Gods of this vast and progressive religion. Humanity existed as a consequence of Divine interaction and had been gifted with the light of Divine Intellect. With all things being full of Gods (1), the interactive relationship between each individual person and the world around them was a visible representation and echo of divine communication. All things moving in accordance with the dance of Love and Strife (2); touching briefly then torn asunder. The fragile mortality of mankind, in eternal motion, was not unlike a small insect in a storm driven by the ancient winds of divine Law. Each life held joy and tragedy that echoed the comic and tragic mythical events of the deathless Gods in their eternal cycle of Creation and Destruction. These mythical feats were expressed in the ancient wisdom of the interconnected nature of action and consequence (3) as a divine deed. This sacred order could also be perceived in the eternal and unchanging qualities of the temporal nature of material existence.

"On those stepping into rivers staying the same other and other waters flow"

Herakleitos (4)

1. Dionysos and the Tragic Goat Song

It must not be forgotten that in Athens the tragedy was a religious ceremony, enacted not so much on the boards as in the soul of the spectators. Stage and audience were enveloped in an extrapoetic atmosphere: religion.

Ortega Y Gasset (5)

The profound understanding of the expressions of the unchanging and the immortal within the changing nature of mortal existence is given form and meaning within human understanding and reason (Logos) through the God of Life, Wine and Theatre; Dionysos, Lord of all living things. Through his sacred Mysteries, Dionysos illustrates the eternal cycle of life (Zoë) that remains unchanging in its central themes or qualities regardless of which specific biographical life (Vios) is being considered. The continuum is greater than any single biography. This motif of the Eternal within the Temporal is simultaneously expressed in the sacred practice of viticulture where the ageless spirit of wine is born from the death of any grape. The Orphics spoke of this Mystery of the immortal essence within mortal existence as the Dionysian spark that animated matter with intelligence and spirit whilst existing entombed within the decaying Titanic nature of the flesh. These reflections on the parallels between mythical motifs, the motions of the Kosmos and nature together with the recurring patterns of human behaviour brought forth the medium of dithyrambs (songs to Dionysos) and its descendent; the theatre. The word theatre derives from the Hellenic *'theatron'* (6) and the verb *'thea'* (view/countenance). This offers the first glimpse (view) of the God Dionysos whose 'mask' or 'countenance' was the *theatron*; a looking glass into the immortal spirit of life. The themes of the theatrical medium illustrate the unchanging essence of life's events that transcend and mark the short-lived nature of each single lifetime. The theatrical themes were performed as portrayals of divine and human deeds that were called Dramas. The word 'Drama' derives from the root word *'drao'* (to act/do/make') and refers as such to an 'action' or 'deed'. This offers the first intellectual understanding of Dionysos behind the mask as not a noun or an object but rather as a verb or an action.

Dionysos begins to sprout according to the conditions of the power which, while young, is hidden beneath the earth, yet produces fine fruits

Porphyry 'On Images' (7)

The late Hellenistic philosopher Porphyry assists this illustration of Dionysos as an active principle through his imagery of sprouting, growth and fruit-bearing. The sprouting and growth may be understood as the 'deed' of a plant whilst the bearing of fruit is symbolic of the consequence of the plants actions. This same pattern was the impetus and inspiration of the art of Tragedy that lay beneath the 'earth' or 'mask' of the exterior theatrical performances. The tragedies are representations of the actions and reactions of its main characters within context to a narrative (usually historical) while the tragic events and climax exemplify the fruits of the protagonists' deeds. The word tragedy derives from '*tragodois*' meaning 'goat song' or 'songs sung by goat-men' (8 & 9) and signifies two central Mysteries of Dionysos.

Firstly, the goat and the child Dionysos are very closely linked in ancient imagery. The goat is the sacrificial substitute for Dionysos in the month of Elaphebolion (10) within the sacred precinct of Dionysos Eleuthereus (the bringer of freedom). The sacrifice of the goat and its relationship to Dionysos embody the revered teaching of the mystical bond between the sacrificer and the sacrifice.

Secondly, the sacrifice of a *tragos* (he-goat) is offered to Dionysos and the vineyard in payment for '*sins against the vine*' (referring to the goat's affinity for grazing upon vines).

> "*Very well, eat my fruit-bearing vines:*
> *The root will still bear enough wine to pour on you when you are sacrificed*"
>
> An epigram by Leonidas of Tarentum (11)

This idea of the death of the goat as the fruits of its erroneous actions or tendencies is central to the primary motif of tragedy within ancient Hellenic theatre. The correlation between the protagonists of a tragedy and the goat seemingly originate from the early goat-skinned choral singers who performed the dithyrambs to Dionysos that preceded the tragic genre.

> *Thus the foundations of tragedy - both in its name and its outer form - were laid in the country and not in the city where the bull sacrifice predominated.*
>
> Dr. Karl Kerenyi - Professor of Classics and the History of Religion

Through the actions of the central characters and by way of the virtues, honour or lives of others that they sacrifice to further their own aims and desires, the tragedy unfolds to reveal that the sacrifices made by the protagonists become the ultimate sacrifice of their own lives or happiness. Accordingly, the sacrificer becomes the sacrificed as punishment for their crimes in whatever form they take and from whichever God they may have offended. Aristotle refers to the plot of a tragedy as its *psyche* (soul) and thus through the soul of the goat song (plot of the tragedy), core Dionysian mysteries are combined into a single fluid medium that expresses simultaneously the true nature of sacrifice and its association with the fruits of actions. An obscure term is still in existence to this day in Greece that refers to a lead actor as the *'megas tragos'* (great goat) in remembrance of this mystic association.

2. The Primal Tragedy

The protagonist of the tragedy through the symbolic title of the 'great goat' thus represents the God and his enemy simultaneously. He is the visual quintessence who symbolises a core spiritual teaching of tragedy. *'Man is his own worst enemy'* and the protagonists demonstrate this truth through the events that support the plot thus illustrating that all action taken is ultimately a deed towards one's own person. This truth about life told via the medium of the Lord of all living things was a central underlying motif within all plots of the ancient tragic genre and formed the basis of the didactic nature of sacred theatre. The Orphics explained the reason for this internal struggle (between man and himself) within each life form through their doctrine concerning the birth and death of the first Dionysos who was the child of Persephone and Chthonian King (12)

And so again came a time when the Lord of the Underworld came upon Kore in the flower of Her maidenhood and descended with Her to the Underworld. There Kore bore the Divine Child called both Dionysos and Iakhos (the Light of God). In Hades, the Lord of the Underworld placed the Holy Kore upon Her throne, where She ruled as Queen and was called upon as Persephone. He placed the Divine Child Iakhos upon His own throne and gave to Him the sceptre of power and proclaimed Him as King. There came a day when the Titans came across the Divine Child King, alone and at play. They gave to Him toys (one of which was a mirror) worthy of Divine Royalty to distract His infant mind. Whilst the young King was busy with His toys, the Titans slew Him and tore His remains into pieces. The Titans consumed their feast except for the kradaios (heart) of the infant God that they had set to one side. It was then that Zeus came upon their festivities and in horror beheld their crime. Enraged, He cast His Lightening upon the Titans until all that remained of them was a sublimated vapour from which ash emerged. From this soot came the substance from which earthly life derived. When this form of life arose it was twofold in nature. One part was made from the remains of the Titans and subject to wickedness and decay. The other part was the Divine body of Dionysos that had been consumed by the Titans before their punishment. This part was heavenly and indestructible. (13)

The mythological pattern of the birth of the Divine Child was the original, although not exclusive, theme of the choral songs *(dithyrambs)* sung to Dionysos. From the genre of the *dithyramb* developed Tragedy and the songs of birth became the tragedies that echoed as reverberations of the primal tragedy; the death and *sparagmos* (rending) of the first Dionysos. The usage of the word 'rend' offers the vital clue to understanding the Divine and mythological seed from which tragedy sprouted and blossomed, both in the suffering of real life and in its reflective medium of the theatre. To rend has a two-fold meaning; to tear apart as well as to distress through grief and despair (14). This dual meaning perfectly illustrates the parallel between the mythical dismemberment of Dionysos together with the grief and despair of theatrical tragedies. This emotional rending was again two-fold. The actions (drama) and words (Logoi) of the actors gave external form to the internal nature of suffering while at the same time emotional responses were evoked from the soul of the spectators engaged directly with the soul (plot) of the tragedy. This union of souls expresses the interactive communion between the spectator/actor with the essence of life and its source; the Lord of all things living. The Orphics represented this mystical reflective medium as the hand mirror gifted to the Divine Child King by the Titans to distract his attention prior to the death by rending. This mirror was believed to have caught the soul of Dionysos and ensured his rebirth. The mythological pattern again is paralleled within the tragic genre of theatre. The emotions of the tragedy reflect images of real life suffering that is common to all humanity at any place or time in history thus illustrating the immortal nature of pure emotion that transcends individual chemical and biographical life and exists beyond death through the continuum of life as a whole. Yet this symbolic mirror affords an even deeper enquiry into the power of the theatrical medium as not only that which acts as a looking glass for life but also that which captures the soul of the spectator and binds it in communion with the soul of Dionysos through identification, empathy and sympathy with heroes and heroines who give form and expression to the plot of a tragedy.

Through this soul communion the spectator is thus afforded the experience of death by emotional rending and purification of their soul through its cathartic effect. This rending by emotions is simultaneously portrayed by the actors and experienced by the soul of the spectators. The rending unfolds along with the plot as the pain and guilt of the protagonists are revealed in full bloom resulting in an emotional split within the spectator between a joyful anticipation of impending justice as well as a compassion for human suffering when the day of retribution arrives. The spectator is further torn asunder by the fearful knowledge that the actions of the protagonist have been the seed of their own destruction and that a single crime or act of *hubris* (overweening pride and arrogance) can set into action a chain of tragic consequences and further crimes for others who are simultaneously innocent victims of the first tragedy and perpetrators of further tragedies from their own reactions.

The Orphics taught that the source of human suffering was the Titanic crime against the First Dionysos and his death by dismemberment. As a consequence of this primal tragedy, the emotions of the life forms that arose from the death of Dionysos would eternally echo the rending of the Divine Child. The two-fold nature of life would thus be bound in the internal struggle to defeat the predator within that sabotages and sows the seeds of self-destruction. This self-defeating nature prone to decay through its destructive essence was capable of all forms of crime, misdeed and *hubris*. In remembrance of the original crime, this mortal aspect of humanity is called the Titanic nature. The spark of the Divine Child that was consumed by the Titans is called the Dionysian nature and exists simultaneously within all life forms as the immortal and creative essence of life. Human and animal nature is thus ever bound by the tension of opposites between the destructive Titanic and the creative Dionysian natures. Creative and destructive forces are in turn moved by Love and Strife. This universal and mythical motif is echoed in the events that form a part of the plot but are not acted out by the protagonists on the stage during the tragedies (15). These off-stage events are motivated by the Prime Movers of Love and Strife in all its forms and sensibilities. This places human nature firmly in a square of opposition between two central universal dualities: Love/Strife and Creation/Destruction. The agents of the rending on the universal, mythical and human levels are thus revealed and the source of suffering disclosed. The tragedies of theatre capture and reflect the soul of this essential conflict that exists within all living things. The square of opposition thus forms the basic framework of any tragedy, both real and theatrical, and displays the core motivations arising from the central internal and external conflict of all protagonists. Through the tragic portrayal of the pure emotions deriving from configurations of the square of opposition within the tragedy, the spectators gain sensibility of the Prime Movers of the Universe as the cause and effect of life in all its aspects.

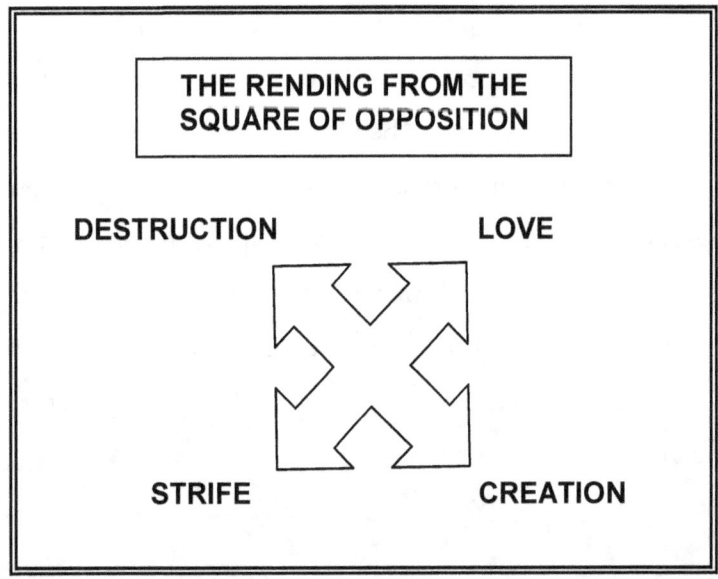

Torn between love and strife while seeking to create or destroy, the protagonists of the tragedy portray the highest and purest form of the Prime Movers that are only sensible to humanity through the emotions that drive them. Thus the soul of the tragedy and the spectator are joined though the reflection of that which is eternal and common to all; the essential emotions to love, to fight, to make and to break. The actor through their portrayal calls forth the essential emotions within both themselves in order to perform and within the spectator in order to watch. The Titanic and Dionysian nature are torn asunder and reduced to the most primal elements of the primordial tragedy. Swept up in the emotions of the tragic protagonists, the spectator recalls the most primitive urges deep within and weeps real tears as the soul of the tragedy performs its greatest deed. For the looking glass of the theatre that is held up to reveal the soul of the tragedy has but one essential function; to evoke this reflective quality (mirror) within the soul of the spectator. As the spectator finds their emotions mirroring (through empathy or reversal) the reactions of the protagonists and sees themselves reflected within the tragic characters and events; reality and illusion unite within a primal truth and the spectator and the protagonist breathe and feel as one being. The spectators and actors, united in eternal nature and yet separated by material form, are thus the perfect vision of the dismembered Dionysos, the tragic victim of the primal tragedy.

3. Rebirth after Rending: Catharsis and Renewal

The very act of living and experiencing life within a society or civilisation dictated to by moral and emotional principles of restraint will cause repressive and dissociative tendencies within its people. Very few communities offer adequate outlets for the negative energies that build up as a natural consequence of living. To purge one of these negative energies was considered purifying and renewing all at once. The Orphics believed that the creative Dionysian nature could be nurtured through the purification of the soul. Theatre with its tragedies offered the purification of the emotions through the catharsis (16) of the soul. The method was simple. A soul enmeshed in tragedy could be purged through the evocation of the primal emotions and through the positive direction of their purgation, the self-destructive impulses would be minimised within the reality of their everyday life. In general terms, catharsis is the means by which emotional tension may be redirected from introverted self-absorption into an out-flowing (e)motion that causes release from tension and renews the spirit at the same time. This cathartic effect expresses one of the reasons why Dionysos was called the Redeeming God (17). The cathartic power of tragic theatre is the acknowledgement of the vehicle of renewal and rebirth being found within the heart. The heart within this context is symbolic and has a threefold meaning. Firstly, the heart is the symbolic seat of the emotions; secondly, the heart or core of a matter indicates the cause of behaviour and thirdly as a colloquial Hellenic pun referring to the phallus as the heart and thus the conduit for the seed of rebirth. The heart is a key symbol in the myth of the dismemberment of the first Dionysos as it is the organ that survives the Titanic consumption. Zeus makes a potion from this heart that he gives to Semele, the second mother of Dionysos, to impregnate her. Thus is born the second Dionysos, God of the Vine, who lives on past the death of the grape in the spirit of the Wine. As the dismembered God, he redeems through the cathartic properties of suffering and from the preservation of the heart the seeds of rebirth are sewn to ensure that what the Titanic nature may destroy, the Dionysian will surely resurrect. This is the mythical analogy for the human instinct to persevere, endure and live on past the horrors of being pulled apart emotionally by death, fear, suffering and pain. It is also a reminder not to lose heart in the face of despair or to allow one's heart to grow cold with bitterness. The heart bears the seed of renewal and if the germ of bitterness and vengeance are planted then only further tragedy may unfold.

4. The Didactic Art of the Redeeming God

'We poets make men better citizens'

Aristophanes (18)

Tragedy made the insensible sensible and gave both form and order to the apparently chaotic causes and effects of human nature and suffering. By means of tragic representation, the poet (playwright in modern terminology) could impart significance to affliction and by giving structure to intense emotional states could facilitate conscious awareness of the incomprehensible. The misfortunes of life could be more easily understood by the mind cultivated in the art of Tragedy and the highly moral nature of the medium allowed for a thorough exploration of both virtue and vice. The development of tragic theatre as a poetic portrayal within religious festivals was directly related to a progressive refinement of its ability to educate at the same time as entertain. This form of recreational edification is called the Didactic Art and was utilised in a highly sophisticated and symbolic manner in sacred theatre to illustrate the tragic consequences of the innate tendencies of human nature. As such the Didactic Art within Tragedy became a form of moral and ethical guidance for its spectators as the means by which coherence of emotions, thought and meaning could be achieved. This alignment between the intellect, the emotions and the spiritual principles of the religion within the spectator was an important factor within the works of the master poet who would often illustrate through the characters of his plays, the tragic consequences of what may happen if the intellect, emotions and actions of a hero are in state of disarray. The tragic work, composed from the structured sequencing of events and characters together with the dramatic standards of performance, would thus enable the poet to direct the sensibilities of the spectator to extend beyond the limits of individual life experience (19) and into the pool of central wisdom. The basic elements of the Didactic Art within theatrical tragedy reveal the tools of the poet and the framework with which the ancient spectator could look deep within this reflective pool of life experience and human memory.

a. The Standard Language of Theatre

The ancient poet was first and foremost an observer of life. Through the objective perspectives that distance offers, the poet could stage this mirror reflection of life within the theatrical medium. By means of the employment of certain measured techniques within the development of tragic theatre, a standard 'language' was developed that gives the spectator the correct context with which to 'view' the work of the poet and the portrayal of the tragedy. The refinement of this standard and symbolic theatrical language enabled the poet to write his work on many levels simultaneously.

Each year the State would commission the great poets of the time to write a trilogy of Tragedy and a single Satire to be performed at the Greater and Lesser Dionysia. The trilogy was in fact a Tragedy in three parts that would trace the chain of consequences set off by the original tragic protagonists through the generations or years that followed the first event. Many of these tragic events mirrored aspects of either the primal tragedy or other mythical/historical tragedies. This continuum of protagonists and events that spanned generations illustrated perfectly the adage that *'this year's harvest is a product of last year's sun'*. The Didactic nature of tragedy reflected both the rituals of the real world and acted as a medium for dramatic representations of many ancient Hellenic maxims all at once. The drama (actions) of a trilogy would follow a particular pattern or set standard to enable the spectator to not be distracted by the 'blood' of a deed but rather to concentrate on the 'tears' resulting from the action. Thus the poet would direct the spectators' attention to the 'fruits' of the events to illustrate that the core of the tragedy was not the deed itself but the consequences and effects thereof. By the means of this standard, the spectator knew what to expect on the most basic level and thus the subtleties of the cycle of action, reaction and reactive actions became more easily apparent. This enabled tragedy to develop into a highly sophisticated and cultivated didactic medium. The costumes, masks, skenes (scenery), gestures, diction and staging were all standardised and stylised to allow even the slightest difference to have a profound effect on the spectator. The very real emotions portrayed within the unrealistic appearances of the masked actors offered a glimpse into the surreal quality of real life tragedy. The true action in any tragic event is what happens beneath the masks of appearances and the theatrical medium symbolised this perfectly. The aim of the poet was to appeal to the soul of the spectator (Dionysian nature) through the spirit, intellect and emotions and not to the Titanic nature through the sensory perception of appearances. This marks the central distinction between the art of sacred theatre and the performance art of modern stage and screen.

b. The Basic Elements of Tragedy

One of the central means by which the spectator was educated at the same time as being entertained was through the basic elements of tragedy as a whole. The first and most obvious of these elements is **Rhesis** (20) referring to a declaration or statement made a protagonist in a tragedy. Rhesis is both a tool of character and plot development for a poet as well as the means by which new ideas or opinions concerning the state of government or humanity may be proposed to the spectator within a contextual setting. Bearing in mind that these tragedies were watched by all leaders and politicians, the Rhesis of a tragedy was an extremely powerful poetic tool that appealed to the intellect of the audience.

The second element appealed to the spectator on a more human level and was called the **Monody**. The Monody refers to the lament within a tragedy that expresses grievous regret usually over a death that occurs. In the strange ironic language of the theatre the lament is almost always a call for the spectator to live without regret by illustrating the tragic effects of remorse once irrevocable change has taken place. Remorse is central to any tragedy as the hero or heroine exemplifies the tragic genre through the lamentation of their regrets.

The regret expressed in the Monody is simultaneously recognition and this refers directly to the third element of tragedy: **Anagnorisis.** The concept of Anagnorisis is one of recognition or discovery (21) and refers to the protagonist's moment of awareness of their true nature as well as the simultaneous acknowledgement of the reality of a situation. Aristotle defines Anagnorisis as *'a change from ignorance to knowledge, producing love or hate between the persons destined for good or bad fortune.'* As the hero or heroine throws themselves down in the lamentation of the Monody, they experience Anagnorisis and will arise either as Elektra or Orestes over the body of their father Agamemnon in the spirit of revenge or in the defeated futility of Andromache as her son is taken from her. On the rare occasion, a tragic figure will arise who acknowledges utterly the power of the Fates and the importance of the tragic event within the larger scheme of life and history. Such is the heroine Iphigenia, daughter of Agamemnon, who must walk freely to be sacrificed on the altar of Artemis or be dragged by the assembled armies. Her recognition and total acceptance of her Fate combined with her willingness to be sacrificed elevates her beyond the purely tragic figure of her mother Clytemnestra who blames and slays her husband Agamemnon in an act of pure vengeance. Thus arises Elektra and Orestes from lamenting over the body of their father and they, in turn, will illustrate the consequences of harvesting fruits that have grown from the seeds of vengeance and will murder their mother Clytemnestra in cold blood. The tragic fruits of vengeance sow their seeds for many a generation and all actions are ultimately cyclic in nature; ever seeking the point of origin yet rippling through life like a drop of water in a calm pool echoing the primal tragedy.

The fourth element of tragedy is very closely related to the Anagnorisis and the resolve by which the tragic hero or heroine arise from their Monody. The ancient concept of **Agon** (22) is central to not only tragedy but also to all forms of competition or conflict. Agon is used generally to denote a contest of any type but may be interpretated to denote the indirect challenge inherent within any act of competition or conflict. How the hero or heroine chooses to meet the challenge of any tragic event, as defined by their Anagnorisis, is indicative of the outcome of the internal conflict between their Titanic and Dionysian natures in the moment of lamentation. Some heroes are defeated at the beginning while others will rise to the challenge in different manners. This is the means by which the poet may appeal to the spirit of the spectator. Agon as a concept is inseparable from Arête (referring to virtue as a principle of personal excellence) and thus the ideal manner in which to meet the challenge of the tragic Agon is through virtuous reaction. By the tendencies inherent within their own natures, the tragic heroes fall short of this ideal as all humans do on occasion. But the utter humanity of the hero complete with all the failings is the truly didactic nature of the tragic protagonist as a model of the tragic consequences that may result from fated misfortune, lack of virtue or from well meaning actions gone awry. Actions based upon virtuous principles but lacking in clarity, reason or the accurate assessment of a situation are often the means by which the protagonists meet their tragic ends. This twist in the plot of the tragedy illustrates admirably that excessive or defective virtue may cause great harm and life is often not very clearly delineated in the definition of right or wrong action within any situation. Many tragic protagonists must face the dilemma of choosing between the lesser or greater evil. Loss is inevitable in Agon and thus the hero in any contest or conflict must face the choice of minimising the harm or following the path of least resistance regardless of the outcome. This choice is the turning point of the tragedy; the Peripeteia that leads to either good or bad fortune for the protagonist.

The Agon of the tragedy will almost always be associated with the fifth element of tragic theatre; the **Peripeteia** referring to a 'reversal' that is best explained by Aristotle (23):

"A change by which the action veers round to its opposite, subject always to our rule of probability or necessity"

Peripeteia was, in the opinion of Aristotle, the most powerful element of tragedy because it revealed a change from one state of being to its opposite state. The living die; the virtuous man acts with vice; joys becomes suffering; poverty befalls the wealthy, love may turn to hate and vengeance just may change into mercy. The Peripeteia of a tragedy was the poetic tool to illustrate the changeability of life's circumstances and thus the true instability of any condition or state of being. The tragic portrayal of human fragility inspires both fear and pity within the spectator. The reversal is yet another manifestation of theatrical mirroring. The eyes of the spectator that find their reflection within the looking glass will always see a reversal of their own image. Left becomes right and right becomes left. The Peripeteia gives this mirror reversal both form and meaning within context to the character development of the protagonist and the plot of the tragedy. Life and fortune can change in a less than a minute and the master poet cautions the spectator not to be complacent.

It is not easy to acknowledge and accept how frail life and humanity really is or how inescapable and irrevocable the power of the Fates and the Gods may be. However, to not recognise this truth of life and believe oneself to be invulnerable to the law of the Gods illustrates one aspect of the sixth element of tragedy; **Hamartia.** Each tragic protagonist has a fatal tendency that burdens and creates bias within their own natures that leads ultimately to a terrible mistake or error in judgement (24). The term Hamartia includes both innate behavioural tendency and any resulting error in judgement within its concept although Aristotle mostly used the word to describe flawed actions or unethical behaviour. Hamartia may take many different forms within the complex personality of a tragic hero as may be illustrated through Oedipus whose Hamartia was simultaneously his hasty and rash temperament (innate) as well as his lack of knowledge of his true parentage through no fault of his own that causes him to unwittingly slay his own father and marry his mother. This sense of Hamartia as being a failing that occurs beyond the power of human control is a crucial element within tragedy. Within ancient Hellas, the power of the

Moirae (Fates) was indisputable and utterly complete. The Fate of a protagonist is tragic only because essentially they are virtuous within their nature before and after the calamity strikes. The protagonist's feelings of anger and revenge seem very just within their own minds. Yet due to the combination of the hero's Hamartia that is both fated and innate, the Peripeteia of the tragedy externalises the challenge of the Agon. Sadly, objectivity and reason are greatly diminished in times of personal crisis and thus the resolve of the protagonist is often founded upon biased opinion and subjective truth. The turning point of the tragic hero is more often than not a path that leads to greater misfortune. The spectator must then watch in horror as the hero, who thoroughly believes in their own virtue and vision of justice, sows the seeds of their own destruction to bear the fruits of their own defeat.

The innate tendencies and errors in judgement that may be defined as Hamartia within the genre of tragic heroes and heroines are closely related to the concept of **Hubris**, the seventh and final basic element of tragedy. The greatest error in ancient Hellas was the act of Hubris and in Athens was considered a crime. Hubris refers to any act where a victim is humiliated or shamed so as to make the offender look superior.

Hubris is to cause shame to the victim, not in order that anything may happen to you, nor because anything has happened to you, but merely for your own gratification. Hubris is not the requital of past injuries; this is revenge. As for the pleasure in hubris, its cause is this: men think that by ill-treating others they make their own superiority the greater. Aristotle (25)

A perfect example of Hubris is the action of Achilles in Homer's Iliad when he mistreats the corpse of Hektor (26). Any act based on self-confidence and pride that humiliated a defeated foe was deemed Hubris as was any mortal who believed themselves to be above the Gods and Divine Law considered being guilty of Hubris. An example is found in the tragedy Hippolytus where Aphrodite is offended by Hippolytus' rejection of Phaedra's love in an act that ultimately leads to the death of the tragic hero (27). Another illustration of Hubris against the Gods may be found in the tragedy named the Bacchantes where the protagonist Pentheus refuses to honour Dionysos and is killed by the God's followers (28). The excessive pride and arrogance of Hubris reveals a deeper understanding of the elements of Agon and Hamartia within context to the tragic medium. The innate pride or self-confidence within the tragic protagonist may more accurately be defined as their Hamartia or the result of their Hamartia. When this Hamartia is externalised into an action, it becomes Hubris. Furthermore, through the act of Hubris the unseen and as yet unmentioned challenger within the Agon is unveiled. For the destruction or virtuous ruin of the protagonist is called more commonly their *Nemesis*. This mythical parallel illustrates the jurisdiction of the Goddess Nemesis, sister to Themis (Natural Law) and mother to the Erinyes (the Furies) who is present each time law is absent. Thus the destruction of the tragic protagonist is truly their fall from the state of virtue and justice that they regard so highly. Once the protagonist has encountered their internal *Nemesis*, their defeat is absolute. Through the Peripeteia (reversal) of Law into Lawlessness, the tragic hero will become what they themselves despise and the circle will be complete. The seed has been sown and the bitter fruits harvested.

Conclusion

The Redeeming Dionysos of Tragedy is a mirror reversal of the more light-hearted Dionysos commonly known only as the drunken God of Wine. In communing with the soul of the Goat-Song, the spectator sees a far more serious side of the God than his accompanying satyrs and nymphs may indicate at first glance. The ecstasy is also agony and the flowing wine is also blood. The mirroring is complete and has unveiled the flesh that exists beneath the mask of appearances. The reflective medium of theatre has revealed the eternal nature of Tragedy that is present in the temporal nature of tragic events. Reality has been exposed from deep within the hidden nature of illusion. The opposites are reconciled and yet from the irrevocable tragedy of the protagonist's *nemesis*, the light of rebirth and renewal shines. The spectator walks away from the theatre unscathed. As the observer of impersonal events, they have been purified by the intensity of pure emotion and have been afforded a new perspective on emotional issues that may only be experienced from a distance. The seed of a new and better way of life has been planted and it is the hope of the tragic poet that the spectator will drink deeply from the pool of human wisdom to nourish and nurture their Dionysian spark. The mirror that shone so brightly is now an inner light that may or may not illuminate the footsteps of the spectator as they make their way back to the ordinary world.

> *"...whose end, both at the first and now, was and is to hold the mirror up to nature; to show virtue her own feature, scorn her own image, and the very age and body of the time his form and pressure..."*
>
> [Hamlet Act III; Scene II] (29)

Prayer to the Muses

'Thanks be to the sweet-voiced Muses of Olympus, daughters of Zeus and Mnemosyne, for the nourishing of souls and the bestowal of reason'

References and Notes:

1. Thales of Miletus: Pre-Socratic philosopher (624-546 B.C.E) considered one of the seven Sages of ancient Greece.

2. Empedocles of Acragas (490-430 B.C.E.)

3. Thomas R. Martin: An Overview of Classical Greek History from Mycenae to Alexander

4. The philosophy of all things being in flux originates from Herakleitos, the Pre-Socratic philosopher. Plato (Cratylus) explains the doctrine of flux: "Heraclitus, I believe, says that all things go and nothing stays, and comparing existents to the flow of a river, he says you could not step twice into the same river"

5. Jose Ortega y Gasset: Meditaciones del Quijote

6. All references to the meaning and roots of Hellenic words are taken from 'The Analytical Dictionary of Ancient Greek' by Makarios P. Pelekes

7. Porphyry 'On Images' translated by Edwin Hamilton Gifford

8. Professor Brian Leahy Doyle: 'A study guide for Sophocles' Antigone'

9. Jane Ellen Harrison Westport: Ancient Art and Ritual

10. Dr K.Kerenyi: 'Dionysos; an Archetypal Image of Indestructible Life'

11. Varo: 'De Rustica'; Leonidas 'Anthologia Palatina; Eunos 'Anthologia Palatina' (excerpt translated by K. Kerenyi from 'Dionysos; An Archetypal Image of Indestructible Life')

12. Dr K. Kerenyi: The Gods of the Greeks

13. Reconstructed by M & L Madytinos from various Orphic fragments taken from K. Kerenyi's 'Gods of the Greeks'; 'Dionysos' and 'Eleusis'; WKC Guthrie's Orpheus and the Greek Religion and GRS Mead's 'Orpheus'. The names of all the toys have not been given in this version of the myth.

14. Funk & Wagnalls 'Standard Dictionary' Volume II

15. All battles, love scenes and actual deaths were not portrayed on stage in Greek Tragedies and were only sung about by the chorus or narrated by the Nuntius (narrator).

16. Aristotle: Poetics (translation by SH Butcher)

17. Orphic Hymn No 50 to Lysios Lenaios (Dionysos at the festival of Lenaia) refers to Dionysos as 'the many-named redeeming God' - Orphic Hymn translated by M Madytinos.

18. Aristophanes: 'Frogs' (405 B.C.E)

19. Oliver Taplin (Lecturer in Greek and Latin at Oxford University): 'Greek Tragedy in Action'

20. Sebastiana Nervegna's review of Simonetta Grandolini (ed), *Lirica e Teatro in Grecia. Il Testo e la sua ricezione. Atti del II incontro di Studi. Perugia, 23-24 gennaio 2003*

21. Northrop Frye: "Myth, Fiction and Displacement" p 25 *Fables of Identity: Studies in Poetic Mythology*

22. Joel Trapido (1949) The Language of the Theatre: I. The Greeks and Romans: Educational Theatre Journal, Vol. 1, No. 1 (Oct., 1949), pp. 18-26 doi: 10.2307/3204106

23. Aristotle: Poetics. Trans. Ingram Bywater. New York: The Modern Library College Editions, 1984.

24. Aristotle. *Nicomachean Ethics*. V.8 1135b12-20

25. Douglas MacDowell: "*Hybris* in Athens." *Greece and Rome* 23 (1976) 14-31.

26. Homer's Iliad, translated by Richard Lattimore

27. Euripides' Hippolytus (also called Hippolytus Unveiled)

28. Euripides' The Bacchantes (also called the Bacchae)

29. William Shakespeare: Hamlet

Bibliography

1. Michael R. Deschenes: The Heart of the Matter: Gods, Grief and Freedom in Aeschylus' Oresteia

2. Dr. Larry A. Brown (Professor of Theatre): Aristotle on Greek Tragedy

3. Michael Best: *Shakespeare's Life and Times*. Internet Shakespeare Editions, University of Victoria: Victoria, BC, 2001-2005.

4. C. Hemingway: Theatre of Ancient Greece (from the Metropolitan Museum of Art)

5. Mark Griffith: Slaves of Dionysos; Satyrs, Audience and the ends of Oresteia.

Solomon in Olympus: The Enduring Connection between King Solomon and Greek Magic by David Rankine

(www.ritualmagick.co.uk)

The connection between King Solomon, the most famous of biblical magicians, and Greek magic, is an enduring one which emphasises the cross-fertilisation of Jewish and Greek magic over the centuries from the ancient world through to the Middle Ages. Three texts spanning around 1700 years particularly exemplify this connection, these being the *Greek Magical Papyri* (C2nd BCE – C5th CE), the *Testament of Solomon* (C2nd CE), and the *Hygromanteia* (C15th CE)

The Greek Magical Papyri

The *Greek Magical Papyri* is a fine illustration of the incorporation of Jewish magical ideas and material into Greek practices in the ancient world. In addition to the use of Hebrew divine names such as Adonai ('Lord') and Sabaoth ('Hosts'), Solomon himself made appearances in some of the charms.

The charm called *'Solomon's Collapse'*[334] emphasises the magical powers associated with Solomon in the PGM. The charm is used to produce a trance in an adult or boy, and the formula is preceded by an oath *"not to share the procedure of Solomon with anyone and certainly not to use it for something questionable"*.

A charm for favour gives an intriguing reference to the eyes of Solomon as part of a list of qualities associated with gods, elevating his status, thus, *"the eyes of Solomon, the voice of Abrasax, the grace of Adonios, the god."*[335] The reference may also be translated as *'glances of Solomon'*, but in either instance the power of sight associated with Solomon is clear.

In three charms against the scorpions of Artemis the name used was a variant of Solomon, i.e. Salaman, and the same Hebrew divine names were used as seen in many other charms, i.e. Adonai and Sabaoth:[336]

> *"Or Or Phor Phor Iao Adaonaei Sabaoth Salaman Tarchchei, I bind you, scorpion of Artemisos, on the 13th."*[337]

---

[334] PGM IV.850-929, trans. W.C. Grese.
[335] PGM XCII.1-16, trans R. Kotansky.
[336] PGM XXVIIIa.1-7, PGM XXVIIIb.1-9, PGM XXVIIIc.1-11, trans. R. Kotansky.
[337] PGM XXVIIIb.1-9, trans. R. Kotansky.

Scorpions were associated with the huntress goddess Artemis through the myth of Orion's death, with the earth goddess Gaea sending a scorpion to kill Orion after he claimed he would kill all the beasts of the earth. This was a well-known association, as seen in references such as *"the Scorpion the helper of Artemis"*[338] by the theologian Tatian the Assyrian (C2nd CE).

A partial charm which is largely lost *For those possessed by daimons*[339] includes the name of Solomon in the fragment *"Atr ... Y Solomon ... is washed"*. The combination of possession and washing clearly recalls the writings of the Jewish antiquarian Flavius Josephus (37-100 CE) in *Antiquities of the Jews*:

> *"(47) He put a ring that had a root of one of those sorts mentioned by Solomon to the nostrils of the demoniac [the possessed man], after which he drew out the demon through his nostrils; and when the man fell down immediately, he abjured him [the demon] to return into him [the possessed man] no more, making still [further] mention of Solomon, and reciting the incantations which he [Solomon] composed. (48) And when Eleazar would persuade and demonstrate to the spectators that he had such a power, he set a little way off a cup or basin full of water, and commanded the demon, as he went out of the man, to overturn it, and thereby to let the spectators know that he had left the man;"*[340]

The Testament of Solomon

Another cross-over between Solomon and Greek magic is in the Jewish magical text, the *Testament of Solomon* (C2nd CE). The *Testament of Solomon* was arguably the first proto-grimoire, giving a catalogue of demons with their controlling angels. In the *Testament of Solomon* the third and fourth Ephesian Letters, *Lix Tetrax*, were used as the name of a wind demon:

> *"But [the demon] answered me: 'I am the spirit of the ashes (Tephras or Lix Tetrax).'"*[341]

The Ephesian Letters (*askion, kataskion, lix, tetrax, damnameneus* and *aision* (or *aisia*))[342] are first mentioned in the fifth century BCE in a Mycenaean inscription[343] and first listed in a lead *defixiones* tablet from Himera (C5th BCE)[344] and an inscribed lead tablet from Phalasarna (C4th BCE).[345]

---

[338] *Address to the Greeks*, Tatian, C2nd CE, trans. J.E. Ryland.
[339] PGM XCIV.17-21, trans. R. Kotansky.
[340] *Antiquities of the Jews*, Josephus, Book 8 Chapter 2:5, verse 42-49, trans. W. Whiston.
[341] *Testament of Solomon* 33, C2nd CE, trans. F.C. Conybeare.
[342] For more on the Ephesian Letters and other voces magicae, see *Hekate Liminal Rites*, d'Este & Rankine, 2009:65-67.
[343] Stone inscription, Mycenae, late C5th BCE, trans. Jeffery.
[344] *Ephesia Grammata at Himera*, Jordan, 2000.
[345] *The Inscribed Lead Tablet from Phalasarna*, Jordan, 1992.

Additionally there was also reference in the *Testament of Solomon* to the *'bonds of Artemis'* in connection with an unnamed demon, the last of a group of seven female spirits who may have corresponded to the star system of the Pleiades. As the demon said she brought darkness, we can speculate she would have corresponded to the sister called Celaeno, whose name meant *black* or *dark*.

As Orion was a companion of Artemis who chased the Pleiades for seven years, the biblical reference in the *Book of Job* connecting the Pleiades and bands/bonds does suggest a connection for this verse in the *Testament of Solomon*:

"*Canst thou bind the sweet influences of Pleiades, or loose the bands of Orion?*"[346]

Significantly this spirit's threat was the one out of all those made by the demons which was achieved. For the reference to the locus referred to the subsequent sacrifice of five locusts to Moloch committed by Solomon to gain the sexual favours of the Queen of Sheba, resulting in the loss of his powers:

"*Likewise also the seventh said: 'I am the worst, and I make thee worse off than thou wast; because I will impose the bonds of Artemis. But the locust will set me free, for by means thereof is it fated that thou shalt achieve my desire <...> For if one were wise, he would not turn his steps toward me.*"[347]

The Hygromanteia

There are at least twenty manuscript versions of the *Hygromanteia*, dating from the period C15th-C19th CE. Several of these manuscripts were significantly bound with copies of the *Testament of Solomon*, and most are introduced by a passage where Solomon addresses his son Rehoboam, establishing his connection to the material.

The fullest versions of this manuscript, such as Harley MS 5596, clearly demonstrate through their contents that this was the bridge between earlier texts like the *Greek Magical Papyri* and the subsequent *Key of Solomon*, which would become the most famous and copied grimoire of the Renaissance (with more than 140 known manuscripts in ten different languages).[348] Unlike other grimoires, the *Hygromanteia* includes the seven Greek planetary gods, who are conjured before the appropriate angel and demon. The use of appropriate planetary incense and the planetary hours are also seen in the earlier *Greek Magical Papyri*. This formula of conjuration of the hierarchy of beings at the appropriate time is described in *A Sacred Book called Unique or Eighth Book of Moses*:

---

[346] *Job 38:31*.
[347] *Testament of Solomon* 41, C2nd CE, trans. F.C. Conybeare.
[348] *The Veritable Key of Solomon*, Skinner & Rankine, 2008:16.

> *"Now [the great name] is [composed of] 9 names, before which you say [those of] the gods of the hours, with [the prayer on] the stele, and [those adjurations of] the gods of the days and of those [angels] set over the weeks, and the compelling formula for these; for without these the god will not listen, but will refuse to receive you as uninitiated, unless you emphatically say in advance the [names of] the lord of the day, and of the hour ... for without these you will not accomplish even one of these things."*[349]

Torijano has argued very convincingly on the connection between Jewish and Greek sources in the *Hygromanteia*.[350] In particular he demonstrates similarities in the material contained within it and the Jewish *Sepher ha-Razim* (The Book of the Mysteries) which may be as early as the C4th CE. Furthermore, he postulates the origins of the *Hygromanteia* being around the C6th CE, with the material migrating from the Byzantine Empire into Southern Italy. This is supported to a degree by the earliest known *Key of Solomon* manuscripts being in Italian, though they are much later, being C16th CE.[351]

In Conclusion

Having only covered three texts, and not even touched on the wealth of amuletic material, it is clear that major magical figures like Solomon (and indeed Moses and others) have an appeal which, like magic, transcends cultural boundaries. This is a subject I have discussed in my co-writing with Sorita d'Este (in works such as *Hekate Liminal Rites*), and which still needs much more exploration to fully express the scope of such cross-fertilisation.

Bibliography

Betz, Hans Dieter (ed). *The Greek Magical Papyri in Translation*. 1992, University of Chicago Press, Chicago

Conybeare, F.C. *The Testament of Solomon*. 1898, in *Jewish Quarterly Review*, October 1898

D'Este, Sorita, & David Rankine. *Hekate Liminal Rites*. 2009, Avalonia, London

Jeffery, L.H. *Further Comments on Archaic Greek Inscriptions*. 1955, in *The Annual of the British School at Athens*, Vol 50:67-84

---

[349] PGM XIII:1-343, trans. M. Smith.
[350] *Solomon the Esoteric King*, Torijano, 2002.
[351] For more on the *Hygromanteia* and its influence, see *The Veritable Key of Solomon*, Skinner & Rankine, 2008:56-63.

Jordan, D.R. *The Inscribed Lead Tablet from Phalasarna.* 1992 in *Zeitschrift für Papyrologie und Epigraphik* Bd.94:191-194

Jordan D.R. *Ephesia Grammata at Himera.* 2000 in *Zeitschrift für Papyrologie und Epigraphik* Bd.130:104-107

Ryland, J.E. (trans). *Tatian's Address to the Greeks.* 1886, in *Ante-Nicene Fathers* Vol 2, Christian Literature Publishing Co, New York

Skinner, Stephen, & David Rankine. *The Veritable Key of Solomon.* 2008, Golden Hoard, Singapore

Torijano, Pablo A. *Solomon the Esoteric King: From King to Magus, Development of a Tradition.* 2002, Brill, Leiden

Whiston, William (trans). *The Works of Josephus.* 1987, Hendrickson

Orphic Hymn to Aphrodite translated by Harita Meenee

Heavenly, laughter-loving Aphrodite, many are your hymns,

revered, creating goddess, born of the sea,

lover of night-long celebrations, of mating in the dark,

mother of necessity, crafty one.

Everything from you derives; you yoked

the world and rule over three realms,

giving birth to all that is in heaven,

on the fruitful earth, in the ocean depths.

Bacchus's revered companion, pleased by feasts,

mother of Eros and his brothers, adorning weddings,

with Peitho the Persuader joyful in bed, offering grace,

secret goddess, obvious and unseen.

Lovely is your hair and noble your father!

Dinner guest at divine weddings, bearer of the scepter.

She-wolf, bringing births, lover of men,

you are the most desired, giver of life,

yoking mortals with unbridled urge

and countless beasts with maddening erotic spells.

Come, divine daughter of Cyprus, joy in your lovely face,

whether in Olympus you may be, goddess and queen,

or in fragrant Syria presiding at the temple,

whether you roam on golden chariot in plains

holding in holy Egypt fertilizing floods,

or on a carriage drawn by swans on salty waves,

you come enjoying the dancing, circling creatures of the sea.

Or if you delight with dark-eyed nymphs on sacred land,

who lightly hop on sandy mounds at the beach,

or if in Cyprus, who nurtured you, O queen,

where pretty maidens and untamed nymphs

throughout the year praise you, blessed one,

along with Adonis, the pure and divine,

arrive, blessed goddess, in your most loveable form,

since I call you with holy words and reverent soul.

Figure 1: Aphrodite emerging from shell. Terracotta figurine, National Archaeological Museum, Athens, Greece. Photo by Harita Meenee.

The Athenian Festivals of Demeter by Melissa Gold

hellenicspiritcanada at gmail.com, Toronto, Ontario, Canada, 2006.

For those who desire to understand ancient Greek religion, especially for those desiring to re-establish it, the information available is simultaneously insufficient and overwhelming. It is insufficient because of the scarcity of both written descriptions and images, in some cases, intentionally so. It is overwhelming because religious practice seems to have informed every aspect of life, and we don't even know how much we don't know. The locality for which we have the most information is Athens, yet even for Athens, the record is incomplete and the overall structure of religion in daily life is difficult to determine. To complicate the picture further, religious practices apparently changed over time, shifting from a primarily agricultural basis prior to the Classical era to a more urban and philosophical one in the fifth and fourth centuries.

Nonetheless, we know that the harvest cycle was especially important in the annual festivals of Athens and its environs. Helene P. Foley, in her background article on the Eleusinian Mysteries in her edition of *The Homeric Hymn to Demeter* (1994), states that "all important rites of Demeter in Attica seem to have been linked (at least loosely) to stages of the agricultural year... In many of these, women played an important or exclusive role" (p. 71). This observation is corroborated by the more extensive work by Allaire Chandor Brumfield in her book, *The Attic Festivals of Demeter and Their Relation to the Agricultural Year* (1981). Moreover, these festivals seem to have a connection with some part of the Homeric Hymn, especially since Eleusis, which was incorporated into Attica, was the site of much of the narrative of the Hymn. I will briefly describe seven female-oriented and agricultural festivals with known or inferred associations to the Hymn and will present the pertinent passages (square brackets contain line numbers from the Hymn; translation by Hugh G. E. White, 1914). Although there were other festivals or observances related to plowing, fertility and such matters, usually honoring other deities, I will limit my discussion to those with an apparent link to the Hymn.

An agricultural year, being cyclical, has no beginning or end, but we must start somewhere, so we begin at the time of plowing, which in Attica was in the fall.

The first festival, then, is the Proerosia in the Athenian month Pyanopsiōn (approximately October). The Proerosia, though technically about the things to be done "before plowing", was actually a harvest festival, in which the main offering was from the "first fruits of the cereals". According to H. W. Parke (*Festivals of the Athenians*, 1977, p.74), the offerings to

Figure 1: Demeter and Persephone with Triptolemus, copy of stone panel from the Telesterion at Eleusis, the original is in the National Museum in Athens; taken July 2006 by Melissa Gold.

Demeter were made to invoke her blessing on the plowing and seeding to come. It is Demeter, after all, "the greatest help and cause of joy to the undying Gods and mortal men" [268-269], who according to the author of the Hymn "made fruit spring up from the rich lands, so that the whole wide earth was laden with leaves and flowers" [471-473].

The festival took place at Eleusis, site of the Great Mysteries and setting of much of the Homeric Hymn to Demeter. The explanation for the rite was that a plague had afflicted the whole of Greece, and the Delphic Oracle said that Apollo ordered a tithe to Demeter of the first harvest on behalf of all Greeks. Thereafter, except for disruptions during the Peloponnesian War, offerings arrived annually from all over the Greek world for the Goddesses' blessings before plowing and seeding, although apparently the residents of Attica did not participate to a great degree (Parke, p. 73). On the other hand, a special and very popular festival of Apollo took place two days after the Proerosia and, among other things, it featured an offering of a mixture of boiled beans—arguably a harvest portion, though it has a myth of origin outside of the Hymn to Demeter. At Eleusis on this day, sacrifice was made to Pythian Apollo, which is construed by modern scholars as a show of gratitude to the Delphic oracle for the foundation of the Proerosia.

To what degree women participated in either of these two festivals is not known, but the next festival was observed exclusively by women. This is the Thesmophoria, a pan-Hellenic festival that, in Athens, lasted five days during the time of the fall planting and included an important women-only component. Although scholars debate what the *thesmoi* were that were borne, the women-led part of the festival involved the procession of all the women of Athens (except for maidens) up to the Thesmophorion, a site probably on the hillside of the Pnyx, and their encampment there, apart from all men, for three days. Among other features of the festival, the women shunned sexual relations, celebrated without wearing wreaths and avoided foods that appear to relate to Demeter, such as pomegranate seeds that had fallen on the ground, for these, apparently, were deemed to be an offering to the Chthonic Deity (Walter Burkert, *Greek Religion*, 1985, p.244). Of these, the Hymn tells us, Hades "secretly gave [Persephone] sweet pomegranate seed to eat, taking care for himself that she might not remain continually with grave, dark-robed Demeter" [372-374].

The women also fasted while sitting on the ground on branches. Foley says that they "imitated 'the ancient way of life' before the discovery of civilization, and mourned, probably in imitation of Demeter, for Persephone" (p.72). Demeter had left the realm of the immortals and found her way to the world of mortals, who are familiar with the sorrow of losing loved ones to Hades, and "sat down and held her veil in her hands before her face. A long time she sat upon the stool without speaking because of her sorrow, and greeted no one by word or by sign, but rested, never smiling, and tasting neither food nor drink, because she pined for her deep-bosomed daughter" [197-201].

The end of Demeter's grieving on this occasion occurred when a servant of her host, "careful Iambe—who pleased her moods in aftertime also—moved the holy lady with many a quip and jest to smile and laugh and cheer her heart" [201-204]. In a similar way, the women ended their mourning in the Thesmophoria with *aischrologia,* derisive language, in imitation of Iambe. The day of fasting and mourning was followed by a day of celebrating and praying for "fair offspring", whether of children or crops, since Demeter presides over not only the cereal crops but also human fertility (Parke, p.87).

Perhaps the oddest feature of Thesmophoria involved a sacrifice of piglets, and not just any piglets but piglets that had previously been thrown into "chasms". A scholar commenting on Lucian's description of the holiday justifies the ritual of casting the piglets as follows: "When the Maiden was carried away by Pluto as she was gathering flowers, at that time in the same place a swineherd Eubouleus was grazing his pigs and they were swallowed up in the chasm with the Maiden. Therefore, in honor of Eubouleus, piglets are thrown into the chasms of Demeter and the Maiden" (Parke, p. 159). Piglets, moreover, were associated with female genitalia, and the organs of both men and women were related to fertility of crops, as illustrations demonstrate (also at the Haloa, see below). Parke conjectures that the corpses, along other items, had been thrown into the caverns earlier in the summer, likely at the Skiraphoria, and retrieved for this festival (see more about Skiraphoria, below). Although placed on the altars at some point, eventually these remains were plowed into the fields to ensure fertility of the crop (Parke, p.83).

The next female-only holiday was the Haloa, in Poseideōn (December). Although the name links the occasion to the threshing floor and harvest, the festival appears to have taken place at Eleusis at the time that the planted seed was threatened by the cold adversity of winter. Parke says that "the purpose would be to stimulate the growth of the corn from seed" (p.99). Foley elaborates, pointing out that "the growth of both human child and the seed occur out of sight", and since women are intimately involved with the one, they are logically associated with the other (p. 74).

Perhaps the main concern at the Haloa was that Demeter, annually mourning for her daughter for the third part of the year that Persephone was obligated to remain underground with her husband, might yet again withhold the growth of plant life. The Hymn describes grief-stricken Demeter as causing "a most dreadful and cruel year for mankind over the all-nourishing earth: the ground would not make the seed sprout, for rich-crowned Demeter kept it hid" [305-307]. If the women failed in placating Demeter, perhaps the Goddess would withhold the growth of the seed again. As at the Thesmophoria, *aischrologia* was practiced at the Haloa, and also the women drank wine and ate representations of sex organs during the feast and priestesses whispered into the ears of the women that they should take lovers. "What began as a phallic rite practiced by women to promote the growth of wheat ended by becoming an all-night orgy of banqueting in an atmosphere of indecency," says Parke (p.99). Dionysus was honored at this time, too, "being in some aspects not only the God of the vine, but of all birth and growth" (Parke, p.107). The Athenian men apparently sat apart and discussed "stories of the introduction of agriculture by Demeter" (Foley, p.74). Foley surmises that bonfire was a likely component of the festivities, as evidenced by the large amount of wood ordered, a not surprising addition given the long hours of darkness and coolness of the season. The large fire, as I see it, is reminiscent of modern holidays with their festivals of light at the winter solstice.

In Anthesteriōn (February), the Athenians held what were known as the "Lesser Mysteries". The month occurred when the new shoots of green and flowers were first seen, as indicated by its name, which derives from the word for "flower." Although originally the Lesser Mysteries had an independent existence, once Athens annexed Eleusis they were coupled with the Great Mysteries: candidates for initiation at the latter were required first to undergo initiation at the former. As at the Greater Mysteries (see below), initiates kept what happened there secret so that, again, our sources for information about them are limited. Parke states that one of the few literary references mentions that the Ilissos River was used for ablutions and the Lesser Mysteries took place at a shrine located near this river. Moreover, legend connected Heracles to these mysteries, explaining that he was unable to take part in the Eleusinian mysteries because he was a "foreigner", so the Lesser Mysteries were instituted on his behalf. Even so, he first had to undergo purification from blood guilt, and carvings show Heracles doing just that, in company with Demeter, Persephone and the Eleusinian torch bearer (who although male, represents torch-bearing Hekate, as in the Homeric Hymn, line 52)—suggesting that purification took place as part of these mysteries (Parke, p. 123).

Whether purification was merely a preliminary or was the main feature of these Mysteries is unclear. However, it is worth noting that many cultures undergo rituals of purification in the spring; the Jewish holiday of Passover, with its practice of extensive cleaning out of home and food stores, and Easter and its custom of purification through self-denial (Lent), both suggest that spring is innately perceived as the logical time to undertake such practices—coinciding with the earliest growth of plants.

In the Hymn, Hades abducts Persephone during the spring while she is "gathering flowers over a soft meadow, roses and crocuses and beautiful violets, irises also and hyacinths and the narcissus" [6-8]. However in future years, she will return in spring. As Demeter tells her, "when the earth shall bloom with the fragrant flowers of spring in every kind, then from the realm of darkness and gloom thou shalt come up once more to be a wonder for Gods and mortal men" [401-403]. We also know that when Persephone returned to her mother the first time, after a long period of mourning by both Goddesses, Demeter "straightway made fruit to spring up from the rich lands, so that the whole wide earth was laden with leaves and flowers" [471-473]. Moreover, Parke mentions that various commentators suggest that the Lesser Mysteries included dramatic representations of the legend of the two Goddesses (Parke, p. 123). All of this suggests that the Lesser Mysteries played an important role both in celebrating and illuminating the divine agricultural myth and also in requesting the Gods' blessings so that the cycle of the grain and of life would continue.

The next agricultural ritual took place in the month of Thargēliōn (May), which takes its name from the festival Thargēlia, a two-day festival honoring primarily Artemis and Apollo. The main offering for this festival is *thargēlos*, a form of sprouted grain bread, probably made of barley. May sees the first harvest of the green cereals, which were offered to Artemis (and to later Demeter or Dionysos or both) as ta thalusia, from the word for "young shoot" or sprouting greenery, *thallos* (Liddell and Scott).

The first day of Thargēlia was, like the Lesser Mysteries, a time of purification. Although the main offerings were to Artemis, as this was Her day, also on the first day a ram was offered to Demeter Chloē, Goddess of green shoots. Ancient authors note that it was unusual to sacrifice a male animal to a female divinity, though they give no explanation for it. Also in the spring, local residents held a festival called Chloia at Eleusis, although this ritual and the one to Demeter in Athens may not be related (Parke, p 149).

The ancients would have recalled that much can happen to destroy a harvest from the time that the first heads of grain appear until the crop reaches maturity: flood, fire, insect plagues or war. The protection and favor of the Goddesses were still important to ensure the cereal reached maturity. Hence it is not surprising that a festival occurred at this point in the agricultural year, when "as spring-time waxed, [the Rharian plain of Eleusis] was soon to be waving with long ears of corn, and its rich furrows to be loaded with grain upon the ground, while others would already be bound in sheaves" [454-456]. Soon, but not yet, so we can understand the foreshadowing in the Hymn as a reminder that a successful harvest is likely but not to be taken for granted. Vigilance and the correct observances are essential.

Skiraphoriōn (June) was the month of the final harvest of the grain and, not surprisingly, another major agricultural festival took place during this month, as part of the three-day long Skira (Skiraphoria). Parke notes that "In the Skira the shaded procession to Skiron which originally concerned Athena and her rival deity on the Acropolis coincided with some mystic ritual of Demeter confined to female participants" (p. 158). At Skiron, a precinct on the road to Eleusis near a sanctuary dedicated to Athena Skiras, Poseidon Pater, Demeter and Kore, the priests and priestesses did something pertaining to the fertility of the crops, since Plutarch mentions that one of the three "sacred plowings" of the Athenians took place at this time. Perhaps then, the "sacred plowing" in Skiraphorion entailed a blessing of the harvest or a thanksgiving for it or both. Coincidentally, the Bouphonia, another of the sacred plowings, occurred two days after this. This entailed a blessing for the oxen in honor of Zeus of the City, although its mythology is separate from the Hymn to Demeter.

The female responsibilities on one day of the festival involved what is probably one of the oddest proceedings in the Athenian year. Parke reasons, based on the note made by the scholar on Lucian's description of holidays, that the *decayed* materials retrieved from chasms and placed on the altars during the Thesmophoria in the fall were probably cast into the chasms during

Skiraphoria; had the materials been thrown into the chasms during the Thesmophoria, no decay would have yet occurred. The scholar's note suggests to me that, even as one agricultural cycle ended, the women were ensuring that the next cycle would begin properly.

The last observance of the agricultural year was actually somewhat external to the cycle of harvest and regeneration, but was essential in reminding people of the reasons for the agricultural rituals. This was the Eleusinian Mysteries, held in Boēdromiōn (September), before the resumption of the annual cycle. No one truly knows all that happened during the nine days of the process, nor will I summarize here what is known. To the ancient Greeks, however, the mysteries were connected to the cereal crop and to life itself.

Two important passages from the Hymn to Demeter demonstrate this. The first occurs just before Demeter casts off her disguise as an old woman in the house of Celeus: "I am that Demeter who has share of honor and is the greatest help and cause of joy to the undying Gods and mortal men. But now, let all the people build me a great temple and an altar below it and beneath the city and its sheer wall upon a rising hillock above Callichorus. And I myself will teach my rites, that hereafter, you may reverently perform them and so win the favor of my heart" [268-274]. The second passage occurs after Demeter agrees to an arrangement wherein her daughter will return to Hades for a third of a year but live with the other immortals for the other two-thirds, after which Demeter allows the annual growth cycle to resume. Then Demeter hastens to the "kings who deal justice", the leaders of Eleusis, and "showed the conduct of her rites and taught them all her mysteries...awful mysteries which no one may in any way transgress or pry into or utter, for deep awe of the Gods checks the voice" [476-479]. Those familiar with the Hymn knew that "right blessed is he among men on earth whom [the Goddesses] freely love: soon they do send Plutus as guest to his great house, Plutus who gives wealth to mortal men" [486-489]. Plutus, or Wealth, was not possible without a bountiful grain harvest.

The Mysteries are believed to have involved re-enacting the events of the Hymn to Demeter, but it is very likely that the six other festivals discussed above also carried out some detail of what Demeter had ordered that "no one may in any way transgress" for fear of losing the favor of the Goddess's heart and thus incurring another "most dreadful and cruel year for mankind over the all-nourishing earth" [305-306].

It is also possible that the women, especially, who had been initiated at Eleusis were in some way obligated to participate in the other rituals, as it is hard to imagine that, in the mind of ancient Athenians, the other grain festivals were entirely separate from the august Eleusinian Mysteries. The Hymn reminds us that "happy is he among men upon earth who has seen these mysteries; but he who is uninitiated and who has no part in them, never has lot of like good things once he is dead, down in the darkness and gloom" [480-482]. Thus it fell upon the women of Athens to ensure that Demeter was honored at all important milestones of the yearly cycle so that Plutus might visit the family in both life *and* death.

For modern people wishing to re-establish ancient Hellenic worship, this is still true. We need to embrace awareness of the agricultural year, wherever we live, remembering the requirements and power of the Goddesses. We also need to remember that the environment does not guarantee that the harvest will always be bountiful, and that mankind shows hubris in how much we ignore the harm we inflict on life of all kinds.

Figure 2: Modern offering to Demeter and Kore in the cave of Plutos at Eleusis; taken July 2006 by Melissa Gold.

Citations:

Brumfield, Allaire Chandor, *The Attic Festivals of Demeter and Their Relation to the Agricultural Year*, Arno Press, New York, 1981

Burkert, Walter, *Greek Religion*, Cambridge, 1977, translation by John Raffan, 1985

Foley, Helene P., ed., introduction, *Homeric Hymn to Demeter*, Princeton, 1994

Liddell, H.G. and R. Scott, *Greek-English Lexicon*, 9th ed., Oxford, 1996

Parke, H.W., *Festivals of the Athenians*, London, 1977

White, Hugh G. Evelyn, translator, *Homeric Hymns*, Loeb, 1914, Edinburgh, 2002

The Lioness by Jane Raeburn

"For, explaining in riddles our commonality with animals, they are accustomed to reveal us according to [names of] animals; so that they call those initiates participating in the same rites lions, and the women lionesses, and the attendants ravens." -- Porphyry, De abstinentia

CHAPTER I: CORAX

1.

The underground room was not large to begin with, and with twelve men inside, it was nearly impossible to imagine one more fitting in. Yet a thirteenth figure cast a shadow at the entrance, almost unseen in the lamplight. The youngest man turned from his station at the left-hand bench and raised his right hand.

"Why have you come here?" he asked, in a way that indicated he already knew the answer.

"To learn the Mysteries," said a soft voice. A few of the men looked up, startled.

"Have you cleansed your body and mind of all impurities?" the next man asked.

"I have."

"How have you cleansed them?" asked the next.

"I have bathed in pure water under the sight of the stars." It was cloudy that night, but this was the formula.

The man closest to the altar was tall, with deep brown eyes, a military bearing and bushy grey eyebrows. He allowed himself a hint of a smile as he asked the next question: "Have you abstained from sexual relations for seven days?"

"I have."

The bald man across from him asked, "What gift have you brought?" At this the new initiate stepped forward, head still covered, and handed a package wrapped in cloth to the youth who had begun the ritual. This was ceremonially passed down to the man who had asked the question. Unwrapped, it proved to be a statue in alabaster, about a foot high, depicting a god with the head of a lion, wrapped in the body of a snake. In the lamplight, the alabaster gave off a golden gleam, and all eyes were drawn to it.

"Leontocephalus," said the bald man with an air of grudging approval. "A worthy addition." He nodded to the next man, who was dark-haired and stoop-shouldered.

"Who brings you to this temple and sponsors your initiation?"

"Gaius Fabius Lepidus." This was the name of the brown-eyed man, and several faces turned toward him. He nodded.

"Under what star were you born?"

"Under the sign of the Ram."

"Are you prepared to set aside your status in the world, and to serve citizen and slave alike as you undergo initiation in the Mysteries?"

"I am."

"Are you prepared to live in accordance with the Mysteries of Mithras, so that all may see you and say 'There goes an initiate of Mithras' with respect in their voices?"

"I am."

"By what name are you called?"

"Flavia Valeria."

2.

As I spoke my name, I took a step into the room, and the men could clearly see my women's robes -- good quality wool, suitable for this wretched Britannic climate, and modestly draped, but clearly female.

A murmur came from some of the men. What was a woman doing in a temple of soldiers? I pretended not to hear. The Pater of the temple, the centurion Decimus Pompeius, had known that Gaius Fabius was proposing his own wife for initiation, and had called for the ritual to go forward. It was not for anyone else to complain.

The men nearest the altar put out all the lamps but one, which was passed to the young man on my left, a surgeon's assistant named Victor. He stood beside me and held the lamp so that its light fell on the mosaic at my feet. Corax, the first degree -- a crow with a caduceus, the snake-twined wand affiliated with Mercury.

"All hail the Corax, protected by Mercury!" I heard the words, but my thoughts were irrelevantly drawn to the pleasant clarity of my husband's deep, familiar voice. Then the rest of the men repeated: "All hail the Corax, protected by Mercury!"

The lights went out, and suddenly I was drenched in cold water. I gasped. Then I gasped again. There was a knife at my throat.

3.

"Kneel," said a booming voice I did not recognize, and I knelt -- carefully, so as not to pitch forward onto the knife. My husband had not told me all of what was to happen, and I was genuinely surprised to find myself wet and cold in the dark.

As I reached my knees, the knife was withdrawn and a fearful crash sounded behind me, as if someone had clapped a pair of cymbals right behind my head. Someone had, and someone was still doing it.

"Thou hast died," shouted the voice in between cymbal clashes. "Thy soul is to be reborn this night." And there, in the dark, still wet and rather deafened, I confess I was frightened.

There was a blissful moment of silence, then the noise began again, deeper. I recognized a drum, a familiar sound, but much closer than was comfortable, resounding madly in that tiny space.

"Be thou purified, emptied of all past associations, that your life may be lived in the light of Mithras, who is the path to salvation." At this last phrase the sound stopped and a light shone forth beneath the statue of the god.

Of course I'd seen him before -- there was a small statue of him in my own house -- but this was different. Illuminated from below, I saw anew the young man's face, turned away from his terrible deed. In silence I looked on Mithras, his cape flying out behind him as he knelt on a bull's back and aimed a knife to kill it. In those long moments I had time to take in other details of the scene -- the small dog leaping up at the bull's shoulder, the snake climbing its side, and a scorpion biting its testes, which seemed like adding insult to injury. Yet even as I had this irreverent thought I also felt something genuine. I knew that Mithras was slaying evil, that in some small way it would be my job to do the same.

"Rise a new man. Woman," said the voice, hesitating just a little, and I suppressed a smile as I stood, my now-clammy garments clinging to my body. I saw that the voice came from Decimus Pompeius. His left hand swept toward the ground.

"Do you swear to learn the mysteries and serve Mithras with your heart, soul and body?"

"I do."

"Do you swear to serve your brothers in this mithraeum, and all who are sworn to Mithras?"

"I do."

"Here, then, is the mask of the Corax, he who has died and been born again. Wear it this night as you perform the duties of the Corax, who serves his elders in the temple." Victor tied the black feather mask over my eyes.

"Receive this wine and know the ecstasy of Mithras." I sipped from the cup handed to me. In Rome I would have spat it out again, but wine was hard to find in the far provinces, and good wine nearly impossible.

"Receive this bread and know the essence of Sol Invictus." The bread was delicious. I should know. I baked it.

"Thou art Corax, the first grade of initiation."

4.

"You won't have to wear the mask every time, just the first night," Victor said helpfully. He was blond, blue-eyed and eager to please, and I stifled the small pang of regret I always felt when a handsome young man treated me like his aunt. They always had. Even in my youth there had been something about me that said to men, "Here is a kindly female figure to whom you can confide your troubles." That was one reason I hadn't married till I was thirty, when most women my age were already starting to think about finding husbands for their daughters.

Victor -- Quintus Volucius Victor, to give him his full name -- was almost young enough to be my son, and it was rather comical to stand with him at the fire outside the temple as he taught me how to serve the higher-ranking men their wine and food. I bore with it patiently until he spilled soup on the ground. "I have served a dinner before now," I observed gently, and we both laughed, for my parties were well-known among the officers of Procolitia Fort.

There were two other Coraxes, a pair of Batavian brothers, Aulus Julius and Manius Julius, who had done most of the work of preparing that night's meal. I had brought bread and wine, the customary offering of a new initiate, but from now on I would join the other three in making and serving the temple dinner, usually a hearty meat dish. Tonight's was a chicken stew, which had simmered in a pot over the fire during the ritual.

"Normally I would instruct you on the cooking of the food," Aulus Julius said politely, with a slight German accent. The brothers were lifelong cavalrymen, and had joined the Mithraeum when Aulus was promoted to command one of the legionary cavalry units. I knew them slightly, for my husband was Procolitia's master of horse. I smiled a little at the thought of these two soldiers in their forties, acting as servants to the other men, some of whom were much younger, but such was the way of the temple. Indeed, one of the men I would be serving tonight -- I, a patrician Roman -- was a freed slave!

"It smells delicious, Aulus Julius," I said appreciatively.

"Ah, so it does, and we are all hungry," said his brother, whose accent was more pronounced. "But we do not eat until all the elders have been served."

"Then we'd best get on with it, right? Show me what to carry."

We processed back into the temple, each carrying a cup of wine. There were seven men on the benches. Aulus Julius, the senior Corax, served the Pater -- Decimus Pompeius, the man who had proclaimed at my initiation -- and the rest of us each served two men. They had spread out so that each was able to recline at least a little on the benches. I was to serve Publius Arminius, a freedman who served as accountant to the Procolitia fort, and my husband, Gaius Fabius. As instructed, I waited to serve them until the higher-ranking brothers had had their wine. "The Pater doesn't care, but Sextus Claudius gets upset if we get it out of order," young Volucius had told me.

"Which one is he?" I knew some of the men, but not all.

"The Heliodromos -- second-in-command," he explained. "Sits next to the Pater." I nodded. I'd seen him in the town, but didn't know much about him. He, too, was blond and blue-eyed, but not handsome -- at least, not unless you like a red face and a bullish chin on a man, and I don't.

Gaius Fabius' turn came, and I served him with the traditional words: "The ecstasy of Mithras fill your heart." He smiled encouragingly at me as he took the cup and drank. Publius Arminius drained the cup at his turn, and smiled beatifically at me. Clearly he would not be complaining about the quality of the wine.

"The knowledge of Mithras fill your soul," we said as we brought each man a plate of the bread, spread with olive oil. Victor was having trouble carrying two plates without disaster, and I showed him the servant's trick of balancing one plate on the forearm and holding it against the body for stability, leaving the other hand free to open doors and handle utensils. He thanked me effusively, and I wondered how he'd reached the age of twenty-two without having observed someone -- a slave? a mother? -- doing this same thing. Like most young men, I supposed, he simply enjoyed food that was put before him, and didn't wonder at how it got there.

"The strength of Mithras move you to good deeds." This was the stew, and it smelled even better now -- or perhaps I was just hungrier. Gaius Fabius complimented me on it, and I nodded to the brothers Julius to indicate it was their doing.

"The sweetness of Mithras send you forth with loving hearts." The last dish was nuts coated in honey.

"The purity of Mithras cleanse and renew you," we said as we went among the men with napkins and bowls of water, cleaning their fingers and faces. Then we withdrew to tidy up from dinner. Victor washed the plates and bowls in a basin of water, and the Julius brothers served out the remaining food into four portions for the four Ravens. As the newest initiate, my job was to scrub the pots -- slaves' work, usually, but the initiates of Mithras each had to serve their time doing menial labor as a sign of their devotion. The men offered to show me what to do. "No need -- I have done it before," I said, and Victor raised an eyebrow. "I may be patrician, but my family was often poor enough that the women did this work," I explained, my hands already busy. Having already been splashed with water that night, I had little concern for getting my garments wet.

"Indeed, I was never so quick or so thorough," said dark-haired Manius Julius admiringly.

"Your mother would probably laugh to see me so clumsy," I told him with a smile. "It has been a long time. Fortuna has favored me of late." Indeed She had. Once an unmarriageable spinster without a dowry, spending my life as a virtual servant to my father and brother, I was now a matron with a family and household of my own. I had made bread today as a mark of devotion, but the bread on my table was baked by slaves and served by a well-trained butler. Best of all, I had a kind and gentle husband.

5.

Gaius Fabius' face was stern as he looked upon the work of the Ravens. "As the Raven serves in the temple, so does he serve Mithras. Are your duties performed?"

"They are," responded Aulus Julius, and already I was beginning to get used to the sight of this respected soldier with a scrubbing-brush in his hand.

"Then bring your dinner into the temple, where you will hear of the Mysteries," he said, and led us back inside.

The temple was a small building with a vaulted roof, set into the side of a hill below the Procolitia fort. It was a fitting place for the cave-like atmosphere that the worship of Mithras required -- dark and quiet, but for the sound of a stream nearby. On the opposite bank, I knew, was a small shrine where the locals and the German women worshiped a water-goddess.

Gaius Fabius seated himself on the right-hand bench and indicated that we were to perch on the opposite side. As we ate, he delivered a lecture, the first of many I was to hear in that room. He was very proper with me in front of others, and addressed me as "Soror" just as he called them "Frater."

"Tonight we have a new initiate, so I will give the lecture of the Raven, which you others have heard before. Yet let it not be time wasted, for as you listen you may find greater depths of knowledge to strengthen your bond to Mithras, to feel his arm beside you in battle and his bright spirit guiding you always.

"Soror Flavia Valeria, you have willingly died and been reborn, joining the ranks of the Corax, the ravens who are the lowest of the low, yet even in their lowness are higher than those who have never known the power of Mithras. Here, then, are your duties.

"Serve your brothers faithfully and well, and lack not in your service to them.

"Attend the temple at the specified times and days.

"Respect your brothers in Mithras, both inside and outside of this temple.

"Learn of the Mysteries and reveal them not to outsiders.

"Use your learning, wisdom and strength to good effect in the world, that others may know you as an initiate and speak of you with respect.

"Obey the Pater and the officers of this temple as your masters.

"Fail not in your duty toward any man, but most particularly in your duty toward your brothers in Mithras, and if one comes to you and gives the sign of Pates and Cautopates, give him your aid as a brother in Mithras, though you know him not."

Here Gaius Fabius gave a peculiar gesture with his left hand. "See how my thumb points upward while my little finger points downward? So go the torches held by Pates and Cautopates, the guardians of this temple." He gestured toward the two statues at the entrance -- one holding a torch aloft, the other pointing it downward. "From sunrise to sunset, and back again to sunrise, you are protected by the light of Mithras. My three fingers are closed in a fist, to signify that I keep sacred the mysteries of this temple." We all practiced the gesture. Victor's hands were the whitest, for he had never worked out of doors.

"If one comes to you and gives this gesture, speak to him privately and ask, 'By the light of the Unconquered Sun, are you my brother?' If he is, he will say, 'By the flight of the Raven, I am.' Know then that this is a true initiate and worthy of your aid.

"Know also that as Ravens you are the messengers of this temple. It is your job not only to prepare and serve the meal we share, but also to summon the brothers of the temple when it is time to meet. When a brother of this temple dies, it will be your duty to summon the others to honor his spirit. For thy patron is Mercury, in whose name are messages brought, and thy symbol is the caduceus, the snake-twined staff of rebirth. In Mercury's name do I tell to thee the lesson of the Raven: In Mithras lies thy salvation."

6.

It was late and I was tired, but we still had to clean our dishes, sweep the temple, tend the lamps and make all ready for the next meeting. Gaius Fabius waited to walk me home -- the only thing he ever did that indicated I was anything other than an equal in the eyes of the mithraeum.

"Was it not as I said, my dear? Did you not truly feel the power of the ritual?"

"I did, husband, and was glad of your presence, for I might have been truly frightened otherwise. Tell me, how did you persuade them to accept me? I did not feel that all there present welcomed a woman."

"Decimus Pompeius is the deciding voice, and he was swayed when I told them of your knowledge of the stars."

"You told them what?"

"You are a talented astrologer, my dear. I have seen you cast many a horoscope, and such knowledge is important to the worship of Mithras."

"A parlor trick, suitable for bored ladies."

"You were right when you cast our son's horoscope."

He meant it kindly, but it was not a cheering thing to say. "Our son." The sad fact was that I could not have children, a fact we had learned after our hastily-arranged marriage. He had returned to Rome in a hurry when his older brother and all his family had died in a house fire, leaving him prosperous yet in need of a wife. His friends had advised him to seek a lady who could better the family's social status.

My brother, coming across his old army buddy at a tavern, had offered my hand almost as a joke, and indeed when I first heard of it I could not believe my new suitor to be in any way serious. I was no doe-eyed beauty of eighteen, but was long past the usual age of marriage, rather too inclined to a sharp tongue, preferring books to parties, with nothing more than a patrician name to recommend me. The dinner my family arranged for him was an embarrassment -- bad wine decanted into good bottles for show, the guest of honor given the best of the meat while I pretended I wanted none, and only one slave to wait on us all. Yet somewhere in between my brother's insincere compliments to my appearance and my father's unspeakably dull accounts of the great deeds of our branch of the Flavii, this suntanned soldier and I had clicked, catching each other's eyes across the table in a moment of near-laughter. Indeed Fortuna had been with me.

Except for this -- the hoped-for sons had not come. We had returned to his unit here in Britannia, and a year went by after our wedding. When my courses arrived yet again, I could not help myself. I wept. "You had better divorce me," I told Gaius Fabius. "I cannot give you a child."

"But I don't want to divorce you," he replied quite reasonably, which for some reason made me cry all the harder. "I will adopt a child, and all will be well."

As it happened, one of his decurions, a Spaniard named Cornelius, had been killed by a rogue horse, leaving behind an orphaned boy. The child's mother had long since died, and he might have spent the rest of his life sweeping out stables if we had not adopted him. Marcus Fabius Cornelius, as the youth was now known, had been trouble from the first. He had terrorized his schoolmates and my slaves for years. He had drunk his father's wine, stolen my jewelry to buy more wine and drunk that. He had raped a local girl, causing an unpleasant scandal at a time when the legions were trying to make peace with our Celtic neighbors.

We had tried our best with Marcus, and we had failed. Early on, I had managed to find a friend of his mother's, and learned the time of his birth. I had been working on a method of casting horoscopes in Britannia, where the positions of the stars are somewhat different than in Rome. The horoscope was ill-favored to say the least -- Venus opposed to his Sun made him self-centered, while Mars opposed to the Moon explained his rudeness and domineering attitude. The tenth house, which ruled his character, was sadly afflicted. Gaius Fabius, finding me at this work, listened in amusement as I read out the horrid details. "Have I married a fortuneteller, then?"

"Of course not, husband -- that is, I have never sat on a street corner, drawing up horoscopes for the foolish. I learned the arts of the Chaldeans for my own benefit, and that of my friends. Indeed, it was one way I managed what little popularity I had back in Rome -- the wealthy ladies of my family remembered me when it was time to find out the brilliant futures of their newborn sons."

"But have not these arts been declared illegal?"

"Who will trouble a woman who putters around with charts and stars, and charges nothing for her work? It is only the charlatans and those greedy enough to advise the Emperor who suffer from this ban. And in the case of our son, it does us little good, for the stars cannot change, only explain."

After that, Gaius Fabius took to consulting me from time to time about matters astrological. Some of his questions were practical and military, but others had to do with the nature of the planetary energies and their influences on human behavior. And four months ago, on Marcus' seventeenth birthday, Gaius Fabius had found a place for the boy in the infantry. "If I can't control him, then maybe a good centurion can." As a high-ranking officer, he was able to arrange for Marcus Fabius to be assigned to the toughest centurion in the fort: Decimus Pompeius, also known as the Pater of the Procolitia Mithraeum.

If I had cast his horoscope instead of my son's, it might have warned me of the news in store.

Anahita: Lady of Persia by Payam Nabarz

The following is based on the Anahita chapter from *The Mysteries of Mithras: The Pagan Belief That Shaped the Christian World*. By Payam Nabarz, Inner Traditions, 2005. It appeared in From a Drop of Water, Avalonia 2009 in this much extended format.

Mighty Anahita with splendour will shine,

Incarnated as a youthful divine.

Full of charm her beauty she will display,

Her hip with charming belt she will array.

Straight-figured, she is as noble bride,

Freeborn, herself in puckered dress will hide.

Her cloak is all decorated with gold,

With precious dress Anahita we shall behold.

-(Original poem based on Kashani's Persian folk songs, from an Avestan invocation to Anahita)

Dusk of Shabe Yalda (Yule) 777 BCE, somewhere on a beach by the Caspian sea. A young Magi (who may later known as the prophet Zoroaster) has been keeping a night vigil. His solitary fire is the only light for miles around and his recitation of Aban Yasht - the hymn to angel-goddess Anahita - the only sound to be heard apart from the waves gently crashing onto the beach:

'Angel-Goddess of all the waters upon the earth and the source of the cosmic ocean; she who drives a chariot pulled by four horses: wind, rain, cloud, and sleet; your symbol is the eight-rayed star. You are the source of life, purifying the seed of all males and the wombs of all females, also cleansing the milk in the breasts of all mothers. Your connection with life means warriors in battle prayed to you for survival and victory.

A maid, fair of body, most strong, tall-formed, high-girded, pure, . . . wearing a mantle fully embroidered with gold; ever holding the baresma [sacred plant] in your hand, . . . you wear square golden earrings on your ears . . .

a golden necklace around your beautiful neck, . . . Upon your head . . . a golden crown, with a hundred stars, with eight rays . . . with fillets streaming down.'[352]

The Magi's prayer is answered by the sea in the form of a vision; as midnight approaches and time slows, the sea parts. A large silver throne appears; on either side of it sits a lion with eyes of blue flame. On the throne sits a Lady in silver and gold garments, proud and tall, an awe-inspiring warrior-woman, as terrifying as she is beautiful. Tall and statuesque she sits, her noble origins evident in her appearance, her haughty authority made clear and commanding through a pair of flashing eyes. A dove flies above her and a peacock walks before her. A crown of shining gold rings her royal temples; bejeweled with eight sunrays and one hundred stars, it holds her lustrous hair back from her beautiful face. Her marble-like white arms reflect moonlight and glisten with moisture. She is clothed with a garment made of thirty beaver skins, and it shines with the full sheen of silver and gold. The planet Venus shines brightly in the sky.[353]

Time passes... history takes place...

---

[352] From verses 126–128 of the Aban Yasht 5.

[353] This description of Anahita is based on her description in Tony Allan, Charles Phillips, and Michael Kerrigan, Myth and Mankind series: *Wise Lord of the Sky: Persian Myth* (London: Time Life Books, 1999), 32.

Figure 1: Goddess Anahita, painting by Akashnath, 2008.

Circa 400 BCE Achaemenian king Artaxerxes II Mnemon (404-359 BCE) inscribes in Ecbatana in his palace:

'Artaxerxes, the great king, the king of kings, the king of all nations, the king of this world, the son of king Darius [II Nothus], Darius the son of king Artaxerxes [I Makrocheir], Artaxerxes the son of king Xerxes, Xerxes the son of king Darius, Darius the son of Hystaspes, the Achaemenid, says: this hall [apadana] I built, by the grace of Ahuramazda, Anahita, and Mithra. May Ahuramazda, Anahita, and Mithra protect me against evil, and may they never destroy nor damage what I have built.' [354]

Artaxerxes II, like other Achaemenian kings, was initiated by priests at a sanctuary of Anahita in Pasargadai during his coronation. Artaxerxes II built the temple of Anahita at Kangavar near Kermanshah as well as many others. The Kangavar was a magnificent temple four-fifths of a mile in circumference, built using cedar or cypress trees. All the columns and floor-tiles were covered with gold and silver. It was perhaps one of the most breathtaking buildings ever built in the Middle East.

Anahita's role as the goddess of water, rain, abundance, blessing, fertility, marriage, love, motherhood, birth, and victory became well established. This goddess was the manifestation of women's perfection. Ancient kings were crowned by their queens in Anahita's temple in order to gain her protection and support. Anahita's blessing would bring fertility and abundance to the country. [355]

Time passes... history takes place... The Achaemenian empires falls to 'Alexander the Accursed'...

Circa 200 BCE sees the dedication of a Seleucid temple in western Iran to *"Anahita, as the Immaculate Virgin Mother of the Lord Mithra"*. [356] The blend of Greek and Persian cultures manifest themselves in the Seleucid dynasty.

Time passes... history takes place...

The Parthian Empire (circa 247 BCE-226 CE) replaces the Seleucid and the Parthians expand the Anahita temple at Kangavar.

---

[354] See: http://www.livius.org/aa-ac/achaemenians/A2Ha.html

[355] Official entry on Anahita by the Embassy of the Islamic Republic of Iran in Ottawa, Canada on their Web site: http://www.salamiran.org/Women/General/Women_And_Mythical_Deities.html

[356] First Iranian Goddess of productivity and values by Manouchehr Saadat Noury - Persian Journal, Jul 21, 2005. http://www.iranian.ws/iran_news/publish/printer_8378.shtml

Figure 2: Bronze head of the goddess Anahita, Hellenistic Greek, 1st century BCE found at the ancient city of Satala, modern Sadak, north-eastern Turkey, now in The British Museum.

Time passes... history takes place...

Mark Anthony marches in to Armenia (circa 37 BCE - 34 BCE), and in one of the latter campaigns reached the Anahita temple at Erez:

'The temple of Erez was the wealthiest and the noblest in Armenia, according to Plutarch. During the expedition of Mark Antony in Armenia, the statue was broken to pieces by the Roman soldiers. Pliny the Elder gives us the following story about it: The Emperor Augustus, being invited to dinner by one of his generals, asked him if it were true that the wreckers of Anahit's statue had been punished by the wrathful goddess. 'No, answered the general, on the contrary, I have today the good fortune of treating you with one part of the hip of that gold statue.' The Armenians erected a new golden statue of Anahit in Erez, which was worshiped before the time of St. Gregory Illuminator.' [357]

Time passes... history takes place...

---

[357] A History of Armenia By Vahan M. Kurkjian, Bakuran. IndoEuropeanPublishing.com, 2008.

The Sassanian Empire is formed ca. 226 CE. The Temple of Anahita in Bishapur was built during the Sassanian era (241-635 CE). The temple is believed to have been built by some of the estimated seventy thousand Roman soldiers and engineers who were captured by the Persian King Shapur (241-272 CE), who also captured three Roman emperors: Gordian III, Phillip, and Valerian. The design of the temple is noteworthy: water from the river Shapur is channeled into an underground canal to the temple and flows under and all around the temple, giving the impression of an island. The fire altar would have been in the middle of the temple, with the water flowing underground all around it. One might interpret this as a union of water—Anahita—with fire—Mithra.[358]

Figure 3: The Temple of Anahita in Bishapur, Iran (Photograph by Jamshid Varza, www.vohuman.org, reproduced with his kind permission.)

The Temple of Anahita in Bishapur, Iran, on the site of the ancient city built by Shapur I, Sassanian Emperor (241 C.E.–272 CE) in celebration of his victory over three Roman Emperors - Gordian III, Phillip, and Valerian.

---

[358] For the Temple of Anahita at Bishapur, see
http://www.vohuman.org/SlideShow/Anahita%20Bishapur/AnahitaBishapur00.htm

Time passes... history takes place...

The Sassanian Empires fades and Islam arrives in Iran.

900 CE. Moslem pilgrims make their way to the 1100 year-old shrine of Bibi Shahr Banoo, the Islamic female saint, near the old town of Rey (South of Tehran). The town of Rey is thought to be 5000 years old, and the site of this shrine with its waterfall is believed by some to have once been an Anahita shrine. It is also close to the Cheshmeh Ali Hill (the spring of Ali Hill), which is dated to 5000 years ago. Perhaps this is an echo of Mithra-Anahita shrines being located close to each other and then becoming linked to later Islamic saints, a process seen frequently in Christianized Europe too; for example, sites sacred to the Celtic goddess Brighid became sites dedicated to Saint Brigit.

Furthermore, according to Susan Gaviri: *Anahita in Iranian Mythology* (1993):

'...it must not be forgotten that many of the famous fire temples in Iran were, in the beginning, Anahita temples. Examples of these fire temples are seen in some parts of Iran, especially in Yazad, where we find that after the Muslim victory these were converted to Mosques.' [359]

Time passes... history takes place...

Pilgrims continue to visit the Pre-Islamic Zoroastrian shrine of Pir e Sabz, or Chek Chek ("drip drip," the sound of water dripping), in the mountains of Yazd. This is still a functional temple and the holiest site for present-day Zoroastrians living in Iran, who take their annual pilgrimage to Pir e Sabz Banu, "the old woman in the mountain," also called Pir e Sabz, "the green saint," at the beginning of summer. *Pir* means "elder," and it can also mean "fire." The title of Pir also connotes a Sufi master. *Sabz* means green. [360]

Pilgrims also continue to visit Pir e Banoo Pars (Elder Lady of Persia) and Pir e Naraki located near Yazd. The Pir Banoo temple is in an area that has a number of valleys; the name of the place is Hapt Ador, which means Seven Fires. [361]

---

[359] *Anahita in Iranian Mythology*, p.7 (1993). This book is in Persian—translation here by Nabarz.
[360] For the temple at Pir-e-Sabz, see http://www.vohuman.org/SlideShow/Pir-e-Sabz/Pir-e-Sabz-1.htm
[361] For the temples of Pir e Banoo Pars and Pir e Naraki, see http://www.sacredsites.com/middle_east/iran/zoroastrian.htm

Time passes... history takes place...

Figure 4: Commemorative gold coin with image of Anahita, 1997.

The Central Bank of Armenia in 1997, issues a commemorative gold coin with an image of Anahita on it. The bank states:

'This commemorative coin issued by the Central Bank of Armenia is devoted to Goddess Anahit. Anahit has been considered the Mother Goddess of Armenians, the sacred embodiment and patron for the crop, fruitfulness and fertility. In 34 BC, the Romans have plundered the country town Yeriza of the Yekeghiats Province in the Higher Hayk, where the huge golden statue to Anahit was situated. They smashed the statue to pieces and shared among the soldiers as pillage. On the turn of the 19th century, a head part of a bronze statue referring to Anahit was found in Satagh (Yerznka region), which is presently kept in British Museum.'[362]

Time passes... history takes place...

The higher social status of women in Iranian society compared to its Arab neighbours has been suggested by some to be due to its long respect for Lady Anahita. Indeed, the first Muslim woman to win a Noble Peace Prize (2003) was from Iran.

Time passes.... history take place..... Yet she is still remembered....

'Tomorrow (21.8.03), I (Jalil Nozari) *will take part in a ceremony to commemorate a very poor, old woman, a relative of mine, who died recently. Her name was Kaneez. The name in modern Farsi has negative connotations, meaning a "female servant." But, in Pahlavi, the language spoken in central Iran before the coming of Islam, it meant "a maiden," a virgin, unmarried girl. Indeed, it has both meanings of the English "maid." Anahita, too,*

---

[362] http://www.cba.am/CBA_SITE/currency/aanahit.html?_locale=en

means virgin, literally not defiled. But this is not the end of story. When I was a child, there was a place in Ramhormoz, my hometown, which now is under a city road. In it, there was a small, single-room building with a small drain pipe hanging from it. Women in their ninth month and close to delivery time stood under this pipe and someone poured water through it. There was the belief that getting wet under the drain would assure a safe delivery of the baby. The building was devoted to Khezer (the green one).[363] Yet, the cult is very old and clearly one of Anahita's. The role of water and safe child delivery are both parts of the Anahita cult. My deceased aunt, our Kaneez, was a servant of this building. The building was demolished years ago to build a road, and Kaneez is no more. I wonder how will we reconstruct those eras, so close to us in time yet so far from our present conditions. It is also of interest that there exist remains of a castle, or better to say a fort, in Ramhormoz, that is called "Mother and Daughter." It belongs to the Sasanides era. "Daughter," signifying virginity, directs the mind toward Anahita. There are other shrines named after sacred women, mostly located beside springs of water. These all make the grounds for believing that Ramhormoz was one of the oldest places for Anahita worshippers.'[364]

Time passes....

Figure 5: Goddess Anahita Sculpture by Jenny Richards (2009); among water lilies, photo by Payam Nabarz.

---

[363] There is a folk tradition about Saint Khezer or Khidar (the green one): if one washes (pours water) on one's front door at dawn for forty days, he will appear. Khider is described as being a friend of the Sufis, and is said to stand at the boundary of sea and land. He is also said to have drunk from the fountain of immortality.

[364] Personal communication from Jalil Nozari, August 20, 2003.

2004 CE. Another seeker meditating by a sea makes an observation on relationships between Mehr and Aban (modern Persian names for Mithra and Anahita.) The Autumn Equinox marks the beginning of the Persian month of Mehr, and the start of the festival of Mehregan. The month of the sun god Mithra is followed by the month of the sea goddess Anahita (according to ancient sources both the partner and mother of Mithra). The month of the sun thus leads into the month of the sea. The sun sets into the ocean. The sunset over the ocean is one of the most beautiful sights there is; as the sun unites with the ocean, the light is reflected upon the water.

Mehr, coming together with Aban, gives rise to a third word: *mehraban*, which translates as "kindness," or "one who is kind." Thus, this metaphorical child of light that comes out of the marriage between Sun and Sea is *kindness*. The child of light is the Inner Light, which is in everyone. The Sun (light of God) and the Sea (divine ocean), united within each person, creates perhaps the most important spiritual quality - that of human kindness.

Time passes...

2777 C.E. Somewhere on a beach by the Caspian Sea. A young Magi has been keeping a night vigil. His solitary fire is the only light for miles around and his recitation of Aban Yasht, the hymn to angel-goddess Anahita, the only sound to be heard apart from the waves gently crashing onto the beach... She is remembered.

Further reading:

The Mysteries of Mithras: The Pagan Belief That Shaped the Christian World, by Payam Nabarz. Inner Traditions, 2005.

Wise Lord of the Sky: Persian Myth, by Tony Allan, Charles Phillips, and Michael Kerrigan. Myth and Mankind series. Time Life Books, 1999

Anahita in Iranian Mythology, (Anahita dar usturah ha-yi Irani), by Susan Gaviri. Tehran, Intisharat-i Jamal al Haqq, (year 1372), 1993.

First Iranian Goddess of productivity and values, by Manouchehr Saadat Noury in *the Persian Journal, Iranian.ws,* Jul 21, 2005.

The Avestan Hymn to Mithra trans. Ilya Gershevitch. Cambridge University Press, 2008.

The Heritage of Persia, by Richard N. Frye. Mazda, 1993.

Textual sources for the study of Zoroastrianism by Mary Boyce. University of Chicago Press, 1990.

Aban Yasht online translation at http://www.avesta.org/ka/yt5sbe.htm

Figure 6: Goddess Anahita Sculpture by Jenny Richards (2009); among water lilies, photo by Payam Nabarz.

Figure 7: Pond, photo by Payam Nabarz.

Figure 8: Sea, photo by Payam Nabarz.

Origin of the Gathas of Asho Zarathustra by Farida Bamji

On the banks of
The River Daitya
One sunny morn
Was Asho Zarathushtra
On Him it didn't dawn
His relationship with
Ahura Mazda was about to born

Like a bolt from the blue
A brilliant Light
Out of no where appeared
Not knowing the apparition
He very much feared
Engulfed by a blinding Halo
What a spectacular sight'
So much so, it blinded His sight

"Who art Thou"?
Queried Asho Zarathushtra
"I am the messenger
Sent to lead you
To Ahura Mazda

In Ahura Mazda's presence
Asho Zarathushtra stood
Totally in awe
Transfixed to boot
Ahura Mazda's voice
Booming loud & clear
"Be calm, Asho Zarathushtra
Do not fear,
I am Ahura Mazda
Your Creator"

The land teeming like termites
Karpans & Idolators
Pillagers & Ravagers
Death & Destruction
Earth Soul crying out
In utter frustration
For Divine Interference
To stop suffering chaos
And excruciating pain

"I have chosen Thee
Asho Zarathushtra
To clear the way
Defeat Evil
Making Truth
And Righteousness
The order of the day"

Each & every day
Atop a mountain high
Against the back drop
Of a clear blue sky
The white fluffy clouds
Silently floating by
As the sun appears a-peeking
The gentle wind
His hair softly caressing
I can almost hear
Asho Zarathushtra chanting:

ýânîm manô ýânîm vacô ýânîm shyaothnem ashaonô
zarathushtrahe, ferâ ameshâ spentâ gâthå gêurvâin!
nemô vê gâthå ashaonîsh, 1
ahyâ ýâsâ nemanghâ ustânazastô rafedhrahyâ manyêush
mazdâ pourvîm spentahyâ ashâ vîspêñg shyaothanâ
vanghêush xratûm manangho ýâ xshnevîshâ gêushcâ
urvânem
(Yasna 28, 2)

"With hands aloft to Thee
I supplicate with submissiveness
For the joy of the Bountiful Spirit
O Lord of Wisdom
Thou 1st & foremost
For all actions to be done
Through Asha (Divine Immutable Law)
As well as for the Wisdom of Thy Divine
Intelligence and cheer unto the soul"

Questions were put forth
Answers were given
Ahura Mazda had a plan
For Asho Zarathushtra's
Divine Mission

After years of contemplation
Along with many conversations
He came to realize
VOHU MANO was a
Powerful Tool
To think & reason
As it would spread
Righteousness & Goodness
To all creations

ýânîm manô ýânîm vacô ýânîm shyaothnem ashaonô
zarathushtrahe, ferâ ameshâ speñtâ gâthå gêurvâin!
nemô vê gâthå ashaonîsh (Yasna 28, 0)

Inspired Thoughts,
Inspired Words,
Inspired Deeds
And the deeds of
Holy Zarathushtra
May the Amesha Spenta
Accept The Gathas

"I bow in reverence to you
O Gathas that teach
The Path of Asha

Ushta te,
Farida Bamji

Avestan quote taken from Mr Joseph Peterson's site: www.avesta.org

The translation from Mr Framroz Rustomjee; The Philosophcal Intrepretations of The Gathas of Holy Zarathushtra

Mehrgan by Farida Bamji

Deep sea divers that

Unravel Natures' mystery

From the depths of

The deep blue sea

Beautiful planktons

Coral reefs, colourful

Slippery snaky eels

Sharks, Otters manatees

Same way I feel

About Zoroastrianism

As slowly steadily

All these rich traditions

Cultures are being

Revealed to me!

In the month Of Mehr

Whence it all began

Rich tradition of Mehrgan:

Such an event was

Zohak a tyrant

An incarnate of the devil

With help of this deity

Heroes Feridoon & Kaveh

Sealed Zohak's fate

By destroying the devil

Victory of Good over Evil

Mehr signifies the

Glorious Sun

Always up at

The crack of dawn

Giver of Light Warmth

As well as Heat

Without which we

Would freeze to death

Without the Golden Eye

The day wouldn't be complete!

Mehr takes relationships

Very very seriously

In dealings with one another

If one fails to

Keep ones' word

Surely from Mehr one

Will surely "hear"

Whether they be Yazatas

Or for that matter Amesha Spentas

They are actually Divine Qualities

Of our beloved Ahura Mazda.

PS:

Even if the world were dark & cold

Where we have to grope our way

With smiles on our faces

And Happiness in our hearts

We can wipe the misery away!

Acknowledgement: Article: Mehrgan by Mrs Dina McIntyre posted on www.vohuman.org.

A Prayer for Initiation by Katherine Sutherland

Here in the hoard of the world,
enclosed and held by heaven and earth,
climbing a ladder through space and time,
a soul on a journey awaits rebirth.

Oh Lord of the Universe, hear this prayer,
ascending in tones sung with an inner voice,
from within the depths of this microcosm,
a templed place rings with songs of choice.

Hear me now, oh Lord of contracts,
to your values now, I promise to hold true,
to be just and fair in every way,
from the words I utter, to the deeds I do.

In the wide green pasture of my life,
I seek and offer you my right hand,
in divine kinship as a sister, I,
shoulder to shoulder with you will stand.

Mithras Reader Vol 1

This edition includes: **Part 1 academic papers:** Continuity and Change in the Cult of Mithra, by Dr. Israel Campos Mendez. Mithra and the warrior group Mithra and the Iranian words and images Introduction to Classes of Manichean, Mithraism and Sufiyeh, by Dr. Saloome Rostampoor. Entheos ho syros, polymathes ho phoinix: Neoplatonist approaches to religious practice in Iamblichus and Porphyry, by Sergio Knipe. Mithraism and Alchemy, by David Livingstone.

Part 2 Arts: 'For example Mithras' part I exhibition by Farangis Yegane.

Part 3 Religious articles: Meeting Mithra, by Guya Vichi. Ode To Mithra, by Guya Vichi. Hymn to the Sun, by Katherine Sutherland. Mithras Liturgy with the Orphic Hymns, by Payam Nabarz.

ISBN-13: 978-1905524099, (Twin Serpents Ltd, 2006).

Mithras Reader Vol 2

This edition includes: **Part 1 academic papers:** Factors determining the outside projection of the Mithraic Mysteries by Dr. Israel Campos Méndez. The Mithras Liturgy: cult liturgy, religious ritual, or magical theurgy? Some aspects and considerations of the Mithras Liturgy from the Paris Codex and what they may imply for the origin and purpose of this spell by Kim Huggens.

Part 2 Arts: 'For example Mithras' part II exhibition by Farangis Yegane. Mithras-Phanes art piece by James Rodriguez. Temple of Mithra in Garni, Armenia, photos by Jalil Nozari. Mithras artistic depiction by Robert Kavjian.

Part 3 Religious articles: MITHRAS SOL INVICTUS Invocation by M. Hajduk. Ode to Aphrodite by Sappho, translated by Harita Meenee. Norooz Phiroze by Farida Bamji. Disappearing Shrines and Moving Shrines by S. David. The Sleeping Lord by Katherine Sutherland. The right handed handshake of the Gods by Payam Nabarz.

ISBN: 978-0-9556858-1-1, (Web of Wyrd Press, 2008).

Notes:

www.ingramcontent.com/pod-product-compliance
Lightning Source LLC
Chambersburg PA
CBHW080832010526
44112CB00015B/2499